Winsome Wisdom

366 Thoughts to Ponder and to Live

Lowell O. Erdahl

Foreword by Marcus Borg
Preface by Paul Sponheim

CSS Publishing Company, Inc., Lima, Ohio

WINSOME WISDOM

Unless otherwise stated, scripture quotations are from the Revised Standard Version of the Bible, copyrighted 1946, 1952 ©, 1971, 1973 by the Division of Christian Education of the National Council of the Churches of Christ in the USA. Used by permission.

Scripture quotations marked (NEB) are from The New English Bible. Copyright © the Delegates of the Oxford University Press and the Syndics of the Cambridge University Press, 1961, 1970. Reprinted by permission.

Scripture quotations marked (REV) are from The Revised English Bible. Copyright © the Delegates of the Oxford University Press and the Syndics of the Cambridge University Press, 1961, 1970. Reprinted by permission.

Scripture quotations marked (REV) are from The Revised English Bible. Copyright © Oxford University Press and Cambridge University Press, 1989.

Scripture quotations marked (RSV) are from the Revised Standard Version of the Bible, copyrighted 1946, 1952 ©, 1971, 1973, by the Division of Christian Education of the National Council of the Churches of Christ in the USA. Used by permission.

Permissions appear on page 403.

Library of Congress Cataloging-in-Publication Data

Erdahl, Lowell O.
    Winsome wisdom : 366 thoughts to ponder and to live / Lowell O. Erdahl ; forward by Marcus Borg ; preface by Paul Sponheim.
        p. cm.
    Includes index.
    ISBN-13: 978-0-7880-2417-7 (alk. paper)
    ISBN-10: 0-7880-2417-5 (perfect bound : alk. paper)
    1. Devotional calendars. I. Title.

    BV4811.E69 2006
    242'.2—dc22
                                                                    2006031094

For more information about CSS Publishing Company resources, visit our website at www.csspub.com or email us at custserv@csspub.com or call (800) 241-4056.

Cover design by Barbara Spencer
ISBN-13: 978-0-7880-2417-7
ISBN-10: 0-7880-2417-5   PRINTED IN U.S.A.

Acknowledgments

Needless to say, a volume of thoughts for which I am thankful is grounded in hundreds of grateful memories. When possible, I have tried to make my thanks personal by referring to these sources. But the origin of many of these thoughts is beyond recall and a general expression of gratitude is the best that I can do. Thank you — thank you — thank you all!

Special thanks go to family and friends who encouraged and supported this project. First among these are our children, Becky, Paul, and Beth, who prompted me nearly ten years ago to start recording thoughts they had heard me quote so often. Thanks to Carol who has been supportive and encouraging all the way. Readers and reactors who reviewed early drafts of the manuscript are also remembered with gratitude. In alphabetical order they are: Myrwood Bagne, Laurel and Pat Gray, George and Vivian Johnson, Verlyn Smith, Paul Sponheim, and Ted Vinger. Since they didn't always agree, I couldn't follow all of their suggestions. Every suggestion, however, was considered and many were heeded. The final decisions were, of course, my own so while I thank reactors for all their helpfulness, none is to be blamed for anything I have written.

I also express profound gratitude to Maxine Enfield for her kindness and skill in typing my dictation through seven drafts. Without such helpfulness this book could not have been written. Thanks also to Paul Nockleby for preparing the manuscript for submission to publishers and for his encouragement throughout the process.

Finally, I struggle for words to express my thankfulness to Marcus Borg and Paul Sponheim who have written the Foreword and Preface. My gratitude not only for these gifts but also for their wisdom, friendship, and encouragement is more than my words can tell.

Day by day,
I know you will provide me
Strength to serve
And wisdom to obey;
I will seek
Your loving will to guide me
O'er the paths
I struggle day by day.

Carolina Sandell-Berg (1832-1903)

Table of Contents

There are, in general, three kinds of content in this book. Many pages seek to share practical wisdom for daily living and aspects of Christian living. There are also pages that focus on specific subjects. As I ordered the pages, it seemed best that those related to specific subjects be grouped together and that those dealing with practical wisdom and Christian living be dispersed throughout the year.

It is my suggestion that you begin reading on January 1 and continue through to the end, no matter what the actual date is.

— Lowell O. Erdahl

Foreword

I am very pleased to write this Foreword. It provides me an opportunity to commend this book of daily reflections and to offer a tribute to its author, Lowell Erdahl, a retired Lutheran bishop.

To begin with the tribute, I like and admire Bishop Erdahl very much. We first met more than ten years ago when he invited me to present a series of lectures to the clergy of his synod. Our paths have intersected many times in the years since, most often in the context of theological education in the church. I have come to know him as a *good man*: hearty, life-affirming, intellectual, compassionate, outspoken, and willing to change and grow. He is an exemplar of what a Lutheran can be, what a Christian can be, and what a bishop can be. As my mother would have said, "Lowell has turned out well."

Lowell and I share a common heritage. We both grew up Lutheran. Though I became an Episcopalian more than twenty years ago, I have been deeply shaped by the Lutheran immersion of my childhood and young adulthood. My wife, Marianne, has said more than once that I will always have a Lutheran heart.

At its best, the Lutheran church's contribution to the larger Christian world is rich. It is marked by a remarkable intellectual and theological tradition: Many of the most important theological and biblical scholars of the past two centuries have been Lutheran. It has a rich heritage of musical composition and performance.

And perhaps its greatest contribution is its emphasis on radical grace. We are saved — made right with God — not by "works," not by something we do, not by measuring up to God's requirements of belief or behavior, but by grace — by God, as a gift. We are, to use a Latin phrase from Martin Luther, *simul justus et peccator* — at one and the same time sinful and yet accepted by God. Radical grace, unconditional grace, means that God accepts us in our "is-ness."

The certainty of radical grace is grounded in Luther's own experience. For years before his experience of grace, Luther agonized about measuring up to what he perceived failures. Luther's problem was not believing in God or the Bible. He believed, and he was terrified. Then, sometime around age thirty, he experienced the radical grace of God, which he articulated in Saint Paul's language of *justification by grace*.

When not at its best, the Lutheran tradition is marked by a distortion of the meaning of "faith" into "believing." When this happens, we are no longer saved by trusting in the radical grace of God, but by believing in the doctrine of justification by grace. Whereas Luther was saved by the experience of radical grace, Lutherans have often believed that we are saved by *believing* in justification by grace. *Believing* then becomes the new requirement that makes us right with God and, of course, believing means "believing the right things." Thus, salvation by "works" creeps back in. Faith as "believing the right things" is now the "work." It is often an anxious work. Have we believed strongly enough? And the world is once again divided into an "in-group" and an "out-group": those who believe correctly and strongly, and those who don't.

Erdahl represents the Lutheran tradition at its best. He understands radical grace. This book of thoughts for each day of the year is deeply shaped by a robust affirmation of grace. We are not to worry about believing or doing what we are supposed to believe or do in order to be accepted by God. Such an orientation leaves us focused on ourselves. Rather, the order is different: We are accepted by God. Now, we are to live our lives as those who have been freed from the anxious project of measuring up to God's requirements.

Taking grace seriously changes our lives. It leads to a commitment to love and compassion. It also leads to a commitment to justice and peace. Erdahl sees the more-than-individual meaning of love and compassion — the political meaning — of a Christianity grounded in the Bible and Jesus. The Lutheran tradition has not always been good at seeing this. It has often been politically quiet and acquiescent, treating the political realm as a separate and secular realm to which we are simply to give our obedience. Of course, there have been exceptions, most famously, the twentieth-century Lutheran saint, Dietrich Bonhoeffer, martyred by the Nazis in the last month of World War Two.

Erdahl belongs among the exceptions. His reflections are marked by a strong concern for justice and peace. He sees that the Bible and Christianity are both personal and political.

There is one more reason I am pleased to write this Foreword. Namely, there is great value in developing a daily spiritual discipline. Along with worship, such a disciple is the most important practice in the Christian life. It is a way of paying intentional attention to our relationship with God.

So it has been in my own life. When I remember to do this, when I discipline myself to do this, I am nourished by it. My life goes better. I am centered, I have better energy, I am better able to be present to the glory and tasks of each day. Most importantly, such a discipline is a way of deepening my (and our) relationship with God. It leads to a deeper centering in the God of grace, that centering which is faith.

The shape of a daily discipline will vary from Christian to Christian. Ideally, it is a specific time set aside each day, typically twenty to thirty minutes long, in which we "remember" God. It commonly will include time for prayer and meditative Bible reading. And it often includes a short reading from outside the Bible as well. This helpful and insightful book, which is written not only for Christian laity and clergy but also for "seekers" of other faiths or no faith, is a reminder to all of the reality of God and what it means to live by the grace of God.

In addition to its clear witness to radical grace, *Winsome Wisdom* contains an abundance of practical wisdom concerning almost all aspects of daily living, including getting along together, married life, sexual fulfillment, decision making, time and money management, and much more.

Bless your Lutheran heart, Lowell. My mother would have been right: You have turned out well. Bless you for seeing and articulating what grace means for our lives and for all of the winsome wisdom for daily living packed into these pages.

— Marcus Borg

11

Preface

Winsome Wisdom is filled to overflowing with the fruit of a lifetime of reading and listening. In 366 daily reflections, the reader meets poets and scientists, pastors and politicians, farmers and philosophers, in a compilation that defies classification. Leo Tolstoy and Mahatma Gandhi join Gerhard Frost and Alvin Rogness, and Dylan Thomas keeps company with Reinhold Niebuhr. The strong voice of Martin Luther is heard frequently. To be a candidate for inclusion one must have thought deeply about life. Lowell Erdahl's gift is to have brought this richness together in one place.

How do claims of Christian faith connect with practical wisdom and social reflections not calling specifically on Christian conviction? *Winsome Wisdom* is marked not only by remarkable range, but also by unusual clarity in its sense of connectedness. The author is aware that none of us knows enough to be an atheist or a dogmatist (January 11), and is driven by the conviction (February 18) that "all truth is God's truth." So equipped, he joins Albert Einstein (October 12) in "holy curiosity," and Walter Brueggemann (June 22) in the exercise of prophetic imagination. This book invites us to think newly (November 17), to "think for yourself" (June 20), and in the process to "unlearn" (June 21) old ideas that are out of touch with reality. Erdahl can bring all of this together because he knows, with E. Stanley Jones, the reality of both Christian unity (October 26) and human unity (October 27). In this strong connectedness, Erdahl will speak to many post-modern people who are weary of modernity's insatiable thirst for specialization.

Lowell Erdahl calls his reader to think about "whatever is true" (Philippians 4:8). But that's not the end of the matter. Each day's reflection concludes with an "affirmation" — for example, in a word of confession or praise. In this, there is what one might call "inner action." But often, that daily last word points outward toward action in the hurting world. It is not strange that it should do so, for the author knows (May 17) that "if it is to be, it is up to me," even as he knows (July 1) that the best we can say at times is "Do what you can and when you can't, don't be afraid to ask for help." Indeed, he learned this from his beloved mother, whose word to her sons was often, "You can do it!" (May 18).

How is the book to be used? In more than one way, I expect. It will "work" well in its primary presentation, as one ponders these things in a daily discipline. But the book also offers a resource on fourteen topics, ranging from marriage to money, from science to sex, from writing to war. The index of names will be particularly helpful as one struggles to remember just how Frost or Tournier put that point. But in whatever way these pages are used, the reader will be informed (for there is knowledge here), empowered (through wisdom), and challenged (closing with a call to action).

For this wonderful book, we are indebted to Lowell Erdahl, to his children (who proposed the book), to his wife, Carol (who is clearly very much with him in this venture), and to his parents (to whom beautiful witness is borne frequently). These family members deserve special mention, and they represent a larger grand gathering of others who call us day by day to think and act for the world's good and God's glory,

— Paul Sponheim

Introduction

About ten years ago, in obvious awareness of the fact that "Dad won't be around forever," our children encouraged me to write down some of the many thoughts that they had often heard me share. In obedience to their request, I began making a list of what I have come to call thoughts for which I am thankful.

Then, for Christmas in 1997, Carol gave me a copy of Leo Tolstoy's *A Calendar of Wisdom: Daily Thoughts to Nourish the Soul* that had just been translated into English for the first time by Peter Sekirin. I devoured this book with such interest that I often read more than one page a day. By the time I finished it (a note on the bottom of the last page indicates that was May 15, 1998), I had decided to try to follow Tolstoy's example by writing this book.

Like Tolstoy's *Calendar of Wisdom*, *Winsome Wisdom* contains a year of readings for every day but the daily format is different. Each of Tolstoy's pages contains three to seven brief quotations that relate to a common theme. Each of my pages focuses on a single thought with a reflection and an affirmation for the day.

Few of the "Thoughts for the Day" in this book are original with me. Most are thoughts received from others, and all really are "thoughts for which I am thankful." They have shaped and guided my life, and it is with gratitude that I am moved to share them with others.

I agree with Marcus Borg, in *Heart of Christianity*, that "Wisdom and knowledge are not identical. Wisdom is more foundational. It is about the two most important questions in life: 'The real' and 'the way.' What is real? And what is the way — how shall we live?"[1] The wisdom in these pages is intended for daily living. It witnesses to reality as I perceive it and to the most meaningful and fulfilling way of living of which I am aware.

Although I am both a personal and professional (although now retired) Christian, I have attempted to write this book for non-Christians as well as Christians. Whether we are religious, nonreligious, or irreligious, we are all seeking meaning in life. We all seek wisdom for daily living and long for resources to live from and purposes to live for. All of us have more to learn and perhaps especially from those whose experiences differ from our own.

All this was brought home to Carol and me when we served as volunteer English teachers in China. Most of our students and most of the Chinese teachers of English with whom we taught had little experience or understanding of Christianity, but it was obvious from the first day that we were all fellow pilgrims in our ventures of living.

Several of those teachers have recently visited us here in the United States. When I told them of my plans to write this book, they asked if they could receive copies as soon as it is printed, which I promised to provide. Therefore, I am aware that in a special way I am writing for them. Their culture is steeped in the wisdom gleaned not just from centuries but from millennia. It humbles me to be invited to share with them these thoughts for which I am thankful.

Whoever you are, I hope that something in this book will be meaningful and significant for you in your venture of living. If that happens, I will be grateful.

---

1. Marcus Borg, *Heart of Christianity: Rediscovering a Life of Faith* (San Francisco: Harper's, 2003), p. 214.

January 1

Take time for reflection.

There is an interesting statement in the apocryphal book of Ecclesiasticus: The Wisdom of Jesus, Son of Sirach, that says, "The wisdom of the scribes depends on the opportunity of leisure; only one who has little business can become wise." The author wonders, "How can one become wise who handles the plow ... and whose talk is about bulls?" (38:24-25).

As an old farm boy I have known people who spent a good deal of time handling the plow and who would occasionally talk about bulls and yet were insightful and wise. Perhaps that is because their time in the fields provided solitude that enabled them to think deeply about the meaning of life. A hectic office or noisy factory, it seems to me, provides less opportunity for quiet reflection than does life on the farm, at least as I remember it.

Whatever may be true in that regard, I affirm the wisdom of this Jesus, Son of Sirach, that our growth in wisdom "depends on the opportunity of leisure" and that we need quiet times to reflect, ponder, and pray.

Affirmation for the Day:
In the ordering of my often too-hectic life, I will remember to take time for reflection.

January 2

"Try to understand and help others understand what it all means."

Today's thought comes from the English preacher, F. W. Robertson. It is part of a longer statement that says:

> *We are here to live and to die. In a few years it will all be over. In the meantime, what we have to do is to try to understand and help others understand what it all means, what this strange and mysterious thing called life contains within it.*

I have shared this statement many times during ordinations and installations of clergy because I think it states clearly a central aspect of a pastor's calling. Clergy are not called to be peddlers of religion but to be sharers of the meaning of life as Jesus helps us to understand it.

Pastors, however, have no monopoly on this calling. Robertson's sermon from which this quote comes was addressed to lay people. It presents a double challenge to each of us. First, to "try to understand" for ourselves and then to "help others understand" what this wondrous thing called life is all about. Whatever our vocation, each of us is created and called to be a learner and teacher of life.

Affirmation for the Day:

In all my pondering, I will ponder the meaning of life and in my giving will seek to share it with others.

January 3

"Wisdom for tomorrow lies beyond the sunset."

Ponder that saying. We need wisdom for today and for tomorrow. From whence does it come? We understand the past to include not only ancient days but everything that has occurred before the present moment. It is obvious that almost all of our wisdom comes from the past. There are flashes of insight that strike us like lightning in the present moment. But most of our wisdom comes from our personal learning across the years and from the wisdom of others who have lived before us. Therefore, we begin this quest for greater understanding, remembering that most "wisdom for tomorrow lies beyond the sunset."

Affirmation for the Day:
I will be open to wisdom from the aged and from the ages.

January 4

"Wisdom does not always come with age, sometimes age comes alone."

I was struck by this statement which was posted on the window of a shop in Juneau, Alaska. I don't know who said it, but I fear that it's often true. Older doesn't always mean wiser.

Some people after twenty years on a job can be described as having had "twenty years' experience," while others have had "one year's experience repeated twenty times." It is sometimes true, as my old friend John Hilbert liked to say, that "Practice makes permanent."

This reminds us that there is a negative truth in the saying that "practice makes perfect." We need to be exceedingly careful concerning what we practice, lest we perfect attitudes and patterns of living that are hurtful to ourselves and to others.

Affirmation for the Day:
I pray that my experience will provide life-giving learning and not bad habits or deadly stagnation.

January 5

Every person is my teacher.

E. Stanley Jones is one of the wisest people I have known. His wisdom came in part from his practice of seeking "to learn something from every person I meet." From my acquaintance with Jones, I believe that he actually tried to do that in his daily encounters with people.

Sometimes his learning involved hearing a new bit of information or gaining a new insight. At other times, it consisted of a renewed appreciation for the significance of a smile or a kind word. Sometimes, the learning grew out of a negative experience and resulted in a personal resolution to refrain from the kind of grouchy complaining that had just been encountered. With Jones, every meeting was an occasion for at least a little learning.

There is an old saying that "experience teaches a dear school but fools will learn in none other." In plain, modern English that means that learning from experience is often exceedingly and sometimes painfully expensive!

We really are foolish if we fail to learn from the wisdom and experience of others. The cost of such folly is often measured in unnecessary misery. We are truly wise when we seek to learn from the learning of others and to profit from observation of their experiences both good and bad.

Affirmation for the Day:
I, too, will seek to learn something from everyone I meet.

January 6

Success is often only an idea away.

The story is told that President John Kennedy's advisors once presented him with three ways of responding to a difficult situation. After considering their recommendations, he rejected them all and asked them to come back with a better idea.

When stymied, we often need to "think outside the box." That is, to step back and take a new look from a different perspective and seek a new understanding, a new plan, a new idea. When we do that, we often discover in our own experience that success is often only an idea away.

Affirmation for the Day:
In every situation, I will be open to a new perspective and a new idea.

January 7

Ignorance may be no excuse but it's often the best one I have.

It is certainly not true, as an old radio jingle put it, that "It pays to be ignorant — to be dumb — to be dense — to be ignorant."

Ignorance is nothing to be proud of, but awareness of ignorance is a mark of wisdom. When we don't know something, we should be smart enough and honest enough to admit it.

This applies not only to great mysteries of life but also to the nitty-gritty issues of every day. When we face and admit our ignorance we are wise. When we fail to do so we are foolish.

Affirmation for the Day:

I will honestly admit my ignorance, first to myself and often to others.

January 8

"When dealing with complex and controversial matters, always remember that you have something more to learn."

Today's thought from Dr. Roger Fisher of Harvard Law School sounds so obvious that it may seem unnecessary to ponder it at all. That would be true, except for the fact that we so frequently forget that thought and act as if we know it all.

It is especially difficult to learn from those with whom we are in disagreement. We dig in our heels, concentrate on presenting our own views, and often fail to listen to, let alone learn from, the person with whom we are arguing.

In such times it is well to back off a bit and to say something like, "I am not sure I understand you correctly. Please help me get what you are trying to say." Or to confess that, "I think that we both have more to learn on this subject. Let's check on some things before we discuss it further."

Affirmation for the Day:

I will seek to be more of a "learn-it-all" than a "know-it-all."

January 9

"Never argue about empirically verifiable facts."

I have tried to follow this rule since first learning it from Dr. Howard Hong at St. Olaf College a half-century ago. I am sure that it has helped me avoid many unnecessary and unwise arguments.

If we can weigh it, measure it, count it, or look it up in an authoritative reference book, why should we argue about it?

We can rightly argue about the meaning of facts but, when they are empirically verifiable, we should not waste our time and that of others arguing about the facts themselves.

Affirmation for the Day:
When facts can be verified, I will refrain from arguing about them.

January 10

Reverence the *mystery.*

There is a line in the Hebrew Bible that says, "The fear of the Lord is the beginning of wisdom" (Proverbs 9:10). The word "fear" in that sentence refers not to anxiety or dread but to reverence and awe. It invites "God-fearing people" to live with a sense of wonder and respectful reverence before the divine presence.

Those who do not believe in God are still challenged to revere the mystery of the wondrous universe and the amazing diversity of life on this little planet. All of us confront the reality in Omar Khayyam's *Rubaiyat* that is translated poetically by Edward Fitzgerald:

> *There was a Door to which I found no Key;*
> *It was a Veil through which I might not see.*

Whether we are religious or irreligious, there is sufficient mystery around and within us to evoke our reverence, wonder, and awe.

Perhaps we should be thankful for mysteries beyond comprehension and confess with Harry Emerson Fosdick that "I would rather live in a world where my life is surrounded by mystery than to live in a world so small that my mind could comprehend it." There is something exceedingly interesting and exciting about living in the midst of mystery. It challenges us to be life-long learners and explorers and is a great inducement to honest humility.

Affirmation for the Day:
I will live today with reverence for the mystery of life, the universe, and God.

January 11

"Nobody knows enough to be an atheist" or a dogmatist.

The first half of our Thought for the Day comes from Dr. Mulford Q. Sibley who was, for many years, a respected professor at the University of Minnesota and a member of the Society of Friends who are also known as the Quakers.

Sibley believed that a rational person could be an agnostic — one who says, "I don't know if there is a God." But when surrounded and inhabited by mystery beyond our comprehension no one knows enough to say, "There is no God."

If it is true that no one knows enough to be an atheist, it is also true that none of us knows enough to be absolutely certain that our beliefs concerning God, or almost everything else for that matter, are the absolute truth.

People who claim such certainty fit my dictionary's first definition of a dogmatist: "An arrogantly assertive person."

We all need convictions strong enough to live and die by but none of us knows everything about anything. The vast mysteries of the universe, of life, and of God compel us to acknowledge our ignorance and lack of understanding. Someday we may understand fully but "for now," as the apostle Paul reminds us, "We see in a mirror dimly" or as "in a riddle" and "know only in part." (See 1 Corinthians 13:12.)

Affirmation for the Day:

I don't know enough to be either an arrogant atheist or an arrogant dogmatist.

January 12

"The older I become, the fewer certainties I require."

The older I become the more I appreciate today's thought from George Sverdrup, a former president of Augsburg College. I no longer need to be certain about everything and can live more comfortably with the mysteries of life.

Luther must have had a similar experience. He quotes himself as having "often said" that "the whole way of life for the Christian person consists in just two things, trust in God and love of neighbor." That's about as basic as one can get. We are to trust that God loves us and then give ourselves with love in caring for others.

I believe that we are created to be loved and to love and that each of us, whether Christian or and non-Christian, is invited and graciously enabled to live with trust in the love of God and with compassionate love toward others.

Affirmation for the Day:

In all my living, I will seek to center on the central certainties.

January 13

One can be both liberal and Christian.

During my growing up years I believed that one could be conservative, even fundamentalistic, and be Christian. I needed to learn that one could be both liberal and Christian. That lesson was forced upon me when I was a student at Union Theological Seminary in New York. Some of the professors and students at that place were far more liberal than any I had encountered at St. Olaf or Luther Seminary. But, to my amazement, they gave evidence of being people of profound faith, prayer, and piety.

Then I studied Harry Emerson Fosdick. I read his sermons and prayers and was deeply moved by his book, *The Meaning of Prayer*. I was captivated by his autobiography titled *For the Living of These Days*, which is a line from his great hymn "God of Grace and God of Glory" that he wrote for the 1930 dedication of Riverside Church in New York. Fosdick confessed (or should I say prided himself) in having never confessed the Creed in public worship. But I found him, as we said in those days, to be "a man of God" and a committed follower of Jesus.

Affirmation for the Day:
Whatever our theology, when we live by the grace of God we are brothers and sisters in faith.

January 14

Our beliefs don't save us, nor do our doubts condemn us.

Our salvation rests in the grace of God, not in our beliefs about God. That also means that we are not condemned because of our doubts and disbeliefs.

I still vividly recall the time of late night wrestling with doubt while a student at St. Olaf College. In the midst of that struggle, I recalled a line from Luther's catechism memorized during confirmation instruction — "I believe that I cannot by my own reason or strength believe in Jesus Christ my Lord or come to him." That was something I could believe! Being stuck in my doubts with no way out, I realized that if the Lord were to have anything to do with me he would have to take me as I was, not only with my sins but also with my doubts. Then, as if a light went on in my dark skull, I realized, "That's what the gospel says!" I had sung it many times but hadn't until then really taken it in.

> *Just as I am, thou wilt receive,*
> *wilt welcome, pardon, cleanse, relieve; ...*
> *Just as I am, though tossed about,*
> *with many a conflict, many a doubt,*
> *fightings and fears within, without,*
> *O Lamb of God, I come, I come.*

After that I still had many doubts and disbeliefs but my understanding and my trust were changed. I had caught a glimpse of what it means to live by the grace of God.

Affirmation for the Day:

I will live by the promise that God loves doubters and sinners.

January 15

We are not saved "by faith."

Both Luther and the apostle Paul talked a lot about being saved "by faith," but if they had been aware of the misunderstanding that statement would cause, I believe they would have consistently stated that we are saved "by grace through faith" (Ephesians 2:8).

If it seems heretical for a Lutheran to reject "justification by faith," I remind you of something C. F. W. Walther, one of the patriarchs of the Lutheran Church-Missouri Synod, said long ago. "The Word of God is not rightly divided when faith is required as the condition of justification and salvation, as if a person were righteous in the sight of God and saved, not only by [I think he should have said 'through'] faith, but also on account of his faith, for the sake of his faith, and in view of his faith" (Thesis 14 from Walther's treatise on Law and Gospel).

This is important because as a confirmation student, and for many years afterward, I thought that faith consisted of believing certain things to be true, and that I had to have such faith to get God to love me. I have since learned that faith is not a matter of accepting certain teachings or doctrines. Such beliefs may accompany faith but they are not faith. One may hold such beliefs without having faith, and one may have faith without holding such beliefs.

Faith is of the heart and not just the head. Faith is basic trust in and openness toward that which William James sometimes called "the More." This means that a reverent agnostic may be a person of faith, while a self-satisfied, self-righteous believer is not!

Affirmation for the Day:
God doesn't love me because I have faith. I can have faith because God loves me.

January 16

"Faith is receptive passivity."

Martin Luther sometimes spoke of faith as "pure passivity." E. Stanley Jones described faith as "pure receptivity." I affirm them both and have put them together in our Thought for the Day. Receptivity is passivity — it dares to trust with openness to receive. Passivity is also receptivity — it welcomes and does not resist the life-giving presence of God with us and within us.

Although it sounds paradoxical, faith is an act of becoming and being passive. It is an act of ceasing to act. It is resting instead of working, trusting instead of trying. As long as we are struggling and striving, we are still depending upon ourselves. Only when we quit trying to do everything on our own do we really start trusting God to do everything that God has promised.

This is how Jesus invites and enables us to live — with trust in and openness toward the presence, pardon, and power of God — trusting that we are held by love that will never let us down, welcoming God's Spirit to inhabit, heal, and empower us.

Lest this be misunderstood, I must immediately point out that passive, receptive faith is only one side of the Christian life. The other side is active, busy, outgoing love.

Affirmation for the Day:
I passively rest in God's love and receptively welcome God's presence.

January 17

"Hope is faith with its face toward the future."

When I have quoted Luther's statement that "the whole way of life for a Christian person consists in just two things — faith in God and love of neighbor," some have wondered, "Whatever became of hope? Doesn't the apostle Paul say, 'And now faith, hope, and love abide, these three ...'?" (1 Corinthians 13:13).

He certainly does, but that doesn't mean that Luther has forgotten about, or even abandoned, hope. That is because, as our thought for today points out, hope is really faith looking forward. Hope is not wishful thinking or naive optimism. Hope is grounded on present trust in the promise that whatever happens, God will be there with the same all-sufficient grace that sustains us now.

This means that even when we are pessimistic we can still be hopeful. Lots of things may go wrong, but we trust that God will bring us through. In such present trust is our hope for the future.

Affirmation for the Day:
Trusting God now, I venture with God into unknown tomorrows.

January 18

Thought for the Day:
"God doesn't help us save ourselves."

Today's thought is a subhead in the chapter on "The Gospel" in J. N. Kildahl's book, *The Holy Spirit and Our Faith*. Kildahl writes about people who believe that:

> *They cannot save themselves, that they cannot convert themselves, that they cannot remake themselves, that they cannot do anything to deserve salvation, but that everything must come from God and that consequently they must be saved by grace. Therefore, they continually pray and implore God to help them, and they hope and wait for Him to help them. They hope that God will help them to become truly penitent, prepared, "worthy to receive faith," "worthy of grace." And this, to be so helped by God is, they think, to be saved by grace.*

In this way, he goes on to say, "we seek to preserve some of our 'honor' and to take a bit of credit for our salvation" since we have "had a hand in it." But he says, "You will never be comforted so long as your eye is turned inward on yourself." Such comfort comes only when we quit asking God to help us save ourselves and let God save us without our help as he is promised in Jesus.

Affirmation for the Day:
Since God saves me without my help, I will rest in God's love and concentrate on helping others.

34

January 19

"Let go and let God."

E. Stanley Jones told a story of two people who went into a church to pray. One prayed "God, give me strength to hang on." The other prayed "God, give me courage to let go."

Someone once gave me a poster of a kitten hanging on a wire by its front paws. The caption read: "Hang in there, baby." When I put it up on the church bulletin board I covered that caption with the words "Let go and let God."

The saying "Let George do it" sounds like rejection of personal responsibility. But if George is a heart surgeon and I need open heart surgery, I had better "let George do it." I certainly can't do it myself! If God is God and has promised to hold us with love that will never let us go and never let us down, "letting go" is far safer and far wiser than "hanging on."

Nevertheless, in our excessive self-centeredness and idolatrous self-reliance, we hold back from total trust in and daily surrender to God. In his book, *The Art of Dodging Repentance*, D. R. Davies provides a vivid simile of our situation: "We cling to the last rag of self as a virtuous woman clings to her last garment." We go to church, sing hymns, confess our faith, say our prayers, and desire to live with the trust and love we see in Jesus. At the same time, a host of excuses, rationalizations, and defense mechanisms hold us back from recklessly giving our lives in trust and surrender to the love and power of God. Yet every day it is as if Jesus takes our hand and says again, "Come on — let go and let God!"

Affirmation for the Day:
In the grace of God every day is a new adventure of trusting, surrendering, letting go, and letting God.

January 20

We are designed to rest and to work.

Immediately after proclaiming that we are "saved by grace through faith" the writer of Ephesians went on to say that we are created "to do the good works for which God has designed us." Another translation says that such "good works" are "to be our way of life." (See Ephesians 2:10 NEB and NRSV.)

As we have noted, Luther liked to say that the whole way of life for the Christian person consists in just two things — passive faith and active love. I believe that every human being is created to live in trust of the love of God, and to be active in loving others.

A great ship cutting through the waves is passive and active at the same time. It rests in the sea and works to reach its destination. So also a lifeguard swimming out to reach a drowning person passively floats while actively working. I like Marcus Borg's statement in his book, *The Heart of Christianity*, that "Faith as trust is trusting in the buoyancy of God." In such trust we don't need to waste our energy in unnecessary efforts to hold ourselves up but can give our attention and our selves to the business of doing good.

Jesus invites us to come to him and to find rest (see Matthew 11:28-30). We are not to live like the white-knuckled airline passenger who said following a flight, "I never let my weight down once!" Dr. Alvin Rogness often invited people to "rest back in the arms of God." But let's never forget that Jesus also commands us to go for him and get to work. (See Matthew 28:18-20.)

This, I believe, is how we are all designed to live — resting in love and working to love.

Affirmation for the Day:
When carried by love, I am free to care for others.

January 21

"We don't make the beans grow by pulling on them."

This statement has stuck in my mind ever since I heard it from psychiatrist Paul Kersten during my internship in Fort Dodge, Iowa, nearly fifty years ago. Kersten reminded us that personal growth can't be coerced. We can sometimes coerce behavior but we can't coerce attitudes, beliefs, and feelings.

When helping to put together a piece of machinery back on the farm, Dad would sometimes say, "Don't force it or you may break it." How many machines and how many people have been broken by unwise and excessive use of force?

The wise gardener in Jesus' parable didn't pull on the branches of the fruitless fig tree. He chose instead to "dig about it and put on manure." (See Luke 13:6-9.) So, too, with human beings — healthful growing and fruitful living come from tender caring and abundant nurture and not from forced coercion.

Affirmation for the Day:

In dealing with beans, machines, and people, I will refrain from excessive, and usually futile, pulling and pushing.

January 22

"Never steal less than a million dollars — to do so is an insult to your character."

Those words were part of the "fifth step" confession of a member of Alcoholics Anonymous. He was a tobacco salesman who, like most of the sales force, had been violating company rules by smoking the samples. When he was a little boy, his father had given him that "Never steal less than a million ..." rule and he now felt guilty and cheap for having failed to keep it. In his "fourth step" reflections he had realized that petty thievery witnessed to a flaw in his character.

If that rule were adjusted for inflation and universally practiced, there would be little thievery in the world. A few fat cats would still be vulnerable but most of us would be home free without ever having been tempted to thievery.

Lest this thought be understood to bless theft of mega-millions, we should note that such stealing by the rich for whom it provides nothing they need, reveals an even more profoundly flawed character and lack of both wisdom and morality.

Affirmation for the Day:

When tempted to theft, large or small, I will remember what stealing will reveal concerning my character.

January 23

Never drink when you need a drink.

"Some folks are so dry," as Phil Hansen liked to say, "that they are a fire hazard." Others use drinks containing alcohol as a beverage because they enjoy it. Then there are others who use it as a drug.

The road to alcoholism begins when someone says or thinks, "I need a drink," and reaches for the bottle. There would be few, if any, alcoholics in the world if nobody ever drank because they needed it!

Therefore, when stressful days and harried lives tempt us to medicate ourselves with alcohol, or with any other drug for that matter, let's remember this rule: When we need it as a drug, let's not touch it!

When we don't need it as a drug we can enjoy it, in moderation, as a beverage.

There is an old saying that doctors who treat themselves have a fool for a doctor. When we seek to solve our personal, emotional, family, and work problems by "prescribing" alcohol, or other drugs, for ourselves we are among such fools.

Affirmation for the Day:
Since I don't want to become an alcoholic, I will never drink when I *need* a drink.

January 24

Thought for the Day:
We can be wrong when we are right.

Many marriages and friendships have come to grief because someone was more concerned about being right than being kind. Imagine a marital argument in which one spouse has the right facts and information but, at the same time, has attitudes and actions that are wrong. Perhaps the person is arrogant and unkind. To tell the truth without kindness can be as wrong as to unnecessarily withhold the truth in the name of being kind.

Since we are often unaware of the impact of our attitudes and actions this touches upon a frightening fact. We see our faces in a mirror, but we neither see nor objectively hear our facial and tonal expressions in intense conversation. Were we to see and hear close-up movies of some of our interpersonal exchanges we might be shocked and even sickened by the experience. Awareness of the possibility that we can be very wrong in our attitudes while being right in our opinions can help save us from the arrogant self-righteousness that poisons many of our relationships.

Affirmation for the Day:
When most convinced of being right, I will seek to be most resistant to temptations to be arrogant and self-righteous.

January 25

Pray and practice the "Serenity Prayer."

Reinhold Niebuhr's theological, social, and political thought influenced thousands but his little "Serenity Prayer" has affected millions. Adopted by Alcoholics Anonymous and adapted slightly, it is taught, prayed, and practiced by "Twelve-Step" programs and by similar recovery groups around the world. As Niebuhr originally prayed it, it goes like this: "God, give us grace to accept with serenity the things that cannot be changed, the courage to change the things that should be changed, and the wisdom to distinguish the one from the other."

As I ponder that prayer, I think our greatest failure is in our acceptance of changeable things we think cannot be changed. To cite a trivial, but illustrative, example: I sat in my office on a hot summer day years ago visiting with a parishioner while a squeaking fan provided a little breeze for our comfort. "Why don't you oil that fan?" the parishioner asked. "I can't," I replied. "It has sealed bearings." "Are you sure about that?" he responded. "Let's have a look." Although embarrassed by my revealed ignorance I was pleased to discover that the fan could be oiled and in a few minutes the squeaks were gone.

We certainly need wisdom to stop knocking our heads against impenetrable stone walls but more often, I think, we need to get busy changing things we had considered unchangeable.

Affirmation for the Day:
I will seek to live, as well as to pray, the "Serenity Prayer."

January 26

"All the water in the world can't sink a ship unless it gets inside."

For several years, all of our children and grandchildren have lived in homes in south Minneapolis that are under some of the flight patterns of the international airport. During outdoor picnics in their backyards our conversations are sometimes interrupted by the sound of jets taking off and landing.

This is troubling to us, but they have adjusted to it so well that they no longer seem to experience much distraction or distress. Our children's and grandchildren's composure reminds me of the truth of our thought for today. Distractions around us don't always have to create distress within us.

It's never easy, and it's sometimes unwise, to be tranquil in the midst of trouble. It is especially difficult to deal with chronic irritations that we can't change. But as Reinhold Niebuhr's famous "Serenity Prayer" suggests, we can accept unpleasant unchangeables "with serenity" instead of endless, internal distress.

Affirmation for the Day:

When sailing on rough seas, I will seek to keep the troubled waters from getting inside.

January 27

Thought for the Day:

Treasure the privilege of being part of a caring community.

Today's thought strikes me most forcefully, not while standing in the pulpit, but when sitting in the pew. When in church as a parishioner I often find myself looking around at the congregation with gratitude for the privilege of being part of a caring community. In my experience, the most caring have been those that are most centered in Jesus.

I know that we are a motley bunch and am quite well acquainted with the foibles and frailties in each of our lives. We gather on Sunday morning as very ordinary people but, at the same time, there is something very special about people who come together to look to Jesus and seek to learn from him how to live.

When our Chinese friends, with whom we had attempted to teach English while volunteering in China, were about to return home after three months in this country, we asked them to tell us about what most surprised and impressed them. At the top of their list was their experience of visiting several Christian congregations. This was new to them, and they were amazed by the vitality of such voluntary communities. They confessed to being moved by the experience and expressed the hope of finding something similar when they were back home in China. We easily take caring community for granted or even brush it off as dull and old fashioned but for them it was new and exciting.

Affirmation for the Day:

When I stop to think about it, I am deeply grateful for the privilege of being part of a caring community.

January 28

God gave each of us two ears and one mouth and we should take the hint.

I don't know who said it but I know that talkers like me need to be frequently reminded to take that hint. I am sure that I have gotten into trouble and misunderstanding more than once because I was talking when I should have been listening.

There is a verse that reminds us to "be quick to listen, slow to speak" (James 1:19). That is ancient advice but it is as up-to-date as our next conversations. It reminds me of a lesson my mother taught me. When I was about to meet some people I didn't know and wondered, "What in the world will we have to talk about?" she replied, "Just get acquainted! Ask about who they are, where they live, what they do, and what they have done. Invite them to tell you about themselves."

When practiced out of a sincere desire to listen and to learn and not as rigid interrogation, that is a great way to start and sustain a conversation. If the other person never reciprocates by making some similar inquiries, the conversation may become one-sided but that is far better than the awkward silence that happens when nobody is smart enough, or cares enough, to make some gentle inquiries.

When we practice what James and my mother teach us, we will learn more and speak less and will likely have more significant things to say when we are speaking. Such listening is an act of wisdom and love.

Affirmation for the Day:

Since people really are interesting, I will seek to listen to and learn from as many as I can.

January 29

Compliments often affect more change than criticisms.

Positive praise of virtues and negative complaints about vices often have a similar effect — they cause the virtue or vice to grow. Complimenting children for being polite and considerate will usually make them become more so. Telling them that they are inconsiderate slobs will provide a label that they may live up to all the more. Apparently, a negative identity is better than none at all. We often will be as we are labeled.

Gratitude affects more change than griping. Gripes are often interpreted as attacks, which make us stubborn and defensive. We dig in our heels and, in self-preservation, refuse to change. When the pressure is removed and we feel accepted as we are, we are free to change.

Coercive efforts to force changes in behavior are notoriously ineffective. Growth comes most often not through exhortation, but through affirmation and encouragement. Years ago, my colleague, Betty Fousek, shared an article on business management that told those who supervised employees that "Every negative criticism should be accompanied by at least seven positive affirmations." I am not sure about the ratio of positive to negative, but I strongly affirm the notion that the positives should significantly outweigh the negatives.

To be sure, honest confrontation is sometimes necessary. Alcoholics are not cured by coddling. None of us would kindly let a child who didn't want to go to the hospital die of a ruptured appendix.

Affirmation for the Day:

I will sometimes use tough-love confrontation but will often use tender-love affirmation.

January 30

When complimenting, say either "I am" or "You are." When complaining, say only "I am."

If today's thought seems confusing imagine some conversations between a married couple. A happy spouse can compliment by saying either "You are terrific!" or "I am thankful to be with you." But it is far wiser for a complaining spouse to say "I am angry" than to say "You are stupid!'

When complaining, the "I am" statement is a confession of personal feeling that invites conversation and may evoke a mutual "I am" of anger or regret. The critical "You are" statement is an attack on the person that is more likely to create defensiveness and counterattack. With either expression, the content of the message is essentially the same, but the response and the effect on the relationship of a confession instead of an attack are often far better.

Affirmation for the Day:

When my feelings are negative, I will be a confessor, not an attacker.

46

January 31

"You haven't had much experience working with someone like this, have you?"

I once counseled with Professor William Smith of Luther Seminary concerning difficulties I was having in a staff relationship. After hearing my story, his first comment was our thought for today, and I share it with you for two reasons.

First, it reminds us of the fact that none of us has sufficient experience to know how to deal wisely with the diversity of people and situations we encounter in life. We need to learn from the experience and insights of others and should be honest and open enough to seek it.

Second, counseling with Professor Smith also taught me, in a personal way that I could never have learned from a textbook, that such conversation can be extremely helpful. Advice columnists often encourage their readers to seek counseling and I have no idea how many do so and are helped by it. I only know that my counseling with Professor Smith, which included my acceptance of the truth of our Thought for the Day, was very helpful to me.

Affirmation for the Day:

When perplexed by people and problems beyond my experience and understanding, I will seek the wisdom of others.

February 1

"The only titles permitted here are 'brother' and 'sister.'"

Years ago, I attended a corporate spiritual retreat, called an Ashram, led by E. Stanley Jones. During the introduction, Jones told us, "At this meeting please check your titles at the door. You may be used to being called doctor, professor, pastor, reverend, bishop, or whatever, but we don't use such titles here. They indicate differences in status with some ranking higher and lower than others. Here we affirm equality. Therefore, the only titles we permit are 'brother' and 'sister.' They remind us that we are all equal."

I shared this in a sermon at University Lutheran Church of Hope and one of the members, thereafter, called me "Brother Lowell" which was just fine with me.

Jesus, as well as Jones, had something to say along these lines. He spoke of those who loved "to have people call them rabbi" and went on to say:

> But you are not to be called rabbi, for you have one teacher, and you are all students. And call no one your father on earth, for you have one Father — the one in heaven. Nor are you to be called instructors, for you have one instructor, the Messiah.
>
> — Matthew 23:8-10

Titles may have their place, but not in communities where all are equal.

In the community of Christ, I am highly honored to be a brother or sister.

February 2

"Look at people and wish them well."

Today's suggestion comes from Dr. John Brantner, a former professor of psychology at the University of Minnesota, who made it very specific, personal, and practical. For example, he encouraged that when sitting in a clinic waiting room we should look around at others waiting to see their doctors and in our thoughts wish each of them well. If we should strike up a conversation with the people next to us, we might even put it into words, saying as they leave for their appointments, "It was good to visit. I wish you well."

Such thinking strikes me as reflecting the caring compassion of Jesus. To love is to will and to work for the good of another. We can love those we don't like, but it is hard to like those we don't love. Making a habit of Brantner's suggestion seems to be an excellent first step toward both loving and liking.

Affirmation for the Day:
With whomever I am, I will seek to practice the art of loving by looking at people and wishing them well.

February 3

Don't play games with names.

Have you had the experience of meeting someone you haven't seen for a long time who begins the conversation by saying, "Hi, you remember me?" and then launches into a lively discussion while you are trying desperately to recall the person's name? After meeting hundreds of people while visiting a different church or two almost every Sunday during my years as bishop I have had such experiences many times and have often been forced to say, "I remember you, but please remind me of your name."

I have always been grateful for people like Jack Parry, a member of University Lutheran Church of Hope, who greeted me with "Hi, I'm Jack Parry" every time we met for at least six months. Needless to say, I've never forgotten his name! Some think it is arrogant to say their names or to wear a name tag. I think it is far more prideful for us to think that we are so important that no one could ever fail to recognize us or forget our names.

Affirmation for the Day:
I will be humble enough to help people remember who I am.

February 4

Dare to let up a little.

Theodor Bovet, author of *A Handbook on Marriage*, wrote long ago that when a husband and a wife have a big argument each may be convinced of being 100 percent right. But, if one is "honest enough to admit to being two percent wrong, the argument is often 100 percent over."

Visualize that argument by imagining two people pulling on a rope in a tug of war while each leans far over the opposite sides of a little boat. What needs to happen to get them back into the boat safe and dry? If either pulls too hard or lets go, one or both will be in the lake. But if one lets up a little and the other wants to stay dry that person must also let up a little. Then, if they continue that process through a series of mutual *letting-up-a-little* moves, they will soon be back into the boat together.

Affirmation for the Day:
When arguments get tense and intense, I will look for ways of being honestly able to let up a little.

February 5

Be vulnerable.

During my years of parish ministry, I photocopied an article, now misplaced, by an author, now forgotten, that I gave to couples preparing for marriage and sometimes used in marriage counseling. The one thing I remember about that article is its title, "Be Vulnerable." I continue to believe it is advice worth remembering.

We would like to be invulnerable — to be spared the anxieties, pains, sufferings, and sorrows of life. But that cannot be, and it is especially impossible for those who choose to love and to be loved.

To love and be loved is to experience the sufferings as well as the joys of the beloved. It is to stand by the bed of a sick child, to hold the hand of a dying spouse, and in hundreds of other ways to be vulnerable to pain and suffering.

To love and be loved is also to open our lives to the greatest of human joys. But joy never comes alone. My wife, Carol, and I began our *Be Good to Each Other* book on marriage with "We wish you joy" followed immediately by a section titled "We promise you trouble." We might have said, "We promise you suffering," for when we love we are vulnerable and in our vulnerability experience both great joy and great suffering.

Affirmation for the Day:
Although it is risky business, I will dare to be vulnerable in loving and being loved.

February 6

"In times of conflict be tough on principles but gentle with people."

Roger Fisher, the author of *Getting to Yes*, put much emphasis on today's thought. For example, he underscored the importance of commitment to the principle of fairness. As a negotiator in situations of intense conflict, he affirmed strong and, if necessary, stubborn insistence that the conflicted parties treat each other fairly.

At the same time, he also underscored the importance of being kind and gentle with people. This included avoidance of personal attacks and accusations, snide and sarcastic comments, and the maligning of people's motives. He encouraged adversaries to thank and compliment each other at every honest opportunity.

Affirmation for the Day:

Like the once-famous character in an ancient ad, I will seek to be "Tough, But Oh So Gentle."

February 7

"Hold each other tightly with an open hand."

I heard today's thought long ago at an open meeting of Emotions Anonymous. The person was speaking of life together in our families and friendships and most specifically of parents relating to their children. After several others had spoken of the frustrations and problems of living with teenagers, she made her little speech about the importance of "holding each one tightly with an open hand," and I have never forgotten it.

Our challenge in parenting and other relationships is to live out, with some balance, both sides of that paradox. To hold tightly with a closed hand would be stifling; to hold loosely with an open hand would reveal lack of both caring and control. We sometimes err by giving our kids too much freedom when they are little and then trying to clamp down when they are older. The ideal for parenting is to keep holding tightly with love that never lets go, while at the same time, gradually opening the hand of control so our children are able to have more freedom and assume greater responsibility.

Affirmation for the Day:
In life together, I will seek to be caring without being excessively controlling.

February 8

Beware of blind spots and sore spots.

We all have optical blind spots. To illustrate this, place a couple of dots about three inches apart on a piece of paper. Close your left eye and keep your right eye focused on the left dot. Hold the paper close to your face and then move it farther away; you will discover that there is a point at which the right dot disappears. You will be able to see the surrounding area but the right dot will be gone.

In a similar way we all have intellectual blind spots. There are things that we don't see. How often have we said to someone, "I don't see what you are getting at"? When that happens we need to, figuratively, open both eyes and take another look, or to ask the person to help us see it from a different perspective.

We also have sore spots in our minds and emotions as well in our bodies. To make a personal confession I think that I can handle most conflict and controversy pretty well but I think that I am sometimes excessively sensitive to some kinds of criticism. Although it is dangerous to psychoanalyze oneself, I think that this sensitivity comes at least in part from life with my father who was a wonderful dad, but who was sometimes excessively critical. I remember, for example, working on certain projects secretly when he wasn't around to criticize.

Others may have sore spots quite different from our own. In intimate relationships like marriage and the family, it is helpful to tell each other about our sore spots so that we can be more understanding of one another. Such sharing may also help with our healing.

Affirmation for the Day:
Awareness of my blind and sore spots will help me see more clearly and feel more correctly.

February 9

In matters of taste there is no disputing.

Our thought for today, which I first heard in Latin (*De gustibus non est disputandum*), and another that is like it — "It is futile to argue with feelings" — are well worth pondering. Keeping them in mind can help spare us from a lot of senseless and often hurtful argument. If you love cooked spinach and I can't stand it, what is there to argue about? If you confess to feeling angry or upset, what good does it do for me to say "You shouldn't feel that way!"?

It can certainly be helpful for mutual understanding for us to tell of our tastes and feelings. Such sharing enables understanding and empathy. But to get into conflict over such differences is almost always hurtful, unnecessary, and unwise.

Affirmation for the Day:
I will seek to respect the tastes and feelings of others and will encourage them to respect mine.

February 10

"Humility is not thinking less of ourselves than of other people, it is not thinking of ourselves one way or the other at all."

This thought from William Temple reminds us that true humility is not self-depreciation but self-forgetfulness. Self-depreciating humility and arrogant superiority have something in common. They are both saturated with self-centeredness and self-preoccupation. Those who think of themselves as being worse than others or better than others are only thinking about themselves.

We can't achieve humility by trying to be humble. True humility happens when we lose ourselves in caring for someone in need or in commitment to a project or cause that is beyond and often much bigger than ourselves. Such humility is not achieved by self-centered trying; it is received as a byproduct of loving, grateful living.

Affirmation for the Day:

I will give up trying to be humble or pretending to be humble and focus instead on people who need me and on causes bigger than my own self-interest.

February 11

"Always be reading something you couldn't have written yourself."

This suggestion from Professor Paul Scherer of Union Theological Seminary in New York, referred to both the perspective and difficulty of things he encouraged us to read. He didn't discourage us from reading things that were easy and affirming of our own convictions, but he warned us against settling with that.

He urged us to read the opinions of those with whom we were in disagreement and to wrestle with writings of such profundity and depth that we had trouble understanding them, let alone having been able to have written them ourselves. Such reading, Scherer said, is essential for life-long learning and growing.

Affirmation for the Day:
I will discipline myself to read things that di
from my opinions and are difficult to underst

February 12

"Seek simplicity and distrust it."

Alfred North Whitehead presented this maxim as "the guiding motto in the life of every natural philosopher" and I believe it is good counsel for ordinary folk as well.

Someone has said that "There are simple solutions to most of life's complex problems and most of them are wrong!" There are times when simple words, such as those asking or receiving forgiveness, or simple deeds as unexpected acts of love, serve to resolve long-lasting grudges and unresolved conflicts. Years of sound reflection and mathematical calculation sometimes result in something as simple sounding as "$e=mc^2$." But most complex problems in life as well as in mathematics require complex and sometimes agonizingly difficult solutions.

We certainly err when we fail to see and then clearly express the simple realities of life, and thereby create unnecessary complexity and confusion. But we also err when we oversimplify and fail to recognize the complex realities of life.

Affirmation for the Day:
I will seek to avoid both "overcomplexification" and oversimplification.

February 13

Many things worth doing are worth doing poorly.

This thought stands against the notion that "Anything worth doing is worth doing well." That's a great saying. It is good advice for careless people who specialize in shoddy work. Our Thought for the Day is certainly not for them.

Today's thought is for perfectionists who are living under the tyranny of impossible ideals. It is for those for whom nothing is ever good enough.

If we are such people, we need to be reminded that there really are lots of things that are better done poorly than not at all. It is certainly better, to cite a couple of obvious examples, for a parent who is a poor cook to feed the children than to let them starve, and for a person with poor spelling and penmanship to write a scratchy note to a friend than never to write at all. If we are obsessive-compulsive perfectionists we need a measure of what someone has called "the courage of imperfection." Without it, we can become paralyzed and do little or nothing at all.

Affirmation for the Day:

While seeking to do most things well, I will be content to do some things poorly.

February 14

"Life by the inch is a cinch. Life by the yard is hard."

This line from E. Stanley Jones reminds me of a chapel sermon by Professor Lowell Satre who taught Greek and New Testament at Luther Seminary. His text was just a few words from Jesus: "Yet today, tomorrow and the next day I must be on my way ..." (Luke 13:33), and his theme was "On Learning to Plod."

Satre illustrated his point by telling of his own experience in completing the requirements for his doctor's degree. He confessed that at the beginning of his doctoral studies he saw multiple tasks and hurdles to be overcome that seemed at times beyond achievement. That's when he learned to plod, to take one thing at a time until little by little over several years the task was accomplished. In thirteen corny words, E. Stanley Jones' aphorism makes the same point.

Affirmation for the Day:

By plodding inch-by-inch, day-by-day, my work will get done.

February 15

Thought for the Day:

There are times to laugh at both ourselves and the devil.

Al Rogness liked to tell the story of a courageous Norwegian pastor who rowed across a stormy fjord to spend the night with a dying parishioner. While rowing home at dawn, he was struck by the thought that word of his compassionate courage would get out and that the congregation and the community would soon be talking about what a wonderful pastor he is. His next thought was of how sinful he was to have such self-centered thoughts. After a few moments of guilt he went on to think of how morally sensitive and spiritually mature he must be in order to be so honestly aware of his sinfulness.

That story reminds us there is no self-centered way out of our self-centeredness. The best we can do is to join the apostle Paul in saying, "Wretched man that I am! Who will rescue me from this body of death?" (Romans 7:24). Then we need to go on to say "Thanks be to God through Jesus Christ our Lord" (Romans 7:25). Embraced by God's love and power, we can laugh at ourselves and the devil, and then quit taking either one more seriously than reality deserves.

Affirmation for the Day:

My repentance will sometimes be with laughter, sometimes with tears.

February 16

Thought for the Day:

"Our trust is created by those in whom we have it."

This thought from Harry Emerson Fosdick reminds us that we do not trust by trying. If someone says, "I am going to try to trust my spouse today" we know that something has gone wrong in the marriage. We trust people because they have given evidence of being trustworthy.

So also with trust in God. Our trust, as Luther liked to say, is "born of the gospel." It is created by the promises of God's love and faithfulness that are assured to us above all in Jesus to whom we look as "the pioneer and perfecter of our faith" (Hebrews 12:2).

To be sure, there is risk in trusting. When trusting God and trusting people we are sometimes like a parachute jumper who is less than 100 percent certain of landing safely, but who, nevertheless, dares to jump trusting life and limb to the parachute. Day by day, enabled by promises of trustworthy love, we make similar leaps of faith as we entrust ourselves to people and to God.

Affirmation for the Day:

I am grateful for trustworthy people and above all for a trustworthy God, who in Jesus invites, creates, and sustains my trust.

February 17

"God has not promised that we will never be disturbed, distressed, or troubled. But God has promised that we will never be overcome."

Today's thought from Julian of Norwich is another reminder that trouble is part of our life experience. It comes with the territory whether we are Christian, pagan, or whatever. And, since God has never promised to spare us from it, we should never take trouble as a sign that God has forsaken or ceased to love us.

The hymn, "Children of the Heavenly Father," is one of my favorites but its line "from all evil things he spares us" is simply not true. It sets us up for disillusionment and despair. It would be better to sing "in all evil things God loves us" and to trust that whatever happens "we will never be overcome."

Those who follow Jesus are spared some troubles that come from living wrongly but at the same time they encounter others that come from Christlike living. Whoever we are, we encounter a lot of troubles that come to good and bad alike. They are part of life in this troubled world. Our hope is not for trouble-free living but in the promise that none of life's troubles or even death itself can separate us from the love of God (see Romans 8:31-39) who has promised, "I will never fail you nor forsake you" (Hebrews 13:5).

Affirmation for the Day:

When troubles come, I will remember that God's love never leaves.

February 18

"All truth is God's truth."

Although I doubt that it is original with him, I credit today's thought to Howard Hong, who taught philosophy at St. Olaf College. This notion is as simple and as profound as it is significant. It frees us to study science and every other discipline with an openness to welcome every reality it reveals without fearing that such knowledge will undermine true faith in God.

It is, of course, true that new knowledge may undermine some of our cherished beliefs. All truth is not our truth. We all have vast areas of ignorance and if reality were fully revealed, we would discover that we believe lots of things that aren't true. To automatically reject everything that seems contrary to our present beliefs may seem to make us defenders of the faith, but it may really be an insult to God.

Affirmation for the Day:
My trust in God frees me to face the realities of life and of the universe.

February 19

When the light goes on, the bugs gather around the light.

All of us are grateful for light that enables us to live well when surrounded by darkness. I think specifically of an outdoor light that illumines the stairway, walk, or backyard so that we can move safely. Those of us who live in places like Minnesota also experience something else when we turn on that outdoor light in the summertime. In a few minutes a swarm of insects is flying around the light.

Something similar often happens metaphorically speaking. I can think of no better example than that of Jesus who said, "I have come as light into the world, so that everyone who believes in me should not remain in the darkness" (John 12:46). We are thankful that the light of Christ still shines in the darkness of our world, and that the darkness has never been able to overcome it. (See John 1:5.) But at the same time we know there is often a fanatic fringe that swarms around Jesus like bugs around a light. Just think of the snake-handlers, self-mutilators, warring crusaders, and torturers past and present who claim the name of Jesus! Many use Jesus to affirm violence, war, and idolatrous nationalism. We are embarrassed to be associated with such people, yet we confess the same Lord.

What then are we to do? I can see no other way than to continue to follow Jesus, to witness to the truth as we understand it in Jesus, and perhaps even to be a bit humbled by the thought that some may regard us to be among the bugs circling around his light.

Affirmation for the Day:

I will walk in the light of Christ even when distressed by those who strike me as bugs swarming around him.

66

February 20

Thought for the Day:

"Set your troubled hearts at rest, trust in God always...."

This line from John 14:1, in the translation of the New English Bible, is one of my favorite Bible verses. Jesus' invitation doesn't just invite us to believe things about God, but to rest our troubled hearts in trust of God, not just sometimes, but "always."

"Always" is a little word with a big meaning. It doesn't leave out any moment of life's joys or tragedies, agonies or ecstasies. There may be times when we feel adequate for almost anything. In times of sickness and sorrow we may feel incapable of anything, but whatever we can or cannot do, Jesus reminds us that we can "always" trust in God.

Affirmation for the Day:

God's abiding love evokes my abiding trust.

February 21

Since we don't like being made fun of, we should not make fun of others.

Some comedians specialize in put-down humor. Some of it is funny and we laugh at it but I doubt that many of us enjoy put-down humor when it is directed at ourselves. Even if we are wise enough to laugh at ourselves, none of us likes to be ridiculed and made fun of.

Therefore, if we believe in following the golden rule by treating others the way we like to be treated, we will seek to eliminate put-down humor from our conversations. When tempted to make a demeaning wisecrack we will keep silent or, even better, make a comment of affirmation or encouragement. Creative "lift-ups" are far wiser and more life-giving than sarcastic and often hurtful "put-downs."

Affirmation for the Day:
I will seek to speak to, and of, others as I wish they would speak to, and of, me.

February 22

Never look down on anybody.

At the close of a long series of counseling sessions with a wonderful, talented, and also deeply troubled person, I was both surprised and gratified to be told, "Thank you, I never felt that you looked down on me."

The surprise came from awareness that I had absolutely no reason to look down on such a person. We were pilgrims together on the road of life and I was honored to have been entrusted to share some of that person's joy and anguish. Therefore, I was also moved to say, "Thank you for sharing some of your life with me."

It was, of course, gratifying to be told that I had apparently avoided being condescending but that was hardly a virtue on my part. Had I felt superior, it would have been a sin for which I should rightly have felt guilty.

Affirmation for the Day:
I will refrain from looking down on anyone and especially not on hurting, suffering people.

February 23

Be kind to those "too unhappy to be kind."

In one of his poems A. E. Housman shares his understanding of those who:

> *Are not in plight to bear,*
> *If they would, an other's care.*
> *They have enough as 'tis: I see*
> *In many an eye that measures me*
> *The mortal sickness of a mind*
> *Too unhappy to be kind.*

Although I don't think that we can credit all the world's un-kindness to unhappy minds, they are certainly a contributing fac-tor. Some people are so burdened with their personal problems that they have little energy or compassion left to care for others. We may think, perhaps correctly, that they would be much better off and far more happy if they would forget their problems and do something to help others. But that can be a cruel prescription to lay on hurting, unhappy people.

Their unhappiness may come from sickness of mind and body or from pains and problems that crowd out joy and gladness. Paul Tournier wrote long ago that it is difficult for the healthy to fully empathize with the sick, and the strong with the weak. It is easy to be judgmental. It is truly difficult to be understanding.

Affirmation for the Day:
I will try to be understanding and gentle with those who are "too unhappy to be kind."

February 24

"Pick your battles carefully."

This bit of advice was given to me by David Preus in our first visit after I succeeded him as pastor of University Lutheran Church of Hope.

As I think of it now, it reminds me of a saying attributed to Benjamin Franklin — "Before you marry, keep your eyes wide open. After you marry, keep your eyes half shut."

Franklin encouraged those considering marriage to approach it with wide-eyed awareness concerning what they were getting into. But once married, they were to ignore and overlook all kinds of things that aren't worth arguing about and hassling over. Such wisdom applies to much of life in addition to marriage. We are wise to save our attention and energy for dealing not with trivia but with things that really matter.

Affirmation for the Day:

In all of life, I will focus on the vital and refrain from fussing over the trivial.

February 25

"Practice the art of standing in other people's shoes."

My first recollection of today's thought is from a talk given by Dr. Fredrik Schiotz when I was a student at St. Olaf College. Most of us have probably heard it in various forms, perhaps most often from the line attributed to Native American wisdom that admonishes us not to criticize anyone "until we have walked at least a mile in that person's moccasins."

As I think of it now, I am prompted to make a double suggestion. First, to practice it when we meet or hear about people with whom it would be difficult for us to deal. In such situations, it is well for us to ask, "If I were that person how would I feel toward me?" and "If I were that person how would I want to be treated by me?"

My second suggestion is to make a list of people who are significantly different from ourselves. For example, as a white, male, married, middle-class, Lutheran, heterosexual American, I can practice the art of standing in other people's shoes by wondering what it would be like if I were black, a woman, or single, or homeless, or Islamic, or gay, or Palestinian, or Israeli, or whatever. We could have been born into circumstances that shaped us into people far different from the people we are today. If we would then desire understanding and respect from those like the person we are today, it is certainly well that we should now seek such understanding and express such respect for others who are different from ourselves.

Affirmation for the Day:

I pray for empathy to feel what others feel, insight to see what others see, and for the wisdom and compassion to relate appropriately.

February 26

Thought for the Day:
"They are hurting more than I am."

Today's thought comes from Doctor Jurgen Moller who was our friend and family doctor during our decade in Farmington, Minnesota. He told me how he had been awakened early one morning (shortly after having fallen asleep after being up half the night delivering a baby) by a phone call from an anxious person with an exceedingly minor medical problem. When I asked how he could be patient with such people he replied, "I try to remember that they are hurting more than I am."

He went on to speak of how important it is for doctors, pastors, and everyone else for that matter, to be gentle with hurting people. He spoke specifically of how difficult it was for him to deal with hypochondriacs who pestered him with calls and visits concerning their imagined afflictions. But "I remind myself," he said, "that hypochondriacs also get sick and die, and that this time the illness might be real." He also confessed that when dealing with such people he often thought of the old joke about a hypochondriac who arranged for the words "I told you I was sick!" to be engraved on his tombstone.

Affirmation for the Day:
I, too, will seek to be gentle with hurting people.

February 27

Thought for the Day:

My freedom to swing my fists ends where your nose begins.

We pride ourselves on our personal and national freedom and grieve for those who lack it.

Over against the fears and legalisms that would enslave us we rejoice that "for freedom Christ has set us free" and take to heart the apostle Paul's encouragement, "Stand firm, therefore, and do not submit again to a yoke of slavery" (Galatians 5:1).

At the same time, we remember that Paul went on to say, "You are called to freedom, brothers and sisters; only do not use your freedom as an opportunity for self-indulgence, but through love become slaves to one another" (Galatians 5:13). That statement expresses what our Thought for the Day seeks to visualize. We are not free to live in ways that are hurtful to others, or even to ourselves. Luther emphasized this fact when he said that in Christ we are the most free, subject to none, and the most bound, subject to all.

Affirmation for the Day:

I rejoice in freedom to be loved and to love, but not to hurt.

February 28

Don't criticize another's viewpoint until you can state it to that person's satisfaction.

Sidney Harris tells us that Lord Acton said a long time ago that one has no right to attack or oppose a contrary view until one can express that view not only as well as but better than its proponents can. In other words, not until we can make a better case for the opposition than it has made out for itself can we be sure that we are knocking down a live enemy rather than a straw man.

I am not sure that it is always necessary to be able "make out a better case" for an opponent's view before criticizing it, but I am sure that we need to be able to describe it clearly enough to evoke a "That's it, you've got it right!" If we can't do that we should back off and do some more listening and learning. If we are deliberately distorting someone's viewpoint we need to be confronted, corrected, and moved to repentance.

Some of the most flagrant violations of such basic fairness and honesty occur in election campaigns where the candidates' primary motivation is too often not to inform or educate but to denigrate another and to elevate oneself. In this regard campaign speeches are a strange breed of rhetoric. The vote-getter's goal is to get people to like them and to dislike their opponents. The result is often deliberate distortion of opponents' viewpoints and failure to honestly discuss their real positions and actual differences.

Affirmation for the Day:

In argumentation, as in all of life, I will seek to be informed, honest, and fair.

February 29

"Come back and sit down!"

Today's thought comes with a story during the Vietnam War. Several faculty members of Luther Seminary met weekly to share personal concerns and pray together. Dr. Edmund Smits had lived under the Soviet occupation of Latvia and had an intense fear and disdain of communism. We held opposing views concerning the Vietnam War. He believed that, like Christ going to the cross, the United States could save the world from godless communism. I thought we were on the wrong side of a war of national liberation.

During one meeting, Dr. Smits became so upset that he got up to walk out of the room which prompted our leader, Bill Smith, to exclaim, "Edmund! Come back and sit down!" Like an obedient child, Dr. Smits turned around, came back, and sat down. We talked some more and then joined hands and prayed together. Over the years we held our differing opinions but never broke our relationship, and again prayed together in the hospital before he died.

There always seem to be some people in the church who talk about leaving over one thing or another. Among current conflicts are differences concerning abortion, war, and homosexuality. If any start to walk out over these issues, I hope that someone will exclaim as did Bill Smith, "Come back and sit down!" and that they will respond like Dr. Smits. When that happens, we affirm our unity in Christ, our acceptance of diversity of opinion, and our respect for one another.

Affirmation for the Day:
I affirm a church so centered and united in Christ that we can talk, work, and pray together in spite of serious differences over significant issues.

March 1

If necessary, count to 1,000.

We've all been encouraged to "count to ten" to avoid responding with hurtful, impulsive anger. Thomas Jefferson gives us advice that goes far beyond that. He is reported to have said, "If you lose your temper, count up to ten before you do or say anything. If you haven't calmed down, then count to 100; and if you have not calmed down after this, count up to 1,000."

That advice reminds me of Jesus' encouragement to "forgive seventy times seven" (Matthew 18:22). Interpreters tell us that means that we should never stop forgiving. In the same spirit, Jefferson's advice can be understood that we should never stop counting until the passion of a vengeful, hot temper has cooled sufficiently to enable us to make a calm, rational response.

It's been said that some people "marry in haste and repent in leisure." If that can be true of marriage it is also true of our spiteful, impulsive speaking and acting. The wisdom of James affirms the wisdom of Jefferson: "You must understand this, my beloved: let everyone be quick to listen, slow to speak, slow to anger; for your anger does not produce God's righteousness" (James 1:19-20).

Affirmation for the Day:
When emotionally upset, I will start counting and refrain from raving.

March 2

Share the good stuff — suppress the bad stuff!

We are all tempted to live the exact opposite of today's thought. When we learn of the misdeeds and misfortunes of others we often receive the news as a "gossiper's gift" and are quick to share it with others. We may be less eager to tell of the virtues and accomplishments of others, especially when they excel our own.

Although it may take concentrated discipline to turn that around, it is certainly worth the effort. We (and our world) would be far better off if each of us took every opportunity to honestly speak well of others and, at the same time, resist the ever-present temptation to become spreaders of negative and often malicious gossip. Here, as in so much of life, the golden rule should be our guide. If we'd like others to tell it about ourselves, we are free to share it. If we'd be displeased by such gossip about ourselves, we should suppress it.

Affirmation for the Day:
I will seek to speak of others as I would like them to speak about me.

March 3

Beware of delighting in people's criticism of others.

When I was a few months into serving my first parish, I must confess that I took delight in hearing some parishioners tell me about the shortcomings of my predecessor and of how much better they liked me. On the other hand, I was not overjoyed when other parishioners told me about how much they missed my wonderful predecessor who was for them the finest pastor they had ever known.

However, as time went on I began to learn that those who didn't like my predecessor were discovering things they didn't like about me, and that those who most deeply grieved his loss were becoming my most supportive friends and co-workers. In that experience, I learned a lesson I've never forgotten.

Affirmation for the Day:
From now on, I will be grateful for the affirmers and wary of the criticizers.

March 4

Compassion is water on the fire of rage.

Today's thought comes from German philosopher, Arthur Schopenhauer, who died in 1860. He said, "Compassion expressed in response to rage is the same as water for fire. When you are in a rage, try to feel compassion for the other person, and then your rage will disappear."

Note that he does not say that compassion will resolve a conflict or result in agreement in opinion. Transformation by compassion is more emotional than intellectual. Differences remain but rage is reduced if not eliminated altogether.

Compassion literally means "to suffer with." To have compassion is to put ourselves in the place of those who suffer. When someone lashes out in rage against us, we should pause long enough to remember that we are dealing with a hurting person. There may be exceptions, but that is a pretty safe assumption. I agree with someone who said long ago: "Be kind, remember that everyone you meet is having a hard time." We are all troubled people in a troubled world and the most troubled may be those who lack the sensitivity and courage to face and admit it.

Affirmation for the Day:
Every human being is a candidate for compassion.

March 5

Feelings of superiority are a sinful possession.

Long before the abolition of apartheid, a black pastor from South Africa named Mannus Buthelizie preached a sermon at University Lutheran Church of Hope that I have never forgotten. He expressed profound gratitude for the help that he and many had received from white Christians in America. He then went on to say with uncommon candor: "There is, of course, something that white people, including most white Christians, have never given up and that is your position of superiority over us."

An amazing nonviolent revolution brought an end to apartheid but it is no secret that many Caucasians continue to feel superior to Africans. It is now decades since the caste system was abolished in India but many Brahmans still consider themselves far superior to "untouchables." Attitudes die hard and a sense of superiority is certainly among the last things we give up.

In our society, this may be especially true in relation to the wealthy to the poor. We may feel deeply and even give generously but how many of us are willing to surrender our superiority and affirm equality with the poor? We claim to believe in Jesus and to seek to follow in his steps but we certainly don't give of ourselves as he did. Jesus "did not regard equality with God as something to be exploited, but emptied himself taking the form of a slave" (Philippians 2:6-7). By that standard, our attitudes of superiority are certainly sinful.

Affirmation for the Day:

I repent of my arrogant superiority and pray for wisdom and willingness to feel and to act accordingly.

March 6

"All suggestions imply criticism."

We may debate the "all" in this thought from psychologist and author Paul Tournier but it is certainly often, and perhaps even almost always, true. It is especially true when we suggest that someone do something other than what they are doing or intending to do.

We are then saying, in effect, "I think you are wrong" or "Since you are not smart enough to think of it yourself I will tell you what to do." Keeping this in mind helps us understand why others aren't always receptive to, and thankful for, our suggestions.

Awareness of our thought for today should not keep us from ever making suggestions. Even when implying criticism suggestions can often be extremely helpful and be much appreciated. But heeding Tournier's wisdom can help us be more wise and gentle in sharing them.

Affirmation for the Day:
When asked for my wisdom, I will seek to share it kindly.

March 7

Don't quarrel over harmless quirks.

A letter to Ann Landers from "a quirky shrink in North Carolina" encouraged readers to be tolerant of the idiosyncrasies and peculiarities of people. It told, for example, of people who refused to eat off paper plates and "insisted on china even at casual events like picnics" and of a man who " will only drink coffee from a cup with a saucer."

This letter prompted not only Ann's affirmation of tolerance, but also her confession that "my oddball quirk is using lead pencils down to the last two inches" and that "you would not believe what my toothpaste tube looks like before I declare it 'used up.' I suspect living through the Depression had something to do with my selective stinginess." Her confession is a comfort to me because I use pencils the same way and am even more stingy with toothpaste tubes. When I can squeeze out no more, I cut the top off the tube and always discover that there is enough left for a week or more of brushing before I need a new tube.

Although she thinks some of them to be a bit weird, I am thankful that my wife doesn't quarrel over my harmless quirks, and I hope that seeing them in myself helps me to be more tolerant of their presence in others.

Affirmation for the Day:
I will try to refrain from making a big deal over little things that really don't matter.

March 8

It's proper for "has-beens" to be humble.

As a "has-been" pastor, "has-been" seminary professor, and "has-been" bishop, I have learned that the world somehow seems to get along without me. This is a humbling experience. Someone once told me that when we think we are indispensable we should put our hand in a bucket of water and then, after pulling it out, look for a hole in the water. That is certainly an imperfect analogy. I can think of a lot of people whose passing left a hole in my life that was not quickly filled by others, but there is some truth to it.

It is also gratifying that others move in to carry on the work we began, and if we are not totally arrogant and self-centered we should be rightly thankful that some of them can do it even better than we did.

We should all be as observant and as humble as was the apostle Paul who noted that one person lays the foundation and someone else builds upon it, one person plants the seed, another waters, and someone else often brings in the harvest. (See 1 Corinthians 3:5-10.)

Affirmation for the Day:
After completing my work, I will affirm others in doing theirs.

March 9

Thought for the Day:

"Neither overestimate others' knowledge nor underestimate their intelligence."

The advice in today's double thought, which was intended especially for writers and speakers, comes from St. Olaf Professor Arthur Paulson. I believe there is wisdom in both admonitions.

We shouldn't assume that others know everything that we know. I am frequently frustrated, for example, by some theological writers who apparently assume that I am so fluent in German, French, Latin, Greek, and Hebrew that they can sprinkle their writing with quotations from all these languages without a translation. Others assume that I have read everything they have read and frequently refer to the views of people I have never studied without telling me who the people are.

As writers and speakers, I believe that it is wiser for us to underestimate people's knowledge and to overestimate their intelligence. This will save us from both writing and talking over their heads, and from writing and talking down to them. There are many very intelligent people who know a lot that we don't know and are ignorant of a lot we know but which they have never studied. If we interpret such lack of knowledge as a sign of intellectual inferiority it may be more true of us than of them!

Affirmation for the Day:

I will try to refrain from expecting too much of people's knowledge and too little of their intelligence.

March 10

"We need not be great in ourselves to stand for something great."

Harry Emerson Fosdick illustrated today's thought by pointing to an ordinary person carrying the colors of a great country. We should think of that when we see a Girl Scout or Boy Scout with no claim to personal greatness carrying the "Stars and Stripes" during a Fourth of July parade.

Fosdick emphasized that each of has what he called "a representative capacity" and can stand for things far greater than ourselves. We can give ourselves to causes and projects far bigger than our own self-interest and which will continue long after we are forgotten.

Sometimes a creative, courageous act makes someone famous as it did for Rosa Parks, whose refusal to budge from her seat on a bus sparked the civil rights bus boycott, but most often such deeds make no headlines. Nevertheless, they are significant acts that count for time and eternity.

Affirmation for the Day:

When feeling weak and insignificant, I will remember my representative capacity.

March 11

"If we yield to all, we will soon have nothing to yield."

This thought is the moral of Aesop's famous fable that tells of a man who had two wives — one much younger and one much older than himself. The younger wife was distressed that her husband looked old enough to be her father, so at every opportunity she plucked out one of his gray hairs. The older wife feared that her husband would be mistaken for her son and when she had a chance she plucked out one of his dark hairs. After a while, the poor husband was completely bald with no hairs left for plucking.

The obvious point of this fable is that we need to stand for something and to not yield to all the wishes and pressures of those around us.

In cynical contrast to Luther's famous "Here I stand" conviction, I once heard a pastor described as "standing here and there" on a significant, controversial issue. That pastor must have appeared, at least to one observer, to yield to opinions on both sides and to lack personal conviction.

Affirmation for the Day:

While respecting the opinions of others, I will have courage to express my own.

March 12

If you amount to anything in life you won't need to know how to spell.

Today's thought was addressed to my twin brother and me from our uncle, whose wife was our first-grade teacher. I recall that she was angry and criticized him for saying it. I think she was right in her criticism. We should be encouraged to learn how to spell and it is certainly arrogant to imply that good spelling is to be required only of those who are unlikely to "amount to anything in life."

Nevertheless, our thought for today conveys a bit of grace and hope for poor spellers like our daughter who is somewhat dyslexic and has had problems with spelling. She thanked me long ago for sharing today's thought with her. She has had a secretary for years and has been able to concentrate on things even more important than good spelling. Her productive life is a reminder to the "spellingly challenged," and to others with similar minor disabilities, that they need not be obstacles to significant achievement. We can learn to rely on spell-checkers and great spellers and can do amazingly well in spite of this deficiency.

Affirmation for the Day:
In all things, I will remember that limitations need not be liabilities.

March 13

A 99 and 98 in the classroom equals two A's; a 99 and 98 on the basketball court equals one A and one F.

As I watch sports events that are often decided by differences measured in inches and split seconds, I am often reminded of a book called *The Verdict of the Scoreboard* by Ade Christianson, a coach and athletic director at St. Olaf during my student days. His teams played to win. At the same time, he was aware of the fact, as expressed in our thought for today, that the win/lose verdicts of the scoreboard declare some to be victors and others to be failures and unjustly tempt to both pride and despair.

Neither he nor I suggest elimination of win/lose contests, but we both affirm experiences in life, like classes that award more than one A for excellence, that can be win/win instead of win/lose.

Affirmation for the Day:

I will be glad to win and sad to lose but will beware of temptations to both pride and despair.

March 14

Jesus affirms the salvation of non-Christians who trust God's mercy.

When asked if non-Christians can be saved I take my answer from Jesus. In one of his most well-known parables he told of a sinful tax collector who prayed: "God, be merciful to me, a sinner!" He was a Jew who entrusted himself to the mercy of God and Jesus said that he went home forgiven. (See Luke 18:9-14.) The preacher who made headlines a few years ago by declaring that "God doesn't hear the prayers of Jews," needed to learn something from Jesus.

Acts 13:43 tells of Paul and Barnabas encouraging "Jews and devout converts to Judaism ... to continue in the grace of God." Their preaching, like Jesus' parable, teaches me that we are not saved by thinking correctly about Jesus. Texts like "No one comes to the Father but by me" (John 14:6) and "There is no other name ... by which we must be saved" (Acts 4:12) don't mean that salvation is only for those who have correct knowledge and beliefs concerning Jesus. They mean that all are saved who trust God's mercy and grace that we believe to be supremely, but not solely, revealed in Jesus. Intellectualizing correctly about Jesus is a good thing but it is not saving faith. Saving faith is trust in the grace of God.

Affirmation for the Day:

The way of salvation is as wide, and as narrow, as the grace of God.

March 15

We will never meet a person God doesn't love.

I credit this conviction to Jesus and believe that one of its many meanings is that we should tell people that God loves them.

When asked if we should preach the gospel to Jews and adherents of other world religions, I answer that we should preach the gospel to everyone — Christian and non-Christian, religious and nonreligious — always remembering that the gospel says, "God loves you!" not "My religion is better than your religion."

When asked, "How do you preach the gospel to Hindus?" a missionary in India replied, "I don't, I preach the gospel to human beings." That answer doesn't provide guidance concerning specific ways of presenting the gospel meaningfully to Hindus, which may differ from how it is best shared with Presbyterians, Lutherans, or Jews, but it witnesses to a profound truth. The good news of God's love is addressed to every human being. Since God loves all, we are to tell all!

Affirmation for the Day:
I love to tell the story of Jesus and God's love.

March 16

The heart of the universe is warm.

This world and the universe around us can sometimes seem cold and heartless. This is especially true when tragedies strike and we are bowed down by sorrow, illness, unjust suffering, and despair. Then it can seem that the universe is a vast machine that cares no more for us than does a bulldozer that crushes everything in its way.

But then we turn to Jesus and to texts of scripture, such as 1 John 4:16 — "So we have known and believed the love that God has for us. God is love, and those who abide in love abide in God, and God abides in them." Such texts invite us to trust that in spite of all of the evidence to the contrary the heart of the universe beats with the compassion of Christ, and that we are held every moment in the embrace of God's love.

Affirmation for the Day:
When icy winds of tragic circumstance chill my soul, I will continue to rest in the promised warmth of God's love.

March 17

Thought for the Day:
The cross is a present event.

Stanley Jones liked to say, "The cross stood not only one day on the hill of Calvary; the cross stands every moment in the heart of God."

Where God's love meets our sin and suffering there is the place of the cross. The cross of Christ is, therefore, both a historical and an eternal event. "The present," said Paul Tillich, "is the moment when eternity touches time." The present is the moment of God's love. God loves us now in this and every present moment.

The cross of Jesus reveals the cost of loving in a sinful, suffering world and witnesses to the anguish in the heart of God who knows our sin and feels our pains and sorrows and still keeps on loving us.

Affirmation for the Day:
When I think of Jesus on the cross, I will think also of the cross in the heart of God.

March 18

"We don't do the dog a favor by cutting off its tail an inch at a time."

There is wisdom in slow and deliberate decision making. We should always look before we leap. There are problems that can be solved by making many little decisions, like putting together pieces of a jigsaw puzzle.

But there is also wisdom and kindness in today's thought that I learned from my dad years ago. Some problems are solved only by making a clear, clean, sharp decision. We can't go on forever "limping with two different opinions" (1 Kings 18:21). Should I stay in school or go to work? Take a job or leave one? Stay married or get a divorce? Move or stay put?

To answer such questions we need to take time to ponder and pray but not to dillydally. We are wise to remember that refusing to decide is also a decision and that indecision can sometimes be the worst decision. Difficult and painful as it is, decisive action is often better than equivocation.

Affirmation for the Day:

With dogs' tails and life's decisions — a clean cut is often better than repeated hacking.

March 19

"Do what would be well if everybody did it."

Today's thought is an expression of the famous "categorical imperative" of Immanuel Kant that says in more lofty language: "So act that the mode of your action may consistently be made universal."

During summer vacations when our children were young we often went camping together, and they observed that I often went out of my way to pick up litter that was scattered around the campground. When the children asked why I did that, I told them, "I am following the categorical imperative of Immanuel Kant," and explained how much better the campground would look if every camper did as I was doing.

Needless to say, that rule applies also to matters more significant than campground trash. Like the golden rule, which teaches us to treat others as we wish to be treated, it relates to almost every aspect of our personal and corporate life and provides guidance for organizations and nations as well as individuals.

Roger Fisher, co-author of *Getting to Yes*, provides a concrete example when he recommends that negotiators be "unconditionally constructive." When others lie we should still tell them the truth; when they are unkind we should still be kind; when they are unfair we should still be fair. However wrongly others may treat us, we are to treat them rightly. Even when their attitudes and actions are degrading and destructive we are still to be "unconditionally constructive."

Affirmation for the Day:
Before acting, I will ask myself: "Would it be well if everyone did what I am thinking of doing?"

March 20

Don't do what you will likely regret.

A man dying of lung cancer told his pastor that his greatest suffering was not from the physical misery of his illness but from the thought that "If I hadn't been a 'damn fool' cigarette smoker, I would now be looking forward to happy times with my children and grandchildren instead of waiting to die." A decision to resist teenage peer pressure might have been temporarily difficult and quitting smoking after being hooked on nicotine more difficult still, but from the perspective of death's door he had no doubt that the decisions he had made were tragically stupid!

His sad story reminds me that Abraham Lincoln tried to practice what might be called "The art of projected hindsight." In decision making, Lincoln would ask himself, "How will what I am thinking of doing appear to people who look back on it five, ten, twenty years from now?" Of course, he couldn't know for sure but asking that question put the decision in a much wider context and helped avoid impulsive actions that 20/20 hindsight would show to be mistaken.

All of us face significant decisions every day concerning food, alcohol, drugs, study, work, personal relationships, and other aspects of life. Remembering that our choices have consequences for good, or for ill, helps us choose more wisely.

Affirmation for the Day:
I pray for wisdom and strength to make decisions that will result in a maximum of gratitude and a minimum of regret.

March 21

Thought for the Day:
Make decisions that can pass the test of publicity.

It is possible to do some things that are so good that we don't wish others to know about them. For example, anonymous donors of large gifts may do so out of sincere desire to avoid excessive adulation. Others may, of course, prefer anonymity to keep people from knowing how rich they are.

I think it is far more likely that we tend to keep things secret, not because they are so good but because we think that others will view them as being bad or foolish. When tempted, it is well to ask ourselves, "Is this something I'd like others, including my spouse, children, and most respected friends and relatives, to know about?" If not, unless it is one of those rare things that are too good to tell, it flunks the test of publicity and we'd best not do it.

Affirmation for the Day:
When contemplating actions, I will ask if they can stand the light of day.

March 22

Live by the diamond rule.

Jesus taught us to live by the golden rule: "In everything do to others as you would have them do to you" (Matthew 7:12).

We often fall short of that rule and treat others as they treat us. I call that living by the "iron rule." It is contrary to both the golden rule and the proverb that says, "Do not say, 'I will do to others as they have done to me; I will pay them back for what they have done'" (Proverbs 24:29).

Then there are times when we live by what might be called the "acid rule" and treat others worse than they treat us, even to the point of returning evil for good.

As we see ourselves in light of these rules we remember that there is a rule for living that is even higher than the golden rule. I sometimes call it the "diamond rule." Jesus taught it when he said "I give you a new commandment, that you love one another. Just as I have loved you, you also should love one another" (John 13:34). We are to treat others as Jesus treats us. That's the highest rule for living this world has ever known.

Affirmation for the Day:
I pray for compassion to treat others as Jesus treats me.

March 23

Thought for the Day:
Jesus sometimes broke the letter of the law to fulfill the purpose of the law.

Legalists were upset when Jesus healed on the sabbath day and complained when his disciples did unlawful work by harvesting handfuls of grain on the sabbath. To which Jesus replied, "The sabbath was made for humankind, and not humankind for the sabbath" (see Mark 2:23—3:6). Jesus understood that the sabbath rules, and all of God's other commandments, were intended to be a life-giving blessing and not life-denying burden. When the sacred religious laws were imposed as a burden, Jesus broke the letter of the law to fulfill their true purpose and affirmed his disciples in doing the same.

Jesus' understanding was helpful to me when I broke the letter of a church rule by participating in the ordination of Anita Hill who was in a committed same-sex relationship. I understood that the rule, which I had affirmed a decade earlier, was made for the ministry and not the ministry for the rule, and chose to break the letter to fulfill its purpose.

Affirmation for the Day:
I will dare to run a red light if doing so will prevent an accident and perhaps save a life.

March 24

"We can tell the size of people by the size of things that upset them."

This thought from a forgotten source from long ago is still true today. And in light of its truth most of us, beginning with me, are often revealed to be little men and little women. I have noticed, for example, how couples with whom I have counseled have often been able to handle experiences of major crisis far better than the little irritations of daily living. That probably tells us that accumulations of little things aren't so little after all, and it may also say something about ourselves and of our need to grow to be a bit "bigger" in our tolerance of minor matters.

The Bible tells us that we are "born to trouble as surely as birds fly upward" (Job 5:7 REV). Most troubles, however, are manageable in one way or another. In dealing with such irritations and problems, I have often reminded myself and our family that "If we have no worse trouble in life, we will do well."

Years ago, my friend, Sue Wolf, told me that her friend, Paul Arnold, had told her, "Take things seriously but don't catastrophize everything." Most of even our serious problems are not catastrophic. We will survive and, in coming through them, might even become wiser, gentler, and more compassionate.

Affirmation for the Day:
I will encourage my emotions to refrain from majoring in minor, or even major but not catastrophic, miseries.

March 25

We may be called to account for all the proper pleasures we have failed to enjoy.

Some Christians seem to regard all pleasure as inherently sinful. But God is on the side of life and Jesus came to give us life "in all its fullness" (John 10:10 NEB). Rejection of proper pleasures must, therefore, be contrary to the will of God.

There certainly are improper pleasures from which we are to abstain. Among them, for example, are pleasures provided to us at the expense of the misery of others. A tyrant who lives in luxury provided by the service of slaves is not enjoying proper pleasures. Nor are we when our joy comes at the expense of another's misery. As residents of an affluent society we rightly wonder if others are suffering to provide our pleasures.

But avoiding sinful pleasures should not keep us from gratefully receiving all of the joy and pleasure God wants to give us. Failing to do so may be a grievous sin of omission.

Affirmation for the Day:

I will joyfully receive all of the pleasures God wants to give me.

March 26

"The secret of happiness is to enjoy small pleasures."

Today's thought from Samuel Smiles (1812-1904), a Scottish writer and social reformer, struck Leo Tolstoy as a bit of wisdom worth remembering and sharing.

Happiness may certainly come from great events like winning a prize, achieving a goal, falling in love, becoming a parent or grandparent, or being given a special honor or recognition. But for most of us those occasions don't come very often nor do they always provide the kind of ongoing joy that is essential to true happiness.

In that regard, I think that Smiles and Tolstoy have something significant to teach us about the importance of enjoying small pleasures — the taste of an apple or an ice cream cone, the beauty of a sunrise or a sunset, times of meaningful conversation with a friend or a loved one, the sound of a symphony or a favorite song, playing or watching a game, the bracing chill of brisk wind and the warmth and comfort of our bed. Each one of these and thousands more are "small pleasures." Enjoying each one in the daily flow of life is certainly one of the great secrets of happiness.

Affirmation for the Day:
I will seek happiness where it is most commonly found — in the joy of little pleasures.

March 27

Every serve is a new beginning.

After having hardly played at all previously, I have taken up tennis in retirement. I am not a great player but think it is a great game. One thing I like about it is that every serve is a new beginning. It is even possible to be down love-40 and still win the game.

This reminds me that the past may predict but does not determine the future. Every day, like every serve, is a new beginning with at least the possibility of good days following bad days. I once watched Jennifer Capriati win a match 7 - 5 after being down 0 - 5. Unlikely? Yes! Impossible? No!

While visiting with Helen Matthiesen on the occasion of her 102nd birthday, I asked, "How old are you now?" She replied by holding up two fingers and saying, "I'm two years old. I'm starting over again!" Even at that age she knew the possibility and joy of a new beginning.

Affirmation for the Day:
Whatever my age, I will remember that every day is a time for new beginnings.

March 28

Thought for the Day:
"We miss 100 percent of the shots we don't take."

Today's thought comes from the famous hockey player, Wayne Gretsky. It is a fitting reminder especially for people who don't like to take risks. Even the greatest athletes miss a lot of shots. The best baseball players fail to get to first base about two-thirds of the time. Hockey and basketball players, who dare to shoot, know that they will often miss.

But as Gretsky points out, those who don't dare to shoot will fail 100 percent of the time. Prudence wisely restrains us from taking wild and crazy shots, but we are in even bigger trouble if fear keeps us from shooting at all. There are times to say, "Let's go for it! We may fail but we'll never know unless we try."

Affirmation for the Day:
I will remember that it is often better to try and to fail than never to try at all.

March 29

The "Word of God" is not the words of God.

As Christians, we often speak of the Bible as "the Word of God" but those of us who do not believe in a dictation theory of inspiration do not regard the text of the Bible as "the words of God." We believe that the words are human words expressing human understandings of God. I believe this to be true even of passages that present direct quotes from God. They are human interpretations and some may be mistaken. I don't believe, for example, that God told Moses that a man who was caught gathering firewood on the sabbath day should be stoned to death. (See Numbers 15:32-36.)

How then do we know God and God's will for our lives? I believe that "the Word became flesh" in the person of Jesus and that while "no one has ever seen God" Jesus has made God known (see John 1:14-18) and that the human words throughout the Bible that affirm what we see and hear in Jesus really are God's "Word" to us. It was such understanding that enabled Martin Luther to say, in debate with his critics, "If you quote the Bible against Christ, I will quote Christ against the Bible!"

Affirmation for the Day:

I thank God for speaking to me through Jesus and through everything in the Bible that affirms the God, and the way of life, we see in Jesus.

March 30

Biblical criticism does not undermine the biblical witness.

When first introduced to historical and textual criticism of the Bible, I was deeply troubled. If the book of Isaiah had at least three authors, if some of Paul's letters were written by someone else, if Jesus didn't say everything he is quoted as saying, if there are hundreds of variants in biblical manuscripts, how could we trust the Bible to be the source of our faith and life?

I think that it was a mistake to label serious historical and textual study of scripture as "criticism" which creates an instant negative impression, but I don't think we need to be afraid of anything that reveals the truth about the Bible.

Professor John Knox, at Union Seminary in New York, was especially helpful. He pointed out that whatever is discovered concerning the authorship or composition of the New Testament, it still stands as the authentic witness of the Christian community to the gospel by which they lived and died. Even if Paul didn't write Ephesians, it still tells us the great good news that "by grace you have been saved through faith" (Ephesians 2:8). Even if Jesus never said, "I am the light of the world" or "I am the bread of life" (see John 8:12; 6:35), we have the witness of the Christian community that knew that Jesus illuminated their world and sustained their lives. Biblical writers used some literary forms and devices that may seem strange and even dishonest to us but they were not so to them. Their lives had been transformed by a great gospel and they tried to share it in ways that would give it the greatest impact.

Affirmation for the Day:

Whatever its history or authorship, I thank God for the life-giving message of the Bible.

March 31

Let's be honest in teaching Bible stories to children.

Many of us were taught in childhood that the stories about Adam and Eve, Noah's Ark, and Jonah living for three days in the belly of a great fish, were accounts of actual events that happened long, long ago. When we began serious Bible study, perhaps as teenagers but more likely in college or seminary, we had to unlearn what we had been taught. Then we learned that if we took these great stories literally we were not taking them seriously.

I know that it is difficult to teach that a story has a profound and true meaning while not being descriptive of historic events, but I think it is possible. In working with confirmation students, I found it helpful to start with the parables of Jesus and then to talk about how others, like Jesus, told similar stories such as the one about Jonah, that are really Old Testament parables. I would always point out that the Bible tells about many things that really happened but that it also contains some great stories that people created to teach important lessons.

Affirmation for the Day:

I will try to impart learning that doesn't require unlearning.

April 1

"The book of Revelation is a happy hunting ground for all kinds of religious fanatics and half-wits."

Today's blunt thought comes from the British theologian, John Sheldon Whale. He said it in a lecture in which he sarcastically dismissed those who understand the book of Revelation to predict all kinds of present and future events. Some authors have made millions by selling books containing such interpretations to gullible people. They are wrong in believing and teaching that "biblical prophecy is history written in advance." For a correct understanding, I recommend *The Rapture Exposed* by Professor Barbara Rossing of the Lutheran School of Theology in Chicago.

The book of Revelation was written to provide comfort and hope to Christians under persecution. It is a book of great promise that witnesses to the ultimate triumph of God's goodness and grace. It is not a book containing detailed previews of specific events in the modern world. It abounds in complex symbolism and all who seek to understand its meaning do well to consult a responsible commentary written by someone who understands its meaning and the purpose for which it was written.

Affirmation for the Day:

I will read Revelation as a book of promise and not prediction.

April 2

Thought for the Day:

Some of God's best gifts are on the bottom shelf.

I recall Gerhard Frost saying that for many years he thought that God's best gifts were on the top shelf and that we had to stretch tall or even climb up a ladder to reach them, but that across the years he had discovered many of God's best gifts are on the bottom shelf, and that we must kneel down to receive them.

A gift is not a reward. A reward is something we attain by personal achievement. A gift is something we obtain because of the generosity of another. We are tempted to regard top-shelf gifts as rewards that we have achieved. It is hard to think that way about bottom-shelf gifts. Kneeling to receive is the opposite of stretching or climbing to achieve. In our kneeling we acknowledge our dependence upon God for all good things including the gift of life itself. We even thank God for receptive capacity to welcome the gifts of unmerited love and power that that enable us to "walk in newness of life" (Romans 6:4).

Affirmation for the Day:

Life with God has far more to do with gifts received than awards achieved.

April 3

"God is not mocked."

Today's thought, which my brother and I often heard from our mother, comes from this verse from the apostle Paul: "Be not deceived; God is not mocked, for you reap whatever you sow" (Galatians 6:7).

I have stressed, and will continue to emphasize, the fact that in the promises of Jesus we are assured that nothing we have done or can ever do, or fail to do, will ever stop God from loving us. I hope to live and die by that promise but at the same time I don't want to imply that I agree with the person who said, "I love to sin and God loves to forgive so we get along just fine!"

God promises to never stop loving us but God does not promise to save us from the consequences of our sin and follies. Bad consequences follow from bad deeds. If I get drunk and crash my car into a tree, God will still love me but I may live the rest of my life as a quadriplegic with lifelong guilt for having killed the person who was riding with me.

After having proclaimed that "Where sin increased, grace abounded all the more," the apostle Paul went on to ask, "Should we continue in sin that grace may abound?" and to answer "By no means! How can we who died to sin go on living in it?" (Romans 5:20; 6:1-2 NRSV).

Affirmation for the Day:
The love of God does not cancel the laws of cause and effect.

April 4

Christian example includes confession of sub-Christian living.

As Christian parents we are to model honesty, kindness, generosity, and a host of other virtues for our children but a memory from childhood reminds me that we are also to provide another kind of Christian example.

When helping Dad repair a fence on the farm where I grew up, I must have done something dumb because it prompted him to lose his temper and to exclaim, "Don't be so damn stupid!" That was hardly a model of Christian virtue. But when he came to me several hours later and confessed, "I am sorry for what I said to you. Please forgive me. You are not stupid and I should not have talked to you that way," he provided an example that still stands strong in memory of what it is to be a Christian example.

Christian example is not just a demonstration of virtue. It also involves confession of our sins and failures and of our need to ask the forgiveness of others.

Affirmation for the Day:

I pray for courage to face my failures and then to say, "I am sorry, please forgive me."

April 5

"When we live below the level of society we will be punished. When we live above the level of society we will be persecuted."

There is truth in this observation from E. Stanley Jones. Those, such as criminals, who live below the level of society, often end up in jail. Those, like Jesus, who live above the level of society often end, literally or figuratively, on the cross.

It is no wonder, then, that most of us escape punishment and persecution by choosing the way of conformity. We fit in, run with the crowd, and do what we can to avoid both punishment and persecution, both prison and the cross. Most of us are more like chameleons than like Christ.

When so tempted, we wisely heed a clear word from the apostle Paul who said, "Do not be conformed to this world, but be transformed by the renewing of your minds that you may discern what is the will of God — what is good and acceptable and perfect" (Romans 12:2).

Affirmation for the Day:
As a follower of Jesus, I pray for wisdom to avoid the punishment that comes from low living and the courage to follow Christ even on high roads that lead to the cross.

April 6

"Evil is *live* spelled backward."

When we hear talk of "evil empires" and "axis of evil" and about "eliminating evil from the world" we rightly wonder what is "evil"? Scott Peck reports that when he asked that question of his eight-year-old son, he replied, "Evil is *live* spelled backward." E. Stanley Jones made the same observation.

Whatever its source, that thought reminds us that evil is that which is contrary to life. It may refer to a life-degrading sin or life-destroying sickness. That which enhances and fulfills life is good. That which degrades life is evil.

Such an understanding of evil doesn't solve all of our ethical problems. Some actions are helpful to some while hurtful to others. In such situations we seek to affirm that which promises the greatest good for the greatest number, and to follow the ancient rule of medical practitioners to seek to avoid doing harm whenever possible.

Affirmation for the Day:

I will seek to turn "evil" into "live" by doing all that I can to be life-giving in my attitudes and actions.

April 7

"Imaginary evil is exciting; real evil is boring."

Our thought for today comes from the wisdom of Simone Weil who says, "Imaginary evil is romantic and varied; real evil is gloomy, monotonous, barren, boring. Imaginary good is boring; real good is always new, marvelous, intoxicating." Her insight reminds me of the observation of Masters and Johnson, the famous sex experts, who pointed out long ago that "the pleasure bond" is commitment and that promiscuity is ultimately boring. It reminds me also that the New Testament acknowledges the "pleasures of sin" but describes them as "fleeting" (Hebrews 11:25).

On the other hand, it is often true that imaginary good doesn't sound very exciting. It sounds like hard work and heavy responsibility. "Do-gooders" aren't always thought of as the happiest people in town but as Weil goes on to point out, they probably are. They have joyous satisfaction in living the lives they are designed to live and of being the persons they are born to be. For them, each day is really a "new, marvelous, intoxicating" adventure that gives others ground for gratitude and provides themselves with the only ultimately satisfying purpose for living.

Affirmation for the Day:
In my living, I will seek to enjoy evil only in imagination and goodness in reality.

April 8

"Be angry but do not sin."

Our thought for today comes from Ephesians 4:26. I once preached a sermon on this text that prompted a member of the congregation to bring me a list of many biblical references that reject anger as sinful. He proved that it is often wrong to be angry but not that anger is never appropriate. There are times to "be angry." We should not assume a sweet piety that denies these feelings. Such pretense is healthy neither for ourselves nor for others.

But this text also says, "Do not sin." That is, we are to experience and express our anger in ways that are not hurtful to ourselves or to others. The verse goes on to say, "Do not let the sun go down on your anger." I understand that to mean that we are to quickly face it, admit it, confess it, and not brood over it. I believe that William Blake got it right in this little poem:

> *I was angry with my friend:*
> *I told my wrath, my wrath did end;*
> *I was angry with my foe:*
> *I told it not, my wrath did grow.*

Confessing anger to God, to a counselor, and often to the person who has angered us provides release and healing. Repressing anger can lead to emotional indigestion and possible explosions that are hurtful to ourselves and to others.

Affirmation for the Day:
I will face my anger honestly and seek to express it wisely.

April 9

Thought for the Day:

"It is difficult to condemn evil in others without increasing the evil in ourselves."

This thought stuck in my memory when I read it years ago in the book, *God in My Unbelief*, by J. W. Stevenson. It reminds us of how easily righteous judgment becomes the kind of self-righteous arrogance that can corrupt and destroy tribes and nations as well as individuals.

Certainly, we are to condemn evil, but never without awareness of the fact that evil also dwells in ourselves. It may even be well, as the old illustration reminds us, to note that when we point a finger of blame at someone else, we have three fingers pointing back at ourselves. Without simultaneous personal repentance, standing in judgment against the sins of others puts us in company with those arrogant, self-righteous Pharisees whom Jesus revealed to be among the worst of sinners.

Affirmation for the Day:

When pointing at evil in others, I will remember to look at my hand.

April 10

God lets evil people do what they are capable of doing.

This reflection is being written on the evening of September 11, 2001 — another tragic day that will "live in infamy!" This morning we watched our television screens in horror as two of the world's tallest buildings collapsed after having been struck by hijacked airplanes. We also saw smoke rising from the Pentagon following a similar attack. We learned a bit later of the crash of another hijacked airliner in Pennsylvania.

While wondering why God permits such tragedies, I recall a comment from Dr. Alvin Rogness who was president for many years of Luther Seminary. Rogness confessed that for much of his life he thought that God "set a hedge" around the lives of evil people saying to them, in effect, "this far, and no farther." But, in light of horrors like the Holocaust, he went on to confess that "I have come to believe that the only limit God has set against human evil is the limit of human ability." This gives freedom to brilliant, barbaric, suicide bombers and in an age of doomsday weaponry might even include the ability to destroy the world.

Affirmation for the Day:

What a wonderful and terrible thing is God's gift of human freedom.

April 11

Remember that God is also angry.

Alvin and Nora Rogness suffered the death of their son in a tragic car accident. "For a long time afterward," said Dr. Rogness, "I was angry with God, but then I began to realize that God is also angry at what caused the tragedy."

Jack Nelson Pallmeyer tells of a similar reaction when he first encountered people suffering from extreme poverty and hunger. He, too, was at first angry with God for permitting such misery. Then his anger turned toward himself and affluent humanity and he began to ponder the anger of God over our greed, indifference, and lack of compassion.

The God we know in Jesus is on the side of life and shares our anger over against all that is life-degrading and life-denying. When we are enraged by evil it is well to remember that God is raging with us and calling us to set wrongs right and to do the things that make for peace, justice, and life in fullness.

Affirmation for the Day:
When angered by evil, I will remember that God shares my anger.

April 12

It's sometimes right to tell a lie.

When a confirmation student asked, "Is it ever right to tell a lie?" honesty compelled me to answer, "Yes!" Then I went on to say that we should tell the truth 99.9 percent of the time but that we might encounter situations when it is right to lie and asked, "Can you think of any?" Some of their answers were a bit far out but some were also instructive: "If someone comes to our house with a gun and says, 'I have come to kill your parents. Are they at home?' It would be right for me to lie to save their lives." Such imagining reminded us of the love and courage of those who lied to the Nazis to save Jews from the Holocaust, and of how we need to ask of our speaking not only "Is it true?" but also "Is it kind and life-giving?"

Examples of occasions when it is right to lie are rare. Examples when it is wrong to lie are many. One of those, for me, is lying to children about Santa Claus. Don't get me wrong — I am not against Santa, but I am against all unnecessary lying, especially to children! We had great fun with Santa when I was a child, but my parents never lied to me. When Santa visited our country school we all knew it was Eddie Monson in the Santa suit.

Christmas celebrates the birth of Jesus who said, "For this I was born, and for this I came into the world, to testify to the truth" (John 18:37). When our children learn that we have lied to them about Santa why should they believe us when we tell them about Jesus? We are to speak "the truth in love" (Ephesians 4:15). Love may rarely compel a lie! Love almost always compels the truth!

Affirmation for the Day:
I will regularly be a loving truth-teller and rarely, if ever, a loving liar.

April 13

Evil is not goodness in disguise.

Some, such as true believers in Mary Baker Eddy's *Christian Science*, deny the reality of evil. They regard sin and suffering as "illusions of the mind" and in effect, understand evil to be goodness in disguise. From my perspective, such thinking is neither Christian nor scientific.

Many who are not Christian Scientists are also tempted toward such thinking. When tragic illness, suffering, and death confront us, someone is likely to say, "We can't see it now but someday we will understand. Now we see only the ragged, backside of the tapestry God is weaving. Someday we will see the beautiful pattern on the other side." To me this is a comforting but dangerous thought. I think the Bible is more realistic. It presents evil as a reality with which we have to deal and proclaims God as our refuge, strength, and hope of final deliverance.

It is even true as someone has said that "It sometimes helps to believe in the devil." Without recognition of the reality of evil that tempts and assails us, we are inclined to blame terrible things on God. Some insurance policies, for example, don't cover tragic events not caused by human negligence that they call "acts of God." I think it would be better if they called them "acts of the devil."

Affirmation for the Day:
While thanking God for all that is good, I pray with Jesus to be delivered from all that is evil.

April 14

"Gambling is immoral because the gambler's expectation of success is based on the hope of the misfortune of others."

Today's thought never occurred to me until I read it in Leo Tolstoy's book. It reminds us that gambling is different from productive enterprises that operate profitably for employees and shareholders without the necessity of anyone losing anything. But with the gambling enterprise, many must lose in order that few may prosper. If I buy a lottery ticket hoping to win $10 million, I am really hoping others will lose $10 million. There is no other source of revenue. This makes gambling different, not only from productive businesses, but also from raffles in which the prizes are donated and all of the proceeds go to a charitable cause. There are risks involved in starting a business or buying stock in a company, but unlike gambling it is not required that many must lose so that a few can win.

Gambling is not only immoral, it is also foolish. I believe it was the French poet and satirist, Voltaire, who said, "The lottery is a tax on stupidity." Others have pointed out that one is more likely to be struck by lightning than to win a big prize! Yet governments continue to promote lotteries that exploit their people by extracting "voluntary taxes" from gullible citizens.

Why then do people gamble? Garrison Keillor may be correct that the large number of senior citizens who gamble "witness to the tedium" in the lives of many.

Affirmation for the Day:

When tempted by tedium, I will do something more intelligent, more moral, more constructive, and more exciting than gambling.

April 15

Thought for the Day:

Discrimination between people is good. Discrimination against people is bad.

Discrimination between people is an act of selective judgment. In selecting a typist, the employer is likely to pick a person who types ninety words per minute over one who types forty. Selective discrimination between people based upon their differing abilities is right and proper.

Discrimination against people is something else all together. To reject someone on the basis of race, religion, sex, sexual orientation, or any other standard unrelated to qualifications for the position is not an exercise of proper judgment but of wrongful prejudice.

Some press this point in their opposition to consideration of race and gender in college admissions. I continue to believe that a case can still be made for such affirmative action, along with many other factors, as a step toward the alleviation of the effects of long-standing prejudice.

Affirmation for the Day:

In all of my dealings, I will seek to practice rightful good judgment and to avoid wrongful prejudice.

April 16

Thought for the Day:
Maybe it's my problem?

In 1879, Leo Tolstoy wrote *A Confession* in which he stated:

> *My life came to a standstill. I could eat, drink, and sleep
> ... but there was no life ... I could not even wish to know
> the truth, for I guessed of what it consisted. The truth
> was that life is meaningless ... I was not yet fifty; I had
> a good wife who loved me and whom I loved, good chil-
> dren, a large estate ... I enjoyed a strength of mind and
> body ... And in this situation I came to this — that I
> could not live, and fearing death, had to employ cun-
> ning with myself to avoid taking my own life.*

In the midst of this misery Tolstoy realized something that each
of us does well to ponder.

> *I understood that I had erred, and why I erred. I had
> erred not so much because I thought incorrectly as be-
> cause I lived badly ... I understood that my question as
> to what my life is, and the answer — an evil — was
> quite correct. The only mistake was that the answer
> referred only to my life, while* I had referred it to life in
> general. [Author's emphasis.] *I asked myself what my
> life is and I got the reply: An evil and an absurdity. And
> really my life — a life of indulgence and desires — was
> senseless and evil, and therefore the reply, "Life is evil
> and an absurdity," referred only to my life but not to
> human life in general.*

Tolstoy learned what Jesus teaches — that when we seek to
save our lives we lose them. Centered in self and captivated by no

greater purpose than self-seeking and self-indulgence, life is ultimately meaningless. Therefore, we again thank God that Jesus calls us to give ourselves in trust and surrender to the grace of God and in love and service to others. In this adventure we begin to live and to be life-giving. To our grateful amazement, we discover, as did Tolstoy, that life has meaning and in spite of many troubles can abound with joy.

Affirmation for the Day:
I thank God for the "way of Jesus" that gives meaning to my life.

April 17

There is a way of distinguishing good from evil.

Leo Tolstoy believed that "Only one clear quality marks an action that is either good or evil: If it increases the amount of love in the world, it is good. If it separates people and creates animosity among them, it is bad." Note that this understanding evaluates our deeds and lives in terms of the effects they have on relationships between people. Good deeds are creative of love and bring people together to live with greater understanding and harmony. Evil deeds create discord and hostility and drive people apart.

My wife, Carol, and I didn't think of Tolstoy's understanding of good and evil when we titled our book on marriage, *Be Good to Each Other*, but it certainly fits! Being good to each other increases the amount of love in a marriage and brings the couple together. Being evil is that which creates animosity and moves them apart. And so it is also in our wider families of community, congregation, denomination, country, and in the worldwide family of Christianity and of humanity itself.

Affirmation for the Day:
Goodness increases love and brings people together; evil creates animosity and drives people apart.

April 18

"Save us from weak resignation to the evils we deplore."

Our thought for today comes from Harry Emerson Fosdick's great hymn, "God of Grace and God of Glory," that he wrote for the dedication of the Riverside Church in New York City in 1930. Each of us, again beginning with me, needs to be saved "from weak resignation to the evils we deplore." We are often good at lamenting the world's sins, while at the same time doing little to correct them. It is true as often said that "For evil to succeed it is only necessary that good people do nothing." If evil is to be overcome, we need to stand against it with our actions as well as with our words. When asked why he refused to obey unjust laws Gandhi replied, "Noncooperation with evil is my sacred duty." From his perspective such "civil disobedience" was really "divine obedience."

I recently viewed a moving documentary presenting William Wilburforce's thirty-year struggle to abolish slavery in the British Empire. Year after year he introduced resolutions in the British Parliament that were continually defeated. But he never gave up and after decades of what sometimes must have seemed futile efforts, slave trading was finally outlawed. Shortly before his death several years later, slavery itself was abolished in the British Empire. That was more than thirty years before the U.S. Emancipation Proclamation and came about without the cost of a civil war.

Affirmation for the Day:

Although I will not live to see it, I pray for strength to continue to work for the abolition of the warring and wasting that continues to threaten our life together.

April 19

There are times to be glad to be wrong.

If it seems strange to rejoice over being wrong, think of examples like these: a patient in a doctor's office with symptoms that have prompted self-diagnosis of cancer; a white-knuckled flier in turbulent weather expecting that the plane is about to crash; a passenger standing on the deck of the *Titanic* that April night in 1912 fearing that the ship will strike an iceberg and sink to the bottom of the sea. Wouldn't all be glad to be wrong?

As confessed elsewhere in these pages, I am fearful for the future of the human family. Our scientific capacity for destruction seems to have developed far faster than our moral capacity to live together in harmony, justice, and peace. Unless we repent and change our ways, I fear that there will be terrible tragedies ahead from which civilization and even humanity may not survive. But I quickly add, I hope I'm wrong and will be delighted if no such tragedy ever occurs.

Affirmation for the Day:
In the grace of God, I confess to being both pessimistic and hopeful.

April 20

"The profoundest thing one can say of a river is that it's on its way to the sea."

When my twin brother and I sat on the banks of the Blue Earth River near Dell in southern Minnesota sixty years ago waiting for a bullhead to bite on our baited hooks, we may have wondered to ourselves and each other, "How long will it take the water flowing past us to travel down the Blue Earth, Minnesota, and Mississippi rivers and out into the Gulf of Mexico?" It took Gerhard Frost's insightful imagination to add meaning to such childhood wonderings:

> *The profoundest thing*
> *one can say of a river*
> *is that it's on its way to the sea.*
> *The deepest thought*
> *one can think of a person*
> *is that he or she is a citizen of eternity.*
> *Moments and years,*
> *years and moments,*
> *pass like sea-bent streams.*
> *And I? I'm carried by the current*
> *of an all-possessing Love.*
> *I'm on my way, God's way for me,*
> *so let it be.*

Affirmation for the Day:

Carried by the stream of God's grace, I, too, will say, "Let it be."

April 21

Light invades the darkness. Darkness does not invade the light.

Our thought for today is one of the most obvious facts in all the world, but I never found comfort in it until I pondered this little poem by Gerhard Frost:

> *If I am asked*
> *what are my grounds for hope,*
> *this is my answer.*
> *Light is lord over darkness,*
> *truth is lord over falsehood,*
> *life is ever lord over death.*
> *Of all the facts I daily live with,*
> *there is none more comforting*
> *than this: If I have two rooms,*
> *one dark, the other light,*
> *and I open the door between them,*
> *the dark room becomes lighter*
> *without the light room*
> *becoming darker. I know*
> *this is no headline,*
> *but it's a marvelous footnote.*
> *And God comforts me in that.*

Affirmation for the Day:
I, too, take comfort from the lordship of light over darkness, truth over falsehood, and life over death.

April 22

"A good liar needs a good memory."

I learned this truth from my dad when I was only a child and must confess that I did not at first understand it. When I asked, "Why is that?" I was told that those who tell the truth need only to recall what happened but that those who tell lies need to also recall exactly what they have told people about what happened. Good (not moral but effective) liars need to keep their stories straight or they will be found out by telling one thing to one person and something else to another or even telling the same person one thing at one time and something else at another.

Dad was big on honesty. Although I doubt that he'd ever heard it, I think he would have agreed with Thomas Jefferson: "Honesty is the first chapter of the book of wisdom." Dad taught my brother and me to use our memories to recall and express the truth and not to waste our brain power trying to remember lies we had told.

Affirmation for the Day:
Since telling lies will overtax my fragile memory, I will specialize in telling the truth.

April 23

Listen to your body but don't always obey it.

There has been much good advice in recent years concerning the importance of listening to our bodies. Paying attention to what our bodies tell us is important and can keep us from becoming run-down or stressed-out. When our bodies give us such messages, we should not only listen but also obey — take a nap, take a break, or take a trip to a doctor or counselor.

There are also times when we should listen but not obey. Those of us, for example, who struggle with the widespread (both anatomical and geographical) American problem of being overweight should disobey our bodies when they tell us to have another candy bar or dish of ice cream. When our bodies voice temptations to overindulge in food or drink or to engage in illicit sexual activity, our minds should be master of our bodily appetites. And when we lack such mastery and our lives are out of control, we should seek the help of a therapist or support group, such as one of the twelve-step programs, to be freed from addiction and restored to sanity.

Affirmation for the Day:
I pray for wisdom to listen to my body and for strength to respond in ways that are healthful and live-giving.

April 24

"Jesus is the part of God we are able to see."

Today's thought comes from E. Stanley Jones who liked to speak of Jesus as "the human life of God" and who was also fond of saying "Jesus is God here" and "God is Jesus everywhere."

When God wanted to reveal to the world his heart and mind and will, he wrapped a bit of his heart and mind and will in the human life of Jesus. It is, as John says at the beginning of his gospel, "No one has ever seen God; God's only Son, He who is nearest to the Father's heart, has made him known" (John 1:18 REV). Jesus is like a window through which we see into the heart and mind and will of God. When asked, "What is God like?" we answer, "God is like Jesus."

Thinking of Jesus in this way reminds me of a thought that has been in my memory for many years after hearing it quoted several times by Alvin Rogness. I don't know its source. It sounds as if it might come from a Christmas poem or hymn: "I do not know how Bethlehem's babe could in the Godhead be; I only know this manger child has brought God's love to me."

Rogness liked those lines and so do I. They cut through the complexity of abstract theology concerning the doctrines of the trinity and the divinity of Christ. When rightly understood these doctrines are helpful but this is essential — we know and trust the God we see in Jesus.

Affirmation for the Day:
Seeing Jesus, I catch a glimpse of the compassionate heart, mind, and will of God.

April 25

Therefore, get to work!

There is an "O Henry type" surprise ending to 1 Corinthians 15. The whole chapter is a powerful proclamation of the resurrection and our hope of heaven. The apostle Paul speaks of death as "the last enemy to be destroyed" (v. 46). The next to last verse says, "Thanks be to God, who gives us the victory through our Lord Jesus Christ" (v. 57).

Then Paul says, "Therefore ..." If we didn't know what comes next and were asked to guess, most of us would likely say, "Rejoice in your hope of heaven!" Other verses invite us to do that, but that is not what Paul says here. He says, "Therefore, my beloved, be steadfast, immovable, always excelling in the work of the Lord because you know that in the Lord your labor is not in vain" (v. 58).

It has been said that "Some people are so heavenly minded that they do no earthly good." But such living is contrary to what Paul affirms. He tells us to get to work with confidence that Christlike service makes a difference that counts for time and eternity.

Affirmation for the Day:

If what I do makes that kind of difference, I'd better get to work!

April 26

"The call to follow Christ is a call to come and die."

This famous line from Dietrich Bonhoeffer is, I believe, true but easily misunderstood. It can be taken in ways that are self-deprecating and even life-denying. I don't think that Bonhoeffer meant it that way. I think he heard Christ calling him to die to his own self-righteous arrogance, self-will, and self-dependence and to be born again as a child of God.

Marcus Borg devotes an entire chapter of his book, *The Heart of Christianity*, to the importance of being "born again" and relates it specifically to the metaphors of "dying" and "rising" in the New Testament. He says, for example, that in Paul's letters "dying and rising with Jesus, dying and rising with Christ, is a metaphor for personal transformation at the heart of the Christian life." In reference to Paul's confession, "I have been crucified with Christ and it is no longer I who live, but it is Christ who lives in me" (Galatians 2:19b-20a), Borg states, "The old Paul is dead. The result is new life: a new Paul has been born, one in whom Christ lives" (p. 109).

In this understanding the death of self as "god," is the birth of self as an authentic human being. We don't live very well as make-believe gods but we can live amazingly well as surrendered-to-God, love-affirmed human beings. Martin Luther saw such daily dying and rising as central to living out the meaning of baptism in everyday renewal of trust and love.

Affirmation for the Day:

In surrender to Christ, daily dying and daily birthing go together.

April 27

"There are millions of Christians in the world but very few followers of Jesus."

That statement shocked me when I heard it long ago in a lecture by Ashley Montague. It may be gross exaggeration but I tremble to think that it may be true. There are certainly millions who call themselves Christians but is it true that there are "very few followers of Jesus"?

Whatever the numbers, there is enough truth in Montague's assertion to make us wince and wonder. And the wondering rightly begins with ourselves! We call ourselves Christians but are we followers of Jesus? In my understanding, Christians are people who live by the grace of God and who seek to live in harmony with the wisdom and compassion of Jesus. I don't think it is possible to live as Jesus lived without trusting in the grace of God, but I think it is possible to trust in the grace of God without living as Jesus lived. If we do that, we may be technically and even truly Christian, but we are certainly not being faithfully Christian.

Affirmation for the Day:

I look to Jesus not only for love but also for leadership.

April 28

"Owe no one anything, except to love one another."

Today's thought and reflection come from the apostle Paul who in this paragraph gives us one of scripture's most clear and succinct summaries of what is central to Christian morality:

> *Owe no one anything, except to love one another; for the one who loves another has fulfilled the law. The commandments, "You shall not commit adultery; You shall not murder; You shall not steal; You shall not covet"; and any other commandment, are summed up in this word, "Love your neighbor as yourself." Love does no wrong to a neighbor; therefore love is the fulfilling of the law.* — Romans 13:8-10

To put it positively, love is life-affirming and life-fulfilling. When we live that way, we do right by people and automatically keep all the commandments. Some criticize the "new morality" of love-centered "situation ethics" but when understood in terms of Christlike love as expressed in this passage from the apostle Paul, we see that it is as old as the New Testament and that it provides guidance in every situation.

Affirmation for the Day:
Whatever the situation, I will seek to live with life-giving, Christlike love.

April 29

"We don't know what is going to happen but we trust that God will be there when it happens."

Today's thought lodged in memory when I heard it from Pastor Rueben Gornitzka years ago.

It is scary to anticipate the unknown future. None of us knows for sure what is going to happen tomorrow or later today or even a few minutes from now.

But scary uncertainties need not immobilize us. We venture into the unknown sustained by promises that assure us that whatever happens God will be there with all of the grace and mercy and power assured to us in Jesus. Tragedy may strike but we will still be held in the love of God who has promised to bring us through.

Someone has said that "Hope is faith with its face toward the future." Hope is faith looking forward. Hope is present trust in the promises of God, facing the future in confidence that whatever happens, God will be there with the same all-sufficient grace that sustains us now. In faith we trust both God's promised presence and God's promised future.

Affirmation for the Day:

Trusting God now, I look forward to venturing with God into unknown tomorrows.

April 30

"A man could go wrong with that kind of money."

Shortly after I was ordained, my dad asked me to tell him about the congregation I was to serve and I told him a lot about the parish and the community. Then, in his shy way, he said, "By the way, how much will you be paid?" I told him that my salary would be $100 a week. He replied, "Don't you mean $100 a month?" "No," I said, "It is $100 a week — $5,200 a year," to which he responded "You better be careful — a man could go wrong with that kind of money!"

Dad was born in a log cabin on a newly homesteaded farm in southern Minnesota in 1882 and remembered "hard times" when lots of people were glad to be working for room and board and a dollar a day. He was grateful to have been spared the sorrow of many who lost their farms during the Great Depression and believed that the temptations of affluence are as much to be feared as those of poverty.

Revelations of the sinful stupidity of some of the super rich who have finagled to pile millions upon millions confirm his wisdom. I am sure Dad would have affirmed the prayer: "Give me neither poverty nor riches; feed me with the food that I need, or I shall be full and deny you, and say, 'Who is the Lord?' or I shall be poor, and steal, and profane the name of my God" (Proverbs 38:9).

Affirmation for the Day:

Whether rich, poor, or in between I will remember that my "life does not consist in the abundance of possessions" (Luke 12:15).

May 1

"Christianity is the most materialistic of all world religions."

Since I am not an expert on all of the world's religions I don't know if this statement, by William Temple, is true in fact but I am persuaded that it is a thought worth pondering. Some religions affirm a spirituality that involves renunciation of material things and especially of physical pleasures. Some Christians, past and present, hold similar views.

True Christianity, however, as Temple and I understand it, affirms the essential goodness of creation and regards material things, including physical pleasures, to be the gift of God. This presents us with both blessing and temptation. We are blessed to receive and enjoy these gifts, but are also tempted to be excessively preoccupied with and dependent upon them. Material things are good but they are not God nor are they intended for us to enjoy alone. We are provided "with every blessing in abundance, so that [we] may always have enough of everything and may provide in abundance for every good work." (See 2 Corinthians 9:8.)

Affirmation for the Day:
While enjoying God's blessings, I will remember that I am called to stewardship, not self-indulgence.

May 2

"Theft consists of holding in my possession that which someone else needs more than I do."

If Gandhi is right in this definition of theft, I am a thief living in what is, in effect, a vast den of thieves. By that definition almost every average, as well as wealthy, American is a thief.

In the context of American affluence it is easy to write off Gandhi as a life-denying ascetic but then I ask myself, "Where did he get that idea?" I don't know for sure but I remember that Gandhi had great fascination with Jesus and I am forced to wonder if he might have gotten it from him? If that is possible I, who profess to be a follower of Jesus, had better not write it off too quickly.

Gandhi's definition of theft prompts me to ask E. Stanley Jones' question: "What right have I to luxuries for myself when others do not have the necessities of life?" I am sure that millions of people would label many of my "necessities" as "luxuries." These are troubling thoughts for me. Does this mean that I am entertaining the wrong thoughts, or that my way of life is out of tune with the way of Jesus?

Affirmation for the Day:

I pray that my troubled thoughts will lead to more Christlike living.

May 3

"Our money is our time and talent in portable form."

If we are persons of empathy and compassion and learn of people far away who are in great need we often feel sorry and helpless. We may even wish that we were capable of going there to relieve their suffering.

Most of us can't personally travel around the world providing such help but today's thought, from Harry Emerson Fosdick, reminds us that our money is a means of going there and doing some good. It really is "our time and talent in portable form." Those people in need are often as close to us as our checkbooks. When we give to serve others something of ourselves travels to those distant places. We are at work through our dollars to feed, heal, teach, and save. In such ways, our money is a means of grace.

On the other hand, it is also true that if we use our money only for self-indulgence, it becomes a means of disgrace.

Affirmation for the Day:

I will remember that how I spend my money reveals how I am spending my life.

May 4

Our money is like the Thanksgiving turkey.

Imagine that it is Thanksgiving Day at our house and family and friends are gathered around the dinner table. Carol sets the stuffed turkey in front of me. I bow my head and piously pray a long prayer thanking God for giving me this turkey and then begin to eat it all by myself. Needless to say, it wouldn't be long before one of our children would say, "Hey, Dad, what are you doing?" To which I would reply, "I'm eating my turkey. It was set before me and is obviously mine to do with as I please."

Although I can't imagine myself doing such a thing, isn't that how each of us is tempted to regard and "devour" money? We know that the turkey belongs to everyone at the table and that our job is to serve it and not just eat it. But when money is set before us, we may forget that it belongs to everyone at God's big table and we are to use it to serve the human family and not just for greedy self-indulgence. Since the turkey belongs to the family, such sharing is not charity. It is just and proper stewardship.

Affirmation for the Day:

I will remember that both my turkey and my money are for serving others and not just stuffing myself.

May 5

Our money is like manure!

Today's comparison is crude and, perhaps to some, offensive, but it is, nonetheless, true — money is like manure! When heaped in a pile, manure is one of the least attractive and most useless things on the face of the earth. It is just a stinking manure pile! But when spread out on a farmer's fields, it enriches the soil and gives life to the land.

So also with money. When piled up by a greedy miser, we see another exceedingly unattractive sight, not only of the heaped-up money but also of the pathetic person who seeks to preserve it and pile up more.

Piled-up wealth beyond any reasonable need is a disgrace. But when spread out to others through acts of generous sharing and service, money becomes a means of grace that gives life, hope, and salvation to those in need.

Affirmation for the Day:
My money is for the needs of many, not just for my many wants.

May 6

Thought for the Day:

"Beware of lending money to relatives and friends."

Today's thought is another warning from my dad, who went on to say, "If you aren't careful you may lose not only your money but also your friendships."

There are certainly times when it is wise and good to provide financial help for friends and family members, but when we give or receive such aid, it is essential that there be a clear understanding concerning whether it is a loan or a gift and what are the specific expectations concerning repayment. If there is confusion, it can result in future conflicts in which each party says, "I thought ..." revealing their understandings and expectations to have been far apart. If there is any possibility of misunderstanding it is best to get the agreement in writing.

Affirmation for the Day:

When dealing with family and friends, good business at the beginning often saves both money and friendship at the end.

May 7

"When we buy what we don't need, we steal from ourselves."

I don't know the author of today's thought but, whatever its source, I believe it is true.

When we buy things that we don't need, we really are stealing from ourselves. We are depleting our bank accounts in exchange for an accumulation of things that fail to satisfy our real needs and in some cases may actually be harmful for us. I think, for example, of the billions spent on cigarettes and other tobacco products that are far worse than useless. Those who buy them are not only stealing their own money but also their own health and years of life. It is sad to think about those millions now in their graves who would be enjoying years of healthy living if they had not robbed themselves of their money, health, time, and finally of life itself.

Even when the things we buy are harmless in themselves, purchasing things when we don't need them deprives us of resources that could be used for what is truly needful, not just for ourselves but also for others.

In his book, *The Hidden Heart of the Cosmos*, Brian Swimme claims that "We are immersed in the religion of consumerism," which he says, "has become the dominant world faith." That may be an overstatement, but it is certainly true that we are all tempted toward idolatrous materialism.

Affirmation for the Day:
I pray for wisdom to refrain from stealing, not only from others, but also from myself.

May 8

Beyond the basics, increasing wealth does not increase happiness.

Two memories prompt our thought for today. One is of a survey reporting that increasing wealth from poverty to sufficiency resulted in a significant increase in personal happiness. But that, increasing wealth from sufficiency to luxury did not significantly increase happiness.

The other is a memory of a television interview with entertainer Steve Allen who confessed that in his own experience accumulating wealth did not increase happiness. To make his point more specific, he went on to point out the obvious fact that "You can only drive one car at a time, eat one meal at a time, sleep in one bed at a time, and wear one suit of clothes at a time."

Accumulating more stuff for occasional use does not proportionately provide more joy. In fact, as indicated by interviews with lottery winners, increased wealth brings problems of its own. They now face the unpleasant task of dealing with family and friends and a host of others looking for handouts and are, of necessity, suspicious that offers of love and friendship may be directed more toward their money than toward themselves.

Jesus had never seen such survey results or talked with Steve Allen, but affirmed their wisdom when he said, "Take heed and beware of all covetousness for a person's life does not consist in the abundance of one's possessions" (Luke 12:15) and when he taught us to pray, "Give us this day our daily bread" (Matthew 6:11).

Affirmation for the Day:
If sufficiency is better than poverty or luxury, I will remember that enough is enough.

May 9

Are we givers or stewards?

Several years ago, I heard Pastor Morris Vaagenes give a brief presentation concerning stewardship in which he asked two questions worth pondering by us all: 1) "How much of what is mine should I give to God?" and 2) "How much of what is God's should I keep and use for myself?"

The first of these is a "givers" question. It sounds pious and the person who asks it may respond with great generosity. We are rightly grateful for all the good that has been done by those who ask the "givers" question and who answer it with lives of generous giving.

But honesty compels facing the fact that "the givers" question is still the wrong question, and that "the givers" giving is not true Christian stewardship. The steward asks, "How much of what is God's should I keep and use for myself?" That puts things in proper perspective. We really don't own anything! It's all God's! "The earth is the Lord's and all that is in it; the world, and those who live in it" (Psalm 24:1). God is the true owner of not only the "cattle on a thousand hills" (Psalm 50:10) but also of all the cash, stocks, and other stuff that we are tempted to consider our own. True stewards live and give as some of us have often sung:

> *We give thee but thine own,*
> *Whate'er the gift may be;*
> *All that we have is thine alone,*
> *A trust O Lord, from thee.*

Affirmation for the Day:
I will seek to live and to give as a trustee and not as an owner.

May 10

"Rich people should be ashamed of their wealth."

I am grateful for the wisdom of Leo Tolstoy and commend to you his book, *A Calendar of Wisdom: Daily Thoughts to Nourish the Soul*, now titled *Wisdom for Every Day*, which has been an inspiration, and model, for this book. I am less than persuaded by some of Tolstoy's convictions that strike me as a bit far out.

- "A truly kind person cannot be rich."
- "In money — in the money itself, in its acquisition, in its possession — there is something immoral."
- "Excessive wealth is worse than poverty."
- "If rich people were truly Christian they wouldn't remain rich for very long."

These thoughts remind me again that Mahatma Gandhi, who was influenced by Tolstoy, expressed a similar conviction when he said that "theft is holding in our possession that which someone else needs more than we do."

What do we make of such convictions? I'm tempted to write them off as the irrational ramblings of religious fanatics but then I remember that Jesus is credited with some similar remarks — "It is easier for a camel to go through the eye of a needle than for someone who is rich to enter the kingdom of God" (Mark 10:25), and "Woe to you who are rich, for you have received your consolation" (Luke 6:24). Might Jesus agree with Tolstoy and Gandhi?

Affirmation for the Day:
Jesus compels me to ask hard questions concerning myself and my wealth.

May 11

"It is as sinful to own land as it is to own a slave."

Following his conversion, Leo Tolstoy became convinced on the basis of verses like "The earth is the Lord's and all that is in it" (Psalm 24:1) and the year of jubilee requirements (see Leviticus 25:1-28; 27:16-25) that land could not be owned in perpetuity and that it is sinful for Christians to claim title to that which ultimately belongs to God.

Perhaps because we own a small amount of land I am not persuaded that it is always sinful for Christians to hold legal title to a bit of the earth. But I think Tolstoy is correct in reminding us that whatever the legal titles we are still only tenants, managers, and stewards of what belongs to God and to those who will live after us.

Tolstoy's strong statement reminds me of another heard long ago from someone who said that "It is a sin to burn petroleum" because it will be needed by future generations for purposes more essential than powering our cars and heating our homes. At the very least, responsible Christian stewardship calls for serious attention to those who urge an end to our dependence upon oil and encourage using sunshine, wind, and other forms of renewable energy to generate electricity and biofuels to power our cars.

Affirmation for the Day:
I will think not only of what is easiest for me today, but of what is best for those who will live after me.

May 12

"The world's fastest growing religion is trans-national capitalism."

Our thought for today comes from Radhika Balakrishman who is professor of economics at Marymount Manhattan College. She affirms the opinion of David Loy who states:

> *The Market is becoming the first truly world religion, binding all corners of the globe more and more tightly into a world view and set of values whose religious role we overlook only because we insist on seeing them as "secular."*

Back before the collapse of the Soviet Union and the growth of capitalistic enterprises in China, many commentators referred to communism as the functional equivalent of a religion. I now find it a bit shocking to hear capitalism being described in essentially the same way. Is it possible that what was true of communism then is also true of capitalism now? Many preachers in those days derided the idolatry and immorality of tyrannical communism. I've not heard similar sermons concerning capitalism but our thought for today makes me wonder if they might be appropriate.

"That upon which you rely with the central confidence of your heart," said Luther, "is your god." If we are worshipers of wealth, and see capitalism as the means of achieving it, we may be adherents of an idolatrous false religion. Being forewarned of "the greed which makes an idol of gain" (Ephesians 5:5), we should certainly beware lest the spirit of capitalism become our religion.

Affirmation for the Day:
Idolatrous capitalism may be no better than "godless communism."

May 13

Bottom lives are more important than the bottom lines.

The billionaire, George Soros, believes that the success of a private enterprise or of an economic system should be measured by human as well as financial factors. He points out that it is not enough to show profit on the bottom line. We must also ask, "What is the effect of this enterprise or economic system on the lives of people? Is it life-giving and liberating, or oppressive and life-degrading?"

In an article on "The Failures of Capitalism," David J. Rothkopf, managing director of Kissinger Associates and a former deputy undersecretary of commerce for international trade, states: "The richest 358 people in the world have a net worth equal to the combined annual income of the poorest 2.3 billion." He goes on to point out that capitalism has not been able to "achieve the just distribution of wealth in society." In effect, he warns against naive, excessive celebration of the victory of capitalism over communism and predicts that someone, somewhere is probably "working to become the architect of reforms that might actually make 'market socialism' a sustainable concept."

Businesses and economic systems that make a few rich while leaving many poor are financial and moral failures.

May 14

"A decent provision for the poor is the true test of civilization."

"Standards of living" are often measured in terms of the percentage of people owning cars, television sets, computers, and the like. Countries that consume large quantities of such stuff are said to have a high standard of living. But Dr. Samuel Johnson, from whom we have our thought for today, invites us to see things differently. By his standard, a country might have a high "consumption of goods standard of living" while at the same time flunking what he calls "the true test of civilization."

That test is especially significant as well as profoundly troubling when we apply it, not only to our country and local communities, but also to the global family. If it is true, as Ched Myers maintains in *The Biblical Vision of Sabbath Economics*, that "the wealthiest twenty percent of the world's population receives almost 83 percent of the world's income, while the poorest twenty percent receive less than two percent," we may be part of a global community that is not yet qualified to be called civilization. If humanity is to become truly civilized, the tragedy of unnecessary poverty must be faced and overcome.

Affirmation for the Day:
Compassion and action for the poor are qualities of Christlikeness and of civilization.

May 15

Practice the art of savoring.

One of my dictionary's definitions of "to savor" is "to taste or enjoy with zest; to relish." God has given each of us capacity for such savoring, and it is foolish, and may be even sinful, for us to fail to exercise and enjoy it.

When it comes to eating, for example, many of us are better at stuffing than savoring. We rush through our meals eating too much and enjoying them too little. Some of us would be better off if we ate half as much in twice the time while savoring every bite of it.

I am also reminded of the advice Theodor Bovet gives in his old classic, *A Handbook to Marriage*. He encourages couples to "make your sexual relations last as long as possible." That implies savoring and, while perhaps too much for some, is certainly far better than the "wham, bam, thank you, ma am" experiences that I heard about far too often in marriage counseling. (When Vivian Johnson gave me feedback on this reflection she asked in a note at the bottom of the page, "Have you heard this? 'There are two things that one should do slowly and eating is one of them!' " When I later confessed that her note is in this book, she credited this great line to our mutual friend, John Yackel.)

Affirmation for the Day:
I thank God for my capacity to savor and will seek to practice the art of savoring.

May 16

No one can take another's place.

In *The Lonely House*, I tell a story from my first parish in which seminary student interns had responsibility for youth work. I once introduced a new intern to a high school student saying, "I would like you to meet Tom Duke. He's taking Wendell Friest's place." To which the high school student replied, "Nobody can take Wendell Friest's place!"

That student was right. We may carry on another's work and complete what someone else has begun, but we do not take another's place. Each of us is a unique human being with a special place in our world and in the lives of people with whom we live.

This fact is forced upon us when death or similar separation take us apart. Other people keep and take their places in our lives. But none of them, not even God, fills the empty place left by the person who is no longer with us. A void remains as a painful reminder of the unique significance of an irreplaceable person.

Affirmation for the Day:
I will remember that each of us has a place no other can fill.

May 17

"If it is to be, it is up to me."

Someone described today's thought as "the most significant ten-word statement of two-letter words in the English language." These ten words are, of course, not literally true of everything. Most things that "are to be" are certainly not "up to me."

But they are true for me concerning some things. If I don't write this book, it will never be written. Others may write a similar book, but if this book is to be, it is "up to me." Nobody can do it for me. Nor can another do the things that only you can do.

In the same paragraph in which the apostle Paul says, "Bear one another's burdens," he goes on to say, "All must carry their own loads" (Galatians 6:2, 5). While thankful for the work of others, we are to take responsibility for doing our own work.

Affirmation for the Day:
When I see what's mine alone to do, I will do it.

May 18

"You can do it!"

Credit today's word of encouragement to our mother who said it to my twin brother and me whenever we expressed doubts or fears concerning an assignment or project that was set before us. She sent us off to school and work with words of assurance that we could meet the challenges of the day.

Nor did my mother limit that counseling to her sons. One of our cousin's first comments on hearing of Mom's unexpected death was, "She always encouraged me." I have sometimes thought that we should have engraved on her tombstone the words "A Person of Encouragement."

Although I never heard her express it in these words, I believe that Mother's "You can do it!" encouragement was based in the belief that God has given each of us enough ability and enough time to do what God wants us to do. We haven't been given ability and time enough to do everything we want to do nor everything others want us to do, but we have enough of both to do what God wants us to do.

When the apostle Paul said, "I can do all things through him who strengthens me" (Philippians 4:13), he was not claiming ability to fly to the moon. Paul was saying, in effect, that in the grace of God, his time and ability were sufficient for doing what God wanted him to do. And, when all is said and done, is there anything more that any of us needs to do?

Affirmation for the Day:
With gratitude for my time and abilities and sustained by God's grace, I will do what I can and not lament what I cannot.

May 19

"Do at least one thing every day that you don't feel like doing."

Today's thought is another suggestion from E. Stanley Jones, and I must confess that it often comes to mind when I am tempted to turn aside from something I don't feel like doing. It might be to write a letter or to make a phone call that I have been putting off, or even to wash the dishes or mop the floor. Maybe there is someone with whom I need to visit to deal with a difficult problem or to seek healing for a broken or painful relationship.

Many of us make "things-to-do" lists to remind ourselves of work to be done. If some of those things don't get done because we don't feel like doing them, it may be well to ponder our thought for today once again, and then put that thought into action.

I strongly affirm the wisdom of Jones' suggestion. It is good discipline and has helped me do a lot of things that I didn't feel like doing.

Affirmation for the Day:

Even when I don't feel like it, if it needs doing, I will do it.

May 20

Transformation of the world begins with personal transformation.

There is a line in the book of Acts reporting that critics of the Christians accused them of "turning the world upside down" (Acts 17:6). That criticism was an unwitting witness to the truth of what those early Christians were doing. From their perspective, the world was in many ways wrong-side-up and they were trying to right it by turning it upside down.

But before those Christians got busy transforming the world, they experienced a personal transformation that had turned their own wrong-side-up lives right-side-up. They credited that transformation to the life-changing power of the Holy Spirit who Henry Pittney VanDusen, president of Union Seminary during my student days, described as "God at hand and God at work." Central to that work was the creation of the moral qualities of Christlikeness that the apostle Paul called "the fruit of the Spirit," which is "love, joy, peace, patience, kindness, generosity, faithfulness, gentleness, and self-control" (Galatians 5:22-23).

Empowered by the Holy Spirit, they now lived by the grace of God and with the values of Christ. Not perfectly, of course, but sufficiently to motivate them to risk their lives to tell others the story of Jesus and God's love and to challenge them to live as Jesus lived.

Affirmation for the Day:
Spirit of God, transform the world, beginning with me.

May 21

Our greater problem is not atheism but polytheism.

When I learned the first commandment, it said, "You shall have no other gods before me." That's still the way it reads in the main text of Exodus 20:3 and Deuteronomy 5:7 in both the old and New Revised Standard Version translations. But there is a little footnote with a big meaning in both places. It reads: "Or besides." We aren't just to put things before God; we aren't even to worship anything alongside of God.

When Moses' brother, Aaron, set up the golden calf for the people to worship, he told the people, "Tomorrow shall be a festival to the Lord" (Exodus 32:5). One day they worshiped an idol and the next day they worshiped the true God.

Isn't that often the way with us? Sunday morning we sincerely worship the true God we know in Jesus. But for most of the rest of the week, the "god" we really worship may be our money, our nation, or ourselves — the little triune god — "me, myself, and I."

In addition to the false gods of money, state, and self, our idol may be the faulty image of the one true God that we hold in our heads. Harry Emerson Fosdick told of visiting with a person who confessed that he didn't believe in God. To which Fosdick replied, "Tell me about the God you don't believe in." After hearing the person's answer, Fosdick confessed that "I don't believe in that God either"! Disbelieving some of our notions about God can be a vital part of an adventure of growing in trust and better understanding of God.

Affirmation for the Day:
I will remember that there are lots of "gods" in whom I should not believe.

May 22

Christ is not lost.

My old friend, Sherm Johnsrud, tells of being accosted on his way through a bus depot by someone who asked, "Have you found Christ?" To which Sherm replied, "I didn't know he was lost!"

That flip answer contains a profound truth. Christ is not lost. We don't have to go somewhere to find the love of God. In Christ the love of God comes seeking us and finds us as we are where we are.

This good news is pictured beautifully in Jesus' parables of the lost sheep and lost coin in Luke 15. They tell of a shepherd and a homemaker who seek diligently until the lost is found. They invite us to stop our frantic seeking or fleeing and to trust that at this very moment we are found by love that will never leave us.

Affirmation for the Day:
Although I may not feel it, I trust that I am found and loved right here, right now, in every place and in every moment.

May 23

Nothing can separate us from the love of God.

As I share this reflection, I am reminded of another comment by Paul Scherer, my teacher and adviser at Union Seminary, who said that there are some texts of scripture that are so clearly and beautifully stated that it is difficult to preach on them. They say it so well that it might be better for us to ponder them than to preach about them. The example he chose to illustrate his point was this passage from the apostle Paul:

> *Who will separate us from the love of Christ? Will hardship, or distress, or persecution, or famine, or nakedness, or peril, or sword? ... No, in all these things we are more than conquerors through him who loved us. For I am convinced that neither death, nor life, nor angels, nor rulers, nor things present, nor things to come, nor powers, nor height, nor depth, nor anything else in all creation, will be able to separate us from the love of God in Christ Jesus our Lord.*
> — Romans 8:35, 37-39

In keeping with Dr. Scherer I will only encourage you to read that text again, to ponder it often, and to live in trust of its great promise.

Affirmation for the Day:

This is our trust and our joy — God loves us now and will love us forever.

May 24

In Christ it is always "Yes!"

While often declaring a clear "No" to our sins and follies, the central proclamation of Christ is an unconditional "Yes!" We often need those "No's" to correct and restrain our wrongful behavior, but we always need that great "Yes!" to affirm our very being.

From parents, teachers, and other significant people, we may have heard a lot of "No's" but it is to be hoped that we have heard a lot more "Yes's." But even if we have been beaten down by a relentless torrent of "No's" from childhood onward there is still one to whose word to us "is always 'Yes.' " We, therefore, thankfully treasure this promise:

> *As surely as God is faithful, our word to you has not been "Yes and No." For the Son of God, Jesus Christ, whom we proclaimed among you, Silvanus and Timothy and I, was not "Yes and No"; but in him it is always "Yes." For in him every one of God's promises is a "Yes."*
> — 2 Corinthians 1:18-20

Affirmation for the Day:
When negations knock me down, Christ's affirmations lift me up.

May 25

The most happiness comes to those who realize they will not always be happy.

It is strange, but true, that life becomes easier when we accept the fact that life will sometimes be hard. This is true of both our inner life and our relationships with others. It is realism and not just pessimism to acknowledge that we will go through some hard times in life. We will fail and others will fail us. Some dreams will never come true. As with the rhythms of nature, day and night, spring and winter, joy and sorrow will be part of our experience.

We sometimes have difficulty getting along with ourselves, and should not be surprised to sometimes be unhappy with others. It is realistic to expect times of misunderstanding, hostility, and resentment in life together. As people who regularly confess our sins, we should not be surprised to see some sign of it in ourselves and in others.

This is not to advocate the despair of thinking that "The only way to avoid disappointment is to never hope for anything." As people of faith we rightly live with great expectations. We expect great things from God and are open to good things from people, but we know that life will never be perfectly happy. We live with what someone has called "the courage of imperfection."

Affirmation for the Day:
I will be open to be surprised by joy and will be realistic in expecting sorrow.

May 26

We live best with those we could live without.

In tribute to love, spouses sometimes say, "I couldn't live without you." Such total dependence is neither healthy nor wise. When another person, be it spouse or parent, child or friend, employer or employee, becomes everything to us, we have in effect made a "god" of that person and have overburdened the relationship with a weight no one can carry.

It is far better to be able to say, "Although it would be extremely difficult, I could live without you. I would grieve a great loss, but I would still go on." In times of grief, it is possible for many to say, "Because of the strength received from the love we shared, I am now able to go on alone." That is a real tribute to the person so deeply missed.

Affirmation for the Day:
I will treasure the depth and joy of wonderful human relationships, but will not depend on anyone as I do upon God.

May 27

Thought for the Day:

Confessing our weaknesses is an evidence and source of strength.

Pretense and not weakness is often our chief source of difficulty. Phoniness and make-believe are seldom signs of strength. Each of us needs at least one person, and one is often enough, with whom we can be open and honest about everything. It is true that some will take advantage of such confession, so caution is in order, but it is usually true that personal sharing brings us closer to, rather than separating us from, one another.

Paul Tournier observed that "Confession is contagious." As we share our weaknesses, others are inclined to share theirs, and deeper, more honest relationships often result. As we risk such confession, we discover the truth of the old saying, "When we share our joys we double them, when we share our troubles, we cut them in half." We also begin to understand the paradoxical words of the apostle Paul, "When I am weak, then I am strong" (2 Corinthians 12:10).

Affirmation for the Day:

In reliance upon God's strength, I will dare to face and confess my weaknesses.

May 28

We are in bondage and yet we are free.

We are often painfully aware of all that we cannot do. At times we seem slaves of our limitations and circumstances. These feelings tell much truth. We are finite creatures who are continually confronted with our limitations. But within the walls of our finitude we have an amazing freedom of choice and self-control. No matter what we can't do, the promises of the love of God remind us that we can still trust God's grace. With such promises it is possible to be hopeful even when helpless.

Beyond freedom to trust, we can also exercise considerable influence over our attitudes and actions. Willpower alone won't make us perpetually pleasant, but most of us can make it a habit of being civil toward our families for the first thirty minutes of the day.

We have some control over what we think and how we feel but it doesn't help to try to not think about something. If told, "I'll give you $1,000 if you don't think of monkeys for ten minutes," we would probably think of nothing else! But we can experience what has been called "the expulsive power of a new affection." That is, we can choose to think of other things that will capture our attention and create new attitudes.

Affirmation for the Day:
I will focus, not on what I can't, but on what I can.

May 29

To enjoy being together we need to be alone.

Solitude is essential for togetherness. Only those who know themselves can know another. Only those who know another can know themselves. As our individuality and community are bound up together, so are our solitude and our togetherness.

Solitude is not loneliness. To be lonely is to feel the pain of separation from love we lack or have lost. To enter solitude is to know the joy of being alone and at home with ourselves, the universe, and God. It is not healthy for us to be always together or always alone. There are times when it is wise to seek spaces of solitude, where we can meet ourselves and be refreshed in silence. At other times, we wisely seek companionship to be enriched by the minds and hearts of others.

Such a rhythm of drawing close and drawing back is vital for our friendships and family life. It is no insult to a marriage, for example, that each spouse seeks time to be alone. If we are to fulfill our roles as spouses, parents, or children, we must keep alive as individuals. Personhood is nurtured in solitude as well as in life together.

Affirmation for the Day:
I will seek to enjoy and be strengthened by both togetherness and solitude.

May 30

"Those who want to save their life will lose it, and those who lose their life for my sake will save it."

These paradoxical words are not true because Jesus said them; Jesus said them because they are true. Here are three examples of their truth in daily living:

- We struggle to sleep but sleep eludes us. The harder we try, the less we sleep. Then we give up, cease trying to sleep, and are soon sleeping soundly.
- A husband and wife seek their own happiness and both are miserable. Then a revolutionary change occurs — each begins to seek the other's happiness and both are more joyful than ever before.
- A couple experience frustration in their sexual relationship. They seek ecstasy for themselves and are repeatedly disappointed. Then they stop trying so hard and begin to be good to each other. With tenderness and love they seek to fulfill each other's pleasure and are surprised by joy.

Jesus' statement is a fact of life: When we greedily grasp for happiness, it escapes us. When we forget ourselves and let our lives be lost in trust of God and in caring for someone else, we are surprised to discover the joy we were so frantically seeking.

Affirmation for the Day:

When I live with even a little of the trust and love I see in Jesus, a voice within says, "This is more like it. This is the life I was designed to live. This is the person I was born to be."

May 31

Victory often comes through surrender.

I have long been fascinated by, and appreciative of, the paradoxical wisdom at the heart of the AA "Twelve-Step" program. I recall being struck, years ago, by discussion at a conference on alcoholism that focused on what was called "the phenomena of surrender in the therapeutic process." It is no secret that for millions of alcoholics, victory has come not through struggle but through surrender, not through trying harder but through acknowledgment of "powerlessness," ceasing to try, and starting to trust "a power greater than one's self."

To acknowledge such helplessness and to speak of "surrender" sounds like an admission of defeat. What could be more hopeless? Yet for millions it has been a vital step toward sobriety and sanity.

There must be something exceedingly significant about this "phenomena of surrender." It has brought new life and joy not only to millions in AA but to thousands more in Emotions Anonymous, Overeaters Anonymous, Sexual Addicts Anonymous, and the other twelve-step programs. It is also a central reality in Christian living and is, I believe, reflective of how we are designed to live — as receptive/responsible, dependent/dependable human beings and not as self-sufficient, make-believe "gods."

When we are surrendered to God, we yield no similar allegiance to any addiction or authority; we stand tall as liberated human beings whose lives witness to this paradoxical but profound truth — victory often comes through surrender.

Affirmation for the Day:

When defeated in my self-centered struggles, I will explore the possibility of victory through surrender.

June 1

"We help people more by sharing our difficulties and defeats than by sharing our victories."

This thought from Paul Tournier reminds me of the help millions have received from the apostle Paul who was bold in confessing his troubles and weaknesses. He tells, for example, of a time when he and his companions "were so utterly, unbearably crushed that we despaired of life itself. Indeed, we felt that we had received the sentence of death." Later in the same letter he goes on to say, "I will not boast, except of my weaknesses," and tells of some kind of lifetime affliction that he calls "a thorn in the flesh" (2 Corinthians 1:8-10; 12:5-10).

Such confession enables us to identify with the apostle Paul and with him to find our strength and hope not in ourselves but in God who delivers us from such deadly perils, and whose grace of mercy and power is always sufficient for us.

Affirmation for the Day:
In the safety of God's grace, I will face and confess my troubles and weaknesses.

June 2

Opposing wrongs doesn't always make us right.

Today's thought is prompted by reflection on the tragic Palestinian/Israeli conflict. I believe that the Palestinians are right to oppose Israeli occupation and oppression but this does not make it right for suicide bombers to kill innocent Israelis. I think it is right for Israel to be concerned for its security but that this does not make it right for Israel to occupy Palestinian territory and bomb and bulldoze innocent Palestinians.

Similar illustrations abound. It is wrong for children to disrespectfully disobey their parents but this doesn't make it right for their parents to beat and abuse them.

Being against crime doesn't justify "three strikes and out" sentences that lock up minor offenders for the rest of their lives. It is as someone has said: "Building more prisons to cure crime is like building more cemeteries to cure AIDS."

In every arena of life being against evil doesn't make us good nor does opposing wrongs make us right. Righting wrongs requires right responses as well as right intentions.

Affirmation for the Day:

I will seek to stand for what's right as well as against what's wrong.

June 3

There is something to be said for "loose living."

There is one kind of loose living that comes commended by Christ. "Do not be anxious about your life, what you shall eat, nor about your body, what you shall put on ... nor be of anxious mind" (Luke 12:22, 29). Jesus invites us to live as "loosely" as the birds of the air and the flowers of the field, that do not fret or frantically cling to life. Yet, God cares for them. "How much more," says Jesus, will God care for you! (See Luke 12:28.)

Such simple pictures and promises, which were among my mother's favorites, may seem an insult to our intelligence. How, in a world like this, can mature reasonable people live with the native trust of birds and flowers? How can we who have come of age live with the confidence of children? One fact makes such trust possible. We are the children of God whom God loves and wants to bless. If this is true, childlike faith is hard-headed realism. If God loves and wills to bless us and we do not trust him, we are not just sinners, we are fools!

My mother was a daily practitioner of this kind of loose living and memory of her joy is still, for me, a witness to the wisdom of Jesus.

Affirmation for the Day:

In this too often uptight world, I, too, will seek to practice this kind of loose living.

June 4

"Don't take the last piece."

To this day, when the platter is passed and there is only one slice of turkey left, I remember today's counsel from my mother. From her perspective, to leave the platter empty would not only embarrass the host for having failed to prepare enough food, but also might deprive someone more needy than ourselves. We were taught to clean our plates, but not the serving platters.

We didn't teach that rule to our children nor do I suggest it as a legalistic recommendation for anyone. I do share it as a witness to the importance of considering the needs of others and as a reminder that it is well to restrain ourselves against all forms of greedy, graspy self-indulgence while at the table or anywhere else.

Affirmation for the Day:
In my living as in my dining, I will try not to embarrass or deprive anyone by overreaching or by overindulgence.

June 5

Love is not enough.

To love is to will and to work for the good of another. But what if the work does more harm than good? Imagine, for example, a pediatrician who truly loves a sick child and who works for health, but because of ignorance or carelessness, misdiagnoses and mistreats the child causing permanent impairment or even death.

I don't blame my parents for leaving without saying, "Good-bye" when I was hospitalized after having had polio and wouldn't see them for weeks. I learned years later that the hospital advised parents to leave without saying, "Good-bye" to their children because it made them so upset. Dr. Steven Koop, in his book on the history of Gillette Children's Hospital, says, "This was a mistake." I have no doubt that my parents loved me, but that didn't keep them from being misled into participating in that mistake.

When our daughter was hospitalized for pneumonia, our family doctor, who was kind and caring, encouraged us not to visit her. He said, "The children get along fine all day, but when parents leave they cry and fuss, and it takes the nurses a couple of hours to settle them down." Perhaps because of my earlier experience we did not heed our doctor's advice.

Affirmation for the Day:
If my loving motives are to become loving deeds, they must be guided by knowledge, insight, and wisdom.

June 6

It's a terrible thing to torture a child.

I doubt that any will argue with our thought for today, but we all need to ask ourselves if we have been the victims or perpetrators of such torture.

I recall a newspaper account of a boy who had been so tormented, bullied, and made fun of, that he took a gun with him to school, stood up in the classroom, and said, "I can't take it anymore," then shot himself to death. This tragic story reminds us that torturers aren't just terrible people who lock children away in dungeons. They may be children themselves who think they are having fun when they torment a classmate with sarcastic, negative comments and put-down humor. They may even be well-meaning parents and teachers who relate to children with what psychologist, Alice Miller, calls "poisonous pedagogy."

In one of her books, *For Your Own Good,* Miller claims that harsh discipline is usually far more destructive than helpful. She believes, for example, that if there had been even one person in Adolf Hitler's childhood who showed him love, respect, and affirmation, the world might have been spared his terrible tyranny.

Affirmation for the Day:
I pray for compassion and wisdom to be, like Jesus, a welcomer and blesser of children.

June 7

"Stuttering is what a person does to keep from stuttering."

I am grateful to have had little trouble with stuttering during my adult years, but it was an immense problem in my childhood. When I heard today's thought, from Wendell Johnson, I was immediately struck by the truth of it. I didn't stutter when I talked with the dog because the dog didn't care. I only stuttered when I tried hard not to stutter, which in those days was most of the time.

I share today's thought for two reasons. First, to encourage parents and teachers to ignore the normal repetitions in their children's speech. Be relaxed and easygoing about their lack of fluency. To quote another line from Wendell Johnson, remember that "Stutterers are people who cannot speak nonfluently." That is, they are self-preoccupied with their lack of fluency and are trying too hard to speak perfectly.

I share it also as a reminder of all of the other performance anxieties related to work, sleep, sex, and many other aspects of life. Anxious fretfulness is utterly counterproductive. There are many things in life that we don't do well when we try too hard to do them. When we live by grace, we don't need to be excessively troubled and self-preoccupied over imperfect speech, imperfect work, imperfect sleep, imperfect sex, or imperfect anything.

Affirmation for the Day:
By the grace of God, I will be more accepting and at ease with imperfections in myself and in others.

June 8

"When you see a nail, pick it up."

That admonition from Dad, from long ago, was directed toward flat tire prevention. He knew from experience that nails left on the drive or in the grass around the machine shed could puncture tires. To spot a nail and fail to pick it up was asking for trouble. To invest ten seconds in picking it up might save an hour or more of wasted time, plus the expense of fixing a flat tire.

For me, the implications of Dad's wisdom reach far beyond nails and tires. Figuratively speaking, I once failed "to pick up a nail" when I rushed home for lunch thinking to myself, as I skidded along the icy sidewalk outside the church door, that I must put some sand and salt on that slippery spot. But, I didn't do it until after one of our church school teachers had fallen and broken her leg. When our church insurance company was reluctant to pay her claim, I told the agent that honesty would compel me to testify that I felt personally negligent for what had happened. I was thankful when payment was made.

It's an old story: "A stitch in time saves nine" and "An ounce of prevention is worth a pound of cure." Jesus even talked about it: "We must work the works of him who sent me while it is day; night is coming when no one can work" (John 9:4).

Affirmation for the Day:
When I see an accident waiting to happen, I will act now to prevent it.

June 9

"We can't be unbaptized."

Donna Adkins was a student in one of my confirmation classes and when she was asked for Luther's answer to the question, "What does baptism mean for daily living?" she couldn't remember. She replied, with her own words, "It means that we can't be unbaptized." I liked, affirmed, and have often quoted her answer.

During my seminary student days and for many years into my ministry, our church placed less emphasis on baptism than it has in recent years. I am, frankly, fearful of a kind of sacramentalism that seems to understand baptism and holy communion not just as wonderful means of grace but as almost the beginning and end of grace itself.

From my perspective, baptism is an enacted one-time promise assuring us that we cannot live beyond the love of God. "We can't," as Donna put it, "be unbaptized!" Similarly, holy communion is what someone has called "God's answer to our forgetfulness" reminding us over and over of the welcome and power of God's grace. These sacramental assurances of God's love do not say that God loves only those who receive them. Therefore, when we partake of these gifts we should do so with gratitude, not arrogance.

Affirmation for the Day:

I thank God for sacraments that give personal assurance that God's promises are true for me and for everyone.

June 10

Economic, racial, and sexual distinctions don't count with Jesus.

The Bible is not a book of always-consistent systematic theology. It contains a diversity of views on many subjects and can be quoted on several sides of many issues.

Texts such as Ephesians 5 and 6, for example, have been quoted to support male dominance, racial discrimination, and even slavery. I understand those texts to be what might be called pastoral counseling in a male-dominated, racist, slave society, but not as an expression of reality revealed in Christ. For such understanding we turn to texts like this:

> *As many of you as were baptized into Christ have clothed yourselves with Christ. There is no longer Jew or Greek, there is no longer slave or free, there is no longer male and female; for all of you are one in Christ Jesus.* — Galatians 3:27-28

This tells us that such economic, social, and sexual distinctions and others like them, do not count with Jesus and, therefore, should not count with us.

Affirmation for the Day:

I understand Christ-centered biblical interpretation to affirm the equality of all human beings.

June 11

"God is able to accomplish abundantly far more than all we can ask or imagine."

I find it helpful to be reminded that God is able to do far more than I think, or can even imagine, that God is able to do. It is gratifying to be assured that the power of God is not limited by the littleness of either my mind or imagination. (See Ephesians 3:20-21.)

It is significant to note that this promise is related not just to God's ability to spin galaxies out in space but refers also to "the power at work within us!" It has to do with what God is able to do in each of our lives. That might tempt us to illusions of grandeur but without such pretension, it can also inspire confident hope and steadfast hard work.

Affirmation for the Day:

Perhaps the apostle Paul was really on to something when he said, "I can do all things through Christ who strengthens me" (Philippians 4:13).

June 12

Everything that happens is not "the will of God."

I am troubled when I hear people describing terrible things as "the will of God." Since reading Lesley Weatherhead's little book, *The Will of God*, years ago, I have refrained from thinking and speaking that way.

Weatherhead says that it is important to distinguish between what he calls 1) the intentional will of God, 2) the circumstantial or permissive will of God, and 3) the ultimate will of God. Number 2 is what God permits but does not desire and Number 3 relates to promises that assure us that all is not lost even when things happen that are contrary to God's will.

To illustrate: Weatherhead believes that God intends us to live long and healthy lives but God permits tragic illnesses, accidents, and death. But with God, even death doesn't have the final word. We are promised that nothing can separate us from the love of God, and that beyond the worst that life and death can do is resurrection unto fullness of life in God's presence.

Weatherhead doesn't answer all our questions or remove all the mysteries. When tragedy strikes we wonder, "Why did God permit it?" but we are wise to refrain from saying, "God did it."

Affirmation for the Day:
I will try to think and speak more clearly concerning the will of God.

June 13

The Lord's Prayer is a model, not a mantra.

I am all in favor of praying the Lord's Prayer as we find it in the New Testament. It is interesting to note that the shorter version is introduced with the words, "When you pray, say" (see Luke 11:2-4), and that the longer version is introduced with the words, "Pray then like this" (see Matthew 6:9-13 RSV). That suggests that we don't have to always repeat the exact words of the text, but can use the prayer as a model. That can keep us from using the Lord's Prayer as a mantra — a sacred formula that is repeated over and over and is believed to possess magical power.

Charles Whiston taught some of us years ago that we can even use the Lord's Prayer to pray for others. Here is an example of an intercessory Lord's Prayer:

> *Our Father in heaven,*
> *Enable Bill and Mary to live with reverence toward you.*
> *Reign and rule in their lives.*
> *Do your will in each of them as it is done in heaven.*
> *Give them the things they need for today.*
> *Forgive their sins and enable them to be kind and for-*
> *giving toward others.*
> *Bring them through their trials and temptations, and*
> *deliver them from every evil.*
> *For you reign in power and glory forever. Amen.*

Affirmation for the Day:
I pray to learn from Jesus not only how to pray, but also to be a person of prayer.

June 14

Church should be a place of warmth and welcome.

When in church, as a child, I was sometimes embarrassed by my mother's singing so loudly and by how she always went out of her way to welcome strangers. Now, in retrospect, I am proud of my mother and wish that everyone would sing as she sang and welcome as she welcomed.

A researcher conducted an experiment to learn how visitors were treated in various congregations. He sat near the front and after worship walked with the congregation to the rear of the church, then turned around and exited by another side aisle. He always asked someone the directions to a room in the building. He then rated the reception he had received according to the following scale: Smile of welcome = 10 points, word of greeting = 20 points, exchange of names = 100 points, invitation to return = 200 points, introduction to a worshiper = 1,000 points, and invitation to meet the pastor = 2,000 points.

Sixty-one percent of the churches scored less than 100 points, 28 percent scored less than 20. In only 11 percent was there an invitation to return!

In parody of a Bible verse, someone has said of some Christians, "Many are cold and a few are frozen." May the gracious warmth of God's love make it impossible for that to be true of any of us as individuals or congregations.

Affirmation of the day:

Warmed by God's love, I will seek to live this verse: "Welcome one another, therefore, just as Christ has welcomed you" (Romans 15:7).

June 15

There are times to meddle in politics.

There are those who discourage pastors, teachers, and others who work with the public, from meddling in politics. This counsel may sometimes be wise, but we dare not make it a general rule. When we care about people, we care about the things that affect their lives. Since political decisions powerfully affect the lives of all of us, it is essential that clergy and laity alike meddle in politics.

Moses sets us a good example. He didn't understand God's commission to be an order to comfort and console his oppressed kinfolk. He understood it as a command to go to Pharaoh and demand their liberation! (See Exodus 3:7-12; 5:1.) Moses meddled in politics and, if we care for people, so will we!

Affirmation for the Day:
Compassion compels my commitment to meddle in politics.

June 16

"Politics is the art of making possible tomorrow what is impossible today."

Politics is often described as "the art of the possible," and there is truth in that. But the Norwegian statesman, Edvard Hombro, makes an important point when he adds that it is also "the art of making possible tomorrow what is impossible today."

The fact of that truth is obvious when we stop to think about it. On the first day of school, it is impossible for a little child to read, but after many days a tomorrow comes when the child is a reader. When the Wright brothers dreamed of flying it was impossible, but through persistent planning and preparation they made it happen and ushered in the era of aviation.

So also in politics. Many of us, for example, dream of a world without war. When that dream seems beyond human capacity, let's remember those who led the way for the abolition of the powerful institution of human slavery. How impossible that task must have seemed to the early abolitionists, but we now thank God for their dedication and perseverance and rededicate ourselves to work for the abolition of the institutions of war and war-making.

Affirmation for the Day:

I will work today to make impossibilities possible tomorrow.

June 17

"We need to be dedicated to at least one task that is beyond fulfillment in our lifetime."

This thought comes from Reinhold Niebuhr. He did not disparage the fulfillment of daily tasks and lifetime goals that give us meaning and the grateful satisfaction of accomplishment. But he went on to point out that we human beings have a kind of transcendence. We are part of something bigger than ourselves, and we need to give ourselves to some cause that we can never complete, but to which we can make some significant contribution, no matter how small.

When we see the world's suffering, hunger, oppression, violence, and war, near at hand or far away, it is certainly obvious that there are enough such tasks to keep all of us busy for the rest of our lives.

Affirmation for the Day:
Though I may never live to see it, I will work for the fulfillment of at least one great goal.

June 18

"Politicians who sacrifice their judgment to the opinion of their constituents betray rather than serve them."

This thought from Edmund Burke is essential to a correct understanding of representative democracy. Our elected representatives are to be thinkers who vote for what they believe to be best, not only for their constituents but also for the wider community, state, nation, and world. They are not just to be mirrors reflecting our views. If that were their calling, we could almost get along without them.

We'd still need some people to prepare bills and proposals, but instead of voting by representatives and senators, internet connections could be established that would enable the citizens to vote directly on every issue. Such pure democracy, however, can be effective only in relatively small groups of well-informed and well-intentioned people. In representative democracy, our elected officials should be encouraged to care more for the next generation than the next election and to vote with majority opinion when they believe it to be correct but to vote against it when they are convinced it is wrong.

Affirmation for the Day:

I will tell my elected representatives: "If I am right, vote with me; if I am wrong, vote against me."

June 19

"Question authority."

Today's thought was frequently seen on bumper stickers and lapel buttons during the time of the Vietnam War. Although I am far from being an anarchist, I believe it was a good slogan then and is still appropriate now.

Paul Scherer, my teacher and adviser at Union Seminary in New York, told us years ago that part of our patriotism as Christians is to be among those who have "the conviction and courage to serve as the conscience of the State." Those who conform and do not question authority can be neither conscientious affirmers nor conscientious objectors. They are like chameleons who take on the color of their environment or like thermometers that reflect its temperature. In Christ we are called to be reformers and transformers more than conformers, more like thermostats than thermometers, more like Christ and less like chameleons.

There is a line in *Work of Love* by Holmes Rolston III, that says, "Sometimes we have to lean into the wind to stand up straight." This evokes for me the visual image of two politicians. One gives unquestioned allegiance to the party and is bent over into subservience by the winds of partisan pressure. The other image is of a politician leaning, when conscience demands it, against the coercive efforts of partisan leadership — even the gale winds of presidential pressure — but standing straight and tall in support of personal convictions concerning what is best for the nation and the world. We wisely support leaders who prize truth and justice above party or presidential authority.

Affirmation for the Day:
When compelled by conscience I will dare to question, and sometimes challenge, authority.

June 20

Think for yourself!

None of us would willingly sell our bodies into slavery to live 24 hours a day under the control of a master. Yet some of us do that with our minds. We run with the herd with our minds enslaved by the thinking of the crowd. It is easy to get used to living a lie when everyone around us is living in the same way.

But that is not the only danger. Even if we question authority and rebel against majority opinion, we are still in danger of letting a group of people, or even one person, do our thinking for us. That's apparently what happened in the church at Corinth where some were saying, "I belong to Paul," or "I belong to Apollos," or "I belong to Cephas" (1 Corinthians 1:12). Paul sets things straight when he says, "Let no one boast about human leaders. For all things are yours, whether Paul or Apollos or Cephas" (1 Corinthians 3:21-22). Paul says, in effect, "Think for yourselves! You don't belong to any of us. We belong to you. We are not your masters. We are God's gift to you. Learn from each of us whatever you can but don't become a slave in your thinking to any one of us."

There is wisdom in that for all of us whether we consider ourselves conservative or liberal, followers of this or that thinker, members of one party or another, affiliates of one religion or another. We are not to give our minds in slavish surrender to any person or human institution.

Affirmation for the Day:
While learning from all, I will think for myself!

June 21

"Old ideas, even when untrue, are often more powerful than new truth that has not yet been accepted."

Our problem is often not just lack of new ideas but that we have been captured by old ideas that are untrue and out of touch with reality. As we look back at history and out around the world we see lots of people who, from our perspective, are imprisoned by old ideas that were never true.

Many affirmed the tyranny of slavery, the oppression of apartheid, and the caste system. Some still affirm racial prejudice, the dominance of women by men, and the poor by the rich, discrimination against homosexuals, and a host of other misconceptions that many of us believe to be out of touch with reality.

But what about ourselves? Isn't it likely that we, even now, are captive to some old falsehoods and in need of accepting some new truths?

Affirmation for the Day:

I will remember my need, not only for learning but also for unlearning.

June 22

"Our prophetic task is to present an alternative perception of reality."

Today's thought comes from Walter Bruggemann's book, *The Prophetic Imagination*, and it reminds us that the central calling of prophets, past and present, is not to predict the future but to expose present realities in order to correct misperceptions.

For example, not long ago it was commonly held that men were to rule and women were to obey. For more than 100 years American women didn't have the right to vote. This was also true in the church. My brother and I recall attending congregational meetings with our father, while our mother and other women who could not vote were in the kitchen preparing the lunch to be served after the meeting. Then prophetic voices were raised in church and state affirming the equality of women and men and, though it took many years, the majority perception was changed and women's suffrage granted.

Many of us continue to believe that majority opinion is often out of touch with reality, and that prophetic voices are needed now as much as ever. Those of us who confess Jesus as Lord regard him also as our chief prophet and clearest guide to the correct perception of reality.

Affirmation for the Day:

I will be attentive to those who present alternative perceptions of reality, and especially those reflecting the reality we see in Jesus.

June 23

"The world perishes not from the dark but from the cold."

As I reflect on this thought from Paul Scherer, I would amend it to say, "The world perishes not *only* from the dark but from the cold." Ignorance and lack of understanding can certainly be destructive and life-degrading. Scherer would, I am sure, agree that darkness can be deadly.

In today's thought, he is emphasizing an equally important and more often-forgotten fact. That is, that people who are brilliant and well-informed but who lack warmth and compassion are among the most destructive people on the planet. Competence void of caring can be crushing. Someone has rightly said that the world's worst "devils" are often those who are intelligent and well educated. Their competence increases their capacity for evil. Brilliance without love can be lethal.

Affirmation for the Day:
As I live in the light and warmth of Christ, I will seek to reflect that light and express that warmth.

June 24

"The power of leaders comes from the cooperation of their people."

Our thought for today comes from political scientist, Gene Sharp, who has spent most of his life studying and advocating non-violent means of overthrowing oppression and tyranny. His basic premise is that nonviolent noncooperation is not just a sentimental way of appealing to someone's conscience but a powerful political force that can topple governments and defeat aggressors.

Sharp is honest in acknowledging that such action often involves costly suffering and, like use of violence and war, is not always wise or successful. At the same time, he points to people like Gandhi, Martin Luther King Jr., and hundreds of others who have demonstrated that it can and does work.

From my perspective, it is a method that should be taught, learned, and used more often. In fact, I believe a nonviolent failure would often be far better in the long run than a violent success. Whatever can be said against it, it does not threaten the survival of the human species, as do doomsday weapons, and it is, I believe, far more in harmony with the way of Jesus than is violence and war.

Affirmation for the Day:

When dealing with tyrants, I will remember the power of nonviolent noncooperation.

June 25

The end of democracy will come when people discover that they can vote themselves money out of the public treasury.

I don't know who said today's thought but it states an obvious truth. If national leaders pander to irresponsible constituents and provide services beyond their willingness or ability to pay, the government will eventually face bankruptcy. If politicians stay in power by promising and passing irresponsible tax cuts without reducing expenditures, mounting deficits will eventually undermine the basic trust essential for vital democracy. The potential for disaster is increased when citizens in direct referenda vote to live on borrowed money to be repaid by their children and grandchildren. I think such behavior by both politicians and citizens is a form of serious child abuse that should be confronted and corrected.

If democracy is to survive and thrive all of us must heed John Kennedy's admonition — "Ask not what your country can do for you, but what you can do for your country."

Affirmation for the Day:

As a responsible citizen, I will encourage and support responsible democracy.

June 26

"Democracy is terrible but all other forms of government are even worse."

Winston Churchill gets the credit for today's thought. It instills humble awareness of the fact that no form of government is perfect. All are in various ways bad but some are worse than others, and democracy is the least worst of them all.

When I shared this thought with our Chinese teacher friends they seemed captivated by it, perhaps especially because it came from an American. They had been schooled in the problems and dangers of democracy and apparently expected me to lift it up as a paragon of perfection. When that didn't happen, we embarked on a lengthy, insightful, respectful discussion of the strengths and weaknesses of both the American and Chinese forms of government.

Affirmation for the Day:

While grateful for democracy, I will be honest about its perils and problems.

June 27

"There is enough good in us to make democracy possible and enough evil in us to make democracy necessary."

My memory of this statement comes from my student days at Union Seminary in New York where I audited two courses from Reinhold Niebuhr. Niebuhr is telling us that there is sufficient wisdom and good will in a community to enable trust in its collective judgment and that, on the other hand, no human being or small group of individuals is good enough to be entrusted with the dictatorial authority to rule a nation. Niebuhr would not go so far as to say, "The voice of the people is the voice of God." He recognized that the majority could be, and were often, wrong but he was still able to affirm representative democracy as the best of all possible forms of government.

If he were with us today, I am sure we would hear his clear prophetic voice warning against the manipulation of the masses by money and the media, and in calling for citizen responsibility lest democracy be degraded by ignorance and greed.

Affirmation for the Day:

With Niebuhr, I will be aware of capacity for goodness and inclination to evil in myself and in everyone else.

June 28

Thought for the Day:
The abused often become abusers.

Many, perhaps even most, of those who were abused as children become caring and compassionate parents and never abuse their children or anyone else. But, there are enough who do become abusers to justify the use of the word "often" in our thought for today. While never commendable, such behavior may be understandable. Open wounds are sensitive to the touch and those who are hurting and not yet healed may lash out in hurtful ways to those who come too near.

Groups and nations that have been victims sometimes become victimizers. Few, for example, suffered as did the Jewish people who were victims of the Nazi Holocaust. As prophetic Jewish commentators such as Marc Ellis, Ned Hanauer, Rabbi Michael Lerner, leader of the Tikkun community, and Rabbis Arik Ascherman and Brian Walt of Rabbis for Human Rights, have pointed out, the government of Israel is now victimizing the Palestinian people and using memories of the Holocaust as a means of gaining support and suppressing criticism, especially in this country, of their own abusive policies and practices. They condemn the violence on both sides of this tragic conflict and affirm both security for Israel and justice for the Palestinian people.

Affirmation for the Day:
When hurting, I will try to refrain from being hurtful.

June 29

"I tremble for my country when I reflect that God is just."

Today's thought comes from Thomas Jefferson who wrote these words in 1782 in *Notes on the State of Virginia*. It is part of a reflection on the institution of slavery and its implications for the future of the new nation. The whole sentence reads:

> *Indeed I tremble for my country when I reflect that God is just: that his justice can not sleep forever: that considering numbers, nature and natural means only, a revolution of the wheel of fortune, an exchange of situation is among possible events: that it may become probable by supernatural interference!*

As Jefferson trembled for the future of "my country," I now tremble for the future not only of this nation but of the entire world. I fear a revolution not spawned by slavery but by poverty and oppression and staged by terrorism, the weapon of the powerless. Since we have achieved sole supremacy in terms of both wealth and military power we can be sure that there are some like the terrorists of September 11, 2001, who are willing to risk daring and desperate means including the loss of their own lives to bring us down.

It is right to defend ourselves against revolutionary terrorism, but I fear there will be no long-term victory in this war unless we use our wealth and power for the alleviation of poverty and oppression and not primarily in self-defense. As God is just, we can do no better than to work for an increase of justice in all the world.

Affirmation for the Day:
I pray "justice (will) roll down like waters, and righteousness like an ever flowing stream" (Amos 5:24).

June 30

Listen to what you say when you talk to yourself.

What do you hear when you listen to yourself talking to yourself? Is the conversation positive and affirming, full of purpose and hope? Or is it negative and self-defeating, full of doom and gloom?

Until I read the book, *What to Say When You Talk to Yourself*, by Shad Helmstetter, I had never heard of what is called the "self-talk movement." Even though I think there is a lot of fluff in this emphasis, I also believe that these people are on to something that is significant for all of us. Living by the grace of God changes lots of things about us, including how we talk to ourselves. That's what happened to the apostle Paul. When he said, "I can do all things through Christ who strengthens me" (Philippians 4:13), he gave us an example of how we should talk to ourselves.

People in twelve-step groups often warn against "stinkin' thinkin'." So did the apostle Paul when he said, "Let the same mind be in you that was in Christ Jesus" (Philippians 2:5), and again, "Whatever is true, whatever is honorable, whatever is just, whatever is pure, whatever is pleasing, whatever is commendable, if there is any excellence and if there is anything worthy of praise, think about these things" (Philippians 4:8). That's a list of topics for healthy conversation not only with others but also with ourselves.

Affirmation for the Day:
In my self-talk, I will tell myself what I hear Jesus telling me.

July 1

"Do what you can and when you can't, don't be afraid to ask for help."

Today's thought comes from Iona Speidel who is a member of University Lutheran Church of Hope. As a child, I had polio which affected one leg and she had a similar affliction that limited the use of one of her arms. As we talked about how we had both managed pretty well, she shared today's thought which is advice she had received from her mother long ago. Whatever our personal limitations, I think it is worth remembering and heeding.

"Do what you can" encourages us, temporarily at least, to forget about our disabilities and to focus on what we are able to do. When we do that we usually discover that there are more things we can do than we have time to get done, and it helps save us from moping around, feeling sorry for ourselves, because we can't do everything others are doing.

"When you can't, don't be afraid to ask for help" — that's often more difficult to do, but is no less important. If we are known as people who do what we can, others are usually willing, and often grateful, to be able to help us in doing what we can't. Since it's often much harder to ask for help than to give it, we should let our reason triumph over our feelings and when necessary give others the privilege and joy of being helpful.

Affirmation for the Day:

I will focus on what I can and not on what I can't, and when I can't, I will turn for help to someone who can.

July 2

How a question is asked often determines the answer that is received.

Sidney Harris tells of two priests who argued over whether it was proper to smoke and pray at the same time. Since they couldn't agree, each wrote to the pope and were surprised when the pope agreed with both of them. When they investigated how this could be they discovered that one had asked, "Is it all right for me to smoke while I pray?" and the pope answered, "No! Smoking is a terrible distraction. Don't smoke when you pray."

The other had asked, "Is it all right for me to pray while I smoke?" To which the pope had replied, "Yes. You are to pray without ceasing and are not to stop praying when you start smoking."

This story is a vivid reminder of the fact that the answers we receive are often dependent on the way the questions are asked.

Affirmation for the Day:

I will watch out for answers, especially in surveys of public opinion, that are strongly influenced by the way questions are asked.

July 3

Thought for the Day:
Capture your thoughts before they fly away.

I once read of an author who was caught up in contemplation of a thought he wanted to remember. Then the doorbell rang and he was compelled to deal with a traveling salesman. When he returned to his desk, he was distressed to discover that the thought he had been contemplating had, as it were, flown away and was now beyond sight or recall. We have all had similar experiences. In the midst of a lively conversation we think of a point we want to make. But when the discussion takes a distracting turn, the thought disappears and we can't bring it back.

Therefore, I believe it is wise to keep note paper and a pencil in our pockets and on our bedstands and to make a habit of jotting down things we want to remember but can quickly forget. These can be thoughts we want to ponder further or to share with others, or simply a listing of things to do that might be forgotten.

Affirmation for the Day:
Since short-term memories are often fleeting, I will seek to capture my thoughts in writing before they fly or fade away.

July 4

Don't give Caesar what belongs to God.

When asked "Is it right to pay taxes to Caesar?" Jesus replied, "Render to Caesar the things that are Caesar's, and to God the things that are God's" (Mark 12:17 RSV). This has usually been understood to affirm paying taxes and submission to governmental authority.

However, it is clear, from the Bible, that our conscience and supreme allegiance belong to God and not to Caesar. When Peter and the apostles were told to stop teaching about Jesus, they replied, "We must obey God rather any human authority" (Acts 5:29).

Colin Morris translates Jesus' words: "Give Caesar what Caesar's got coming and give God what God's got coming." He suggests that Jesus' hearers understood this as would Jews living under Nazi tyranny if told, "Give Hitler what Hitler's got coming and give God what God's got coming." Morris, therefore, believed that Jesus' answer to the question was an emphatic "No!" and that those who later accused Jesus of forbidding payment of taxes to Caesar may have gotten that idea from the event reported in Mark 12:13-17. We can debate about that, but there can be no doubt that absolute allegiance and total submission to governmental authority is not proper patriotism but sinful idolatry.

Affirmation for the Day:
When I say the Pledge of Allegiance, it will be to "one nation *under* God" not to "one nation over God."

July 5

"To fulfill God's design means entire abandonment to him."

When I read Oswald Chambers years ago, I was struck by his emphasis on the importance of an almost reckless surrender to, dependence upon, and openness to the Spirit of God that he calls "abandonment." My devotional book, *Joyful Living*, begins with these quotes from his book, *My Utmost for His Highest*:

- *Abandonment to God is of more value than personal holiness.*
- *When we are abandoned to God, he works through us all the time.*
- *In our abandonment we give ourselves to God just as God gives himself to us, without any calculation.*
- *When you get through to abandonment to God, you will be the most surprised and delighted creature on earth; God has you absolutely and has given you your life.*
- *We never know the joy of self-sacrifice until we abandon in every particular ... as soon as we abandon, the Holy Ghost gives us an intimation of the joy of Jesus.*

Such surrender to any human authority would be self-denigration. The surrender of abandonment in trust and openness to the love of God is self-discovery and self-fulfillment! When we give ourselves to God, God gives us back and lifts us up to "walk in newness in life" (Romans 6:4).

Affirmation for the Day:

Day-by-day I give myself away in abandonment to God who gives himself to me.

205

July 6

Make room for the mystical.

Clear-headed, rational Christians often feel uneasy and uncomfortable when they hear people sing and speak of how Jesus "walks with me and talks with me and tells me I am his own." That may sound a bit too sweet and sentimental for some of us, but it witnesses to the mystic dimension of Christian living that I believe to be vital for each of us. It was so for Luther. We can read about it in books like *Luther and the Mystics* that tell of how Luther was influenced by people like Tauler and Meister Eckhard. They affirmed personal experience of the living God, and often spoke of Christ being born anew in each of our lives.

Come to think of it, many of us have prayed for this experience. Here is our prayer in the words of Phillips Brooks' beautiful Christmas carol:

> *O holy child of Bethlehem,*
> *Descend to us, we pray;*
> *Cast out our sin, and enter in,*
> *Be born in us today.*

Affirmation for the Day:
With Luther and millions more, I will be open to the mystery and marvel of the mystical.

July 7

We can be blessed by what we can't understand.

Our thought for today is certainly true in the natural world. I don't think anybody fully understands light or gravity but we all enjoy the sunshine, couldn't survive without photosynthesis, and are held in our places by a force beyond comprehension. We don't need to understand radio waves to listen to the news or enjoy a symphony. Even when marveling at computer technology that is far beyond my comprehension, I can be blessed by an email from a friend far away.

In the life of faith, I am reminded again of these lines Al Rogness liked to quote — "I do not know how Bethlehem's babe could in the godhead be. I only know that manger child has brought God's love to me." I don't know the source of that little rhyme but I appreciate its wisdom. I think it expresses the essential meaning of the incarnation. In Jesus, the love of God reaches out to touch, welcome, invade, and indwell our lives. We can't fully comprehend the mysteries of the Trinity and the Incarnation but we can rest in, and rejoice in, God's love.

Affirmation for the Day:
I thank God that I am not saved by my theology but by God's love.

July 8

"Jesus is my friend. I on him depend."

This thought comes from my mother. As I recall my childhood and youth, I am struck and moved by how Mother lived with a kind of primitive profundity. She was a farmer's wife with little formal education. She didn't flaunt her religion or impose it on anybody, but she certainly lived and rejoiced in it. It was all so natural and free from either self-consciousness or self-righteousness.

I still get misty-eyed when I remember the hymns she sang in the kitchen and recall looking out the window on an early morning and seeing her kneeling in the woodshed door with her arms lifted in praise as she greeted the sunrise and a new day.

Mother would have flunked a test in systematic theology but I'd give her an A in knowing how to live. She trusted that Jesus was her friend and she did "on him depend." She lived her faith in confident trust combined with outgoing warmth and compassion, and for that I will always be grateful.

Affirmation for the Day:
I pray to live with joy and compassion that comes from dependence on the friendship of Jesus.

July 9

Thought for the Day:

Trust 100 percent in God and never trust 100 percent in anyone else.

If that seems too harsh on the human side, remember that none of us is 100 percent trustworthy. That's not because we are mean or malicious but because we are limited, finite, and, for example, forgetful. If I ask Carol, whom I trust profoundly, to mail a letter for me, I would be disappointed but not utterly shocked or surprised if she would confess to me a week later that she had forgotten to mail it and had just found it in her purse. We are all frail and fallible and often need to be reminded to do things we have promised to do.

While believing that we shouldn't put 100 percent trust in any human being, including ourselves, I also think we make a far greater mistake if we don't trust anybody. I have often said that if we often get conned we are too trusting and if we never get conned we are too suspicious and untrusting.

Refusing to trust out of fear of being betrayed is like refusing to hope out of fear of being disappointed. It is far better to risk betrayal and disappointment than to live grimly without trust or hope.

Affirmation for the Day:

Without trusting anyone as God, I will trust many as honest and dependable human beings.

July 10

Thought for the Day:
"Marry a good friend."

In our *Be Good to Each Other* book, my wife, Carol, and I affirm today's thought which comes from a column by Ann Landers.

We believe that mutual sexual attraction is a necessary but insufficient condition for marriage. It is right and proper for couples contemplating marriage to look forward to lots of great times in bed together, but it is also true that if one or both discover that they really don't like each other and have very little to talk about at the breakfast table or on a long trip in the car, having great times in bed is not likely to last very long.

Mental, emotional, physical, and spiritual intimacy are all vital aspects of a long-term relationship of love. For marital fulfillment, sexual attraction and personal friendship are best experienced together.

Affirmation for the Day:
When contemplating marriage, I will look for someone to enjoy at breakfast as well as in bed.

July 11

Keep the three candles burning.

During many weddings, there is a little ceremony that involves lighting a unity candle. There are two lighted candles standing beside a large center candle. At the appropriate time the bride and groom each take one of the lighted candles and light the center candle. Then sometimes they blow out the candles they are holding and put them back in the candle stands. Whenever that happens I wince to see their individuality symbolically going up in smoke.

Therefore, I always encouraged couples to leave all three candles burning as a symbol not only of their new unity in marriage but also of their continued individuality. They have affirmed a new togetherness and commitment to shared life together, but they are still Bill and Mary and not just "Mr. and Mrs. Somebody."

I've been displeased with some of the poetry quoted at weddings, but have always appreciated these lines from Kahlil Gibran:

> *Let there be spaces in your togetherness,*
> *And let the wind of the heavens dance between you.*
> *Sing and dance together and be joyous, but let each*
> *   one of you be alone.*
> *Even as the strings of the lute are alone though they*
> *   quiver with the same music.*

Affirmation for the Day:
Whatever my marital state, I will remember that I am still an individual and will keep my personal candle burning.

July 12

"Pity is a wonderful Christian virtue but a very poor basis for marriage."

Although I have no idea how it related to art history, I recall today's thought from an aside in Arnie Flaten's class at St. Olaf. Flaten had a reputation not only for being a great artist and teacher of art but also as one who knew what it is to live by the grace of God and who affirmed care and compassion for hurting people. It was, no doubt, in that context that he shared today's thought that I still remember a half-century later.

There are many worthy motives for marriage. I think Flaten is right that pity is not among them. We should not marry someone because we feel sorry for a lonely, hurting person. Marriage is an adventure of mutuality and not a form of "Operation Rescue."

Affirmation for the Day:
When looking toward marriage, I will beware of being misled by a "Savior" mentality.

July 13

We wish you joy and promise you trouble.

Today's thought comes from the first page of our *Be Good to Each Other* book on marriage. We say it not to be negative but to be realistic. In the book, we tell of something Uncle Absalon Erdahl said during his golden wedding celebration with Aunt Sarah: "In all these fifty years, Sarah and I have never thought of separation or divorce but we have thought of murder on several occasions." I heard that the year before I got married and must confess that it helped give me realistic expectations.

Carol and I once gave a talk on marriage at the Holden Village Retreat Center near Lake Chelan, Washington. Among other things we told that "We met on the debate team and have been at it ever since!" We confessed to having had bad days and misunderstandings. After our talk, an older woman thanked us and said, "I am glad I heard you today. My husband died five years ago and I have often thought of the problems we had in our marriage. But after hearing you two, I think our marriage wasn't so bad after all!"

Affirmation for the Day:
In marriage, as in all of life, I will expect both joy and trouble.

July 14

Half the troubles in life come from being married and half from being single.

We quote this thought in *Be Good to Each Other*. It comes from a long-forgotten source and is one with which we do not agree. We think that at least half of life's troubles have nothing to do with whether we are single or married. They are human problems that come to single and married people alike.

Therefore, if pressed concerning percentages we think it would be more correct to say that one-fourth of life's problems come from being married, one-fourth from being single, and one-half from being human. Those numbers, of course, are more symbolic than real and should not be taken literally.

The point of pondering today's thought is to help us avoid the mistake of one divorced person who told me that "When I was married I blamed all my problems on my spouse. I now realize that many of them were just part of living in this troubled world."

Affirmation for the Day:
I will try to live with the problems of life without blaming everything on others.

July 15

"A good marriage is ninety percent civilized business management and ten percent romance."

When I have shared today's thought, which comes from an older book called *Mirages of Marriage*, by William Lederer and Don Jackson, some couples have responded with, "That doesn't sound very exciting!" But it depends on how we apply those percentages. Ten percent of 24 hours provides 2.4 hours for romance every day which should be about enough for even the most romantic couples! Whatever the percentages, times of joyful romancing will likely be highly supportive of the "business management" side of the relationship.

On the other hand, cooperative sharing of "business management" including such mundane tasks as shopping, taking out the garbage, working on the budget, and similar responsibilities of life together will almost certainly increase, extend, and enhance those times of romance.

Affirmation for the Day:

I will remember that regular romancing and responsible management support and sustain each other.

July 16

Some relationships are "the moral and emotional equivalent of marriage."

In our book, *Sexual Fulfillment*, Herbert Chilstrom and I wrestled with the question of what constitutes marriage. There are relationships of love, faithfulness, and public lifelong commitment that are "the moral and emotional equivalent of marriage." Such thinking is not new. Luther said of priests, who were forbidden to marry:

> *From the bottom of their hearts both are of a mind to live together in lawful wedded love, if only they could do it with a clear conscience. The two are certainly married in the sight of God. And I say that where they are so minded, let the priest take and keep her as his lawful wedded wife and live honestly with her as her husband, whether the pope likes it or not, whether it be against canon or human law.*

"Married in the sight of God" strikes me as synonymous with "the moral and emotional equivalent of marriage," which we relate to all couples living together in committed relationships. If Luther understood homosexuality as we understand it today, and heard the testimony of gays and lesbians who thank God for their committed lifelong relationships, I think that he would say, as we do, that they are, in effect, "married in the sight of God" and would affirm the blessing of such unions.

Affirmation for the Day:

What Luther said then gives me a hint concerning what he might say now.

July 17

When we pick an apple we shake the tree.

I am increasingly persuaded of the truth of this thought in each of our lives. It witnesses to the fact that our words and deeds have effects for good and ill far beyond our immediate awareness. When we scan our personal histories, each of us can recall relationships that have been hindered or healed by things said and done or unsaid and not done by people who were, and sometimes still are, unaware of the significance of those events.

I once read of a person who was killed when a slate fell from a roof where it had been placed over 100 years before. Investigation revealed that the worker who had installed the slate had failed to use one of the fasteners that was meant to keep it in place. Although long dead, that worker's mistake brought death and sorrow to people of whom he never thought or dreamed.

Each of us has also been blessed by the words and deeds of many people who were never aware of having such influence in our lives.

Affirmation for the Day:
I rightly tremble at the thought of the unknown effects of my life, for better and for worse, in the lives of others.

217

July 18

Promises are to be kept and sometimes broken.

This reflection on promises will consider two quotations. The first is from Robert Service's poem, "The Cremation of Sam Magee" — "A promise made is a debt unpaid." That statement reminds us that debts are to be paid and promises kept.

The second quotation is from Abraham Lincoln who, when confronted with having broken a campaign promise, replied, "A promise I should never have made in the first place is better off broken than kept."

If promises are debts to be paid and if it is a mistake to keep mistaken promises, how do we know which to keep and which to break? Deciding may sometimes be difficult, but it seems clear that we should do what is best for others and not just for ourselves. We should pay our promises as we pay our debts even when costly to ourselves. But if we now see that keeping a promise will do more harm than good, we should admit our mistake and break it.

Affirmation for the Day:

I will almost always be a promise-keeper, but when love and wisdom require it, I will dare to be a promise-breaker.

July 19

Thought for the Day:

"We are sometimes like roadside signs that correctly point the way but never move to go there."

That confession, from long ago, comes from Dr. Jurgen Moller, who was then our family physician. We were discussing the health effects of smoking and he had just told me that "every cigarette takes nine minutes off a person's life" and I had asked him, "Why, if smoking is so terrible, do so many doctors and nurses still smoke?" He first referred to the addictive power of nicotine and how difficult it is for many to quit, then used the road sign analogy to emphasize the fact that doctors who were smokers should still be heeded when they counseled their patients to abstain from smoking.

Many of us pastors fail in many ways to practice what we preach. We encourage love and yet are sometimes spiteful and unkind. We invite confident trust in the promises of God but are often anxious and afraid. We speak of the importance of taking time for family and friendship but yield to temptations that keep us from doing so ourselves. Like those stationary signs, we may be stuck in the mud of old habits and hurtful ways of living. That doesn't mean our message is false and should be rejected. Truth-telling and faulty living can go together.

Affirmation for the Day:

I will try to practice what I preach and, when I fail, will continue to preach, including to myself.

July 20

"The grand old constellations still stand firmly in their places."

On a night of meteor showers, many panicked and feared that the sky was falling and that the world was coming to an end. Some wondered how Abraham Lincoln could remain so calm in the face of such catastrophe and found comfort in his observation that "The grand old constellations still stand firmly in their places."

We live in a shaky world and there is much to fear. Nations rise and fall. We stumble and fall. People in whom we trust fail us and we fail them. Stocks go up and down. Health fails. None of us knows if we will be alive next week, next year, or even tomorrow. We, too, may panic and fear that the sky is falling.

But in the midst of it all, God's "grand old constellations" of promise still stand firmly in their places. Among them are such as these from the letter to the Hebrews:

I will never fail you nor forsake you.
— Hebrews 13:5

Jesus Christ is the same yesterday, today and forever.
— Hebrews 13:7

Therefore let us be grateful for receiving a kingdom that cannot be shaken, and thus let us offer to God acceptable worship with reverence and awe.
— Hebrews 12:28 (RSV)

Affirmation for the Day:
When the sky seems to be falling, I will look to the "grand old constellations."

July 21

Thought for the Day:
There may be times for pious profanity.

I was shocked by these three comments: First, from Fritz Norstad, my professor of pastoral care at Luther Seminary: "There are times to say, 'To hell with it!' " Second, from the renowned Christian psychotherapist, Paul Tournier: "Neurotics are people who can't say, 'Damn it.' " Third, from an active member of my first parish: "My God is too big to worry about my getting mad and saying, 'God damn it,' now and then."

While being neither an advocate nor practitioner of profanity, I now confess to wondering if these people weren't on to something significant. At the very least, they are certainly to be commended for their honesty. Being able to candidly express our anger and frustration is likely far healthier than bottling it up, which can be harmful to our own and others' emotional, mental, and physical health.

Such exclamations remind me of Luther's exhortation to "sin boldly but believe more boldly still" and also of his comment that "Curses of the blasphemers may sound more pleasing to the ears of God than some of the prayers of the pious." He was probably thinking of the self-righteous Pharisee's prayer, "God, I thank you that I am not like other people" (Luke 18:11).

I am also reminded that death is to be damned. (See Revelation 20:14.) Does this suggest that it is proper for a Christian whose life has been devastated by an untimely death or similar tragedy to pray (not to curse but to pray!) "God damn it!"?

Affirmation for the Day:
When the words fit the reality and the feeling, I will dare to think — and sometimes say — and even pray them.

July 22

Those who wait for the Lord shall renew their strength.

Many years ago, my aunt rode with me from the church to her home following the funeral for her husband who had died unexpectedly. When I said, "Good-bye and God bless you," she responded by saying, "The Lord has never failed me and I am sure he will not fail me now." Then she quoted these words from memory: "Those who wait for the Lord shall renew their strength, they shall mount up with wings like eagles, they shall run and not be weary, they shall walk and not faint" (Isaiah 40:31).

Such confident trust had sustained her for nearly eighty years. Now in the time of great loss and sorrow it sustained her still.

Affirmation for the Day:

I, too, will trust in God who "gives power to the faint and strengthens the powerless" (Isaiah 40:29).

July 23

Thought for the Day:
"Forgiveness does not remove feelings of guilt."

When we have acted in ways that are hurtful, it is appropriate to feel guilty. In such times we rightly seek the forgiveness of God and those whom we have wronged and may be surprised to discover, after being assured of forgiveness, that we still feel guilty. Today's thought, from Paul Tournier, helps us to understand and live with continued feelings of guilt.

If we have done something that was really hurtful to someone, we should regret it for the rest of our lives. Forgiveness does not remove such feelings of regret. Forgiveness assures us that we are still loved and welcomed into the embrace of God's grace. That love frees us from having to deny our hurtful behavior and, in that sense, may even cause us to feel our guilt more deeply and to receive forgiveness more gratefully.

Affirmation for the Day:
However painful my feelings of regret, I thank God for still loving me.

July 24

"We should neither be so proud that we think we have no sins nor so proud that we think our sins are too big for God to forgive."

There is certainly arrogance in thinking that we are so perfect that we have no sins to be forgiven. But as George Aus, another of my Luther Seminary professors, reminds us in our thought for to-day, there is also another kind of pride that considers our sins too big for God to forgive.

Charles Spurgeon tells of a time when he wondered if God's forgiveness was sufficient for his many sins. Then he imagined a little fish going to the great fish that was lord of the deep and say-ing, "I have decided to drink the sea," to which the wise old fish replied, "That's fine, there is enough for you!" By that imaginative exchange Spurgeon was reminded that "There's a wideness to God's mercy like the wideness of the sea" and that "Where sin increased, grace abounded all the more" (Romans 5:20).

Affirmation for the Day:

When my sins seem too big for God to forgive, I will renounce my pride, remember that little fish, and be reassured of God's abounding grace.

July 25

Our worst sins may be, not among the things of which we are most ashamed, but among those of which we are most proud.

Most of us would be terribly ashamed if others knew certain things about us. But we are highly honored to be recognized for the great things we have done.

Then we read a text like this:

> *Thus says the Lord: Do not let the wise boast in their wisdom, do not let the mighty boast in their might, do not let the wealthy boast in their wealth; but let those who boast boast in this, that they understand and know me, that I am the Lord; I act with steadfast love, justice and righteousness in the earth, for in these things I delight, says the Lord.* — Jeremiah 9:23-24

Jesus also reminds us that there are things that people prize and praise that are "an abomination in the sight of God." (See Luke 16:14-15.)

And then we wonder — are our greater sins closer to our arrogance and pride than to our shame and guilt? Are they among the things of which we are most ashamed or among those of which we are most proud?

Affirmation for the Day:

When honored, I will wonder, "Is this recognition for my goodness or for my sin?"

July 26

It's hard to forgive and to be forgiven.

When seriously wronged, we know that it is not easy to forgive. When we have trouble forgiving someone, we do well to ponder Jesus' parable about a person who was forgiven a multimillion dollar debt and yet refused to forgive someone who owed him a few dollars. (See Matthew 18:23-35.) That story reminds us that God doesn't just forgive us of some things but of everything that is in need of pardon. It can help us take ourselves less seriously and to be more forgiving toward others.

On the other hand, if we have seriously wronged someone, we have also learned in the painful school of experience that it is not easy to be forgiven. To admit our wrong and to ask someone to forgive us is among the most difficult and humbling things we ever do. When we are in need of forgiveness, I see no alternative to enduring the embarrassment and pain of entrusting ourselves to the love and mercy of the person we have wronged, and honestly and humbly, ask for it.

Affirmation for the Day:
I pray for compassion to forgive and for courage to confess and ask for forgiveness.

July 27

Sex is God's gift for our good.

Near the end of the Bible's first account of creation, it says that "God created humankind ... male and female" and "God saw everything that he had made, and indeed it was very good" (Genesis 1:27, 31). Our sexuality is one among many of God's "very good" gifts.

In our book, *Sexual Fulfillment for Single and Married, Straight and Gay, Young and Old*, Herbert Chilstrom and I ask, "If sex is God's gift for our good, what's it good for?" We answer, "Sex is good for life! Sex is life-giving both in terms of procreation and re-creation. Sex is the means God has chosen to give new life. Sex is also one wonderful means, among many, by which God has chosen to give love, joy, and pleasure to our lives."

As we rightly rejoice that God has given us brains to think, eyes to see, and ears to hear, we also give joyful thanks for God's good gift of our sexuality.

Affirmation for the Day:
I thank God that sex is among God's many good gifts.

July 28

Intimacy of mind and heart is even closer than intimacy of body.

Today's thought is not to minimize the closeness of sexual relations, which, at best, are beautiful and wonderful. It is rather to put proper emphasis on the even closer closeness that comes through sharing of what is deepest in our hearts and minds. These intimacies go together, and it is doubtful that we can have the most fully satisfying physical intimacy without similar depth of mental, emotional, and even spiritual intimacy.

If this is to happen, we need to be trusting and vulnerable in our life together. We need to risk letting down our defenses, daring enough to tell of our hopes, fears, and dreams in ways that let our partners know who we really are. This is often difficult to do but is made easier by a kind and caring partner who helps us feel safe enough to be open and honest. In the security of such love, we can open doors to mental and emotional intimacy in ways that are often a prelude to letting go physically in a more free and joyful sexual relationship.

Affirmation for the Day:

In life together, I will seek to encourage and enable sharing of what is in our deepest hearts.

July 29

The sexiest part of a person is the brain, not the body.

To put it bluntly, our most significant sex organ is not between our legs but between our ears, and the greatest "turn-ons" are not visual, but verbal. Even the visual is not primarily on bodily appearance. As I once heard someone say, "The sexiest thing about a woman is not how she looks to me, but how she looks at me!"

This is not to disparage physical attractiveness that can certainly be a sexual enhancement, but it is not central. In counseling with couples, I learned that some who were extremely attractive physically had miserable sex lives, while others who would never win a beauty contest, had active, life-giving sexual relationships.

We should all do our best to be healthy and attractive physically but lack of perfection in that department need not keep us from sharing the words, signals, and thoughts that lead to joyful sexual fulfillment.

Affirmation for the Day:
Whatever my body has or lacks in sexual attractiveness, I will be thankful for my brain.

July 30

Thought for the Day:
We do not choose our sexual orientation.

I did not choose to be heterosexual but by the time I was a teenager I had discovered that some girls were sexually attractive. The word "heterosexual" was not part of my adolescent vocabulary but there was no doubt that I was one.

After years of abysmal ignorance, I finally began to get acquainted with gay and lesbian people, and was amazed to learn that their experience was similar to mine except that they discovered themselves to be sexually attracted to people of the same sex. They didn't choose their orientation any more than I did. In fact, many of them at first denied, rejected, and struggled to change the reality they had discovered. Some discovered that they were sexually attracted to both genders. They didn't choose that, either, but it did give them a choice concerning specific people with whom they could relate sexually.

The dynamics of sexual, and affectional, attraction are extremely complex and difficult to understand. I don't know what creates sexual orientation but I believe that it is pretty well established by adolescence, if not earlier, and there seems to be little that can be done to significantly change it.

Affirmation for the Day:
I thank God for the possibility of living well with the sexual orientation I have been given.

July 31

Thought for the Day:
The Bible says nothing concerning homosexuality as we understand it today.

I once believed that the Bible declared homosexuality to be an abomination. Careful study of scripture and the testimony of gay and lesbian Christians have compelled me to change my mind. It is clear that the Bible condemns lustful, exploitive same-sex activity but it says nothing concerning homosexual orientation, which wasn't analyzed until hundreds of years after the Bible was written.

To conclude from the Bible's condemnation of certain sinful practices that all homosexual activity is sinful is, I believe, as unfair as it would be to conclude from a book describing heterosexual rape and child abuse that all heterosexual activity is sinful.

It seems likely that most of the sinful same-sex activity to which the Bible refers was perpetrated by heterosexuals involved in behavior such as the abuse of prisoners and having sexual involvement with children. I agree with the Bible's rejection of such practices but disagree with those who misuse the Bible to condemn people of homosexual orientation and all same-sex activity.

In his book, *MANY members yet ONE body*, Professor Craig Nessan of Wartburg Theological Seminary wisely calls for room in the church for both "traditional" and "contextual" (as affirmed in this reflection) interpretation of the biblical texts that speak of same-sex activity. Failure to provide such room would, I believe, be contemptuous of some of our best biblical scholarship.

Affirmation for the Day:
I will beware of irresponsible use of biblical texts to condemn that which they don't address.

August 1

The Bible says nothing concerning committed same-sex couples.

There is no account in the Bible of couples who lived in committed, faithful, lifelong, same-sex relationships for which they gave thanks to God. For perhaps the first time in the history of church and community such couples are making their love and commitment public and are asking for our acceptance and affirmation.

Although the Bible says nothing specifically concerning committed same-sex relationships, it has much to say concerning relevant Christian morality. The apostle Paul, in a text quoted earlier, sums it up when he says:

> *Owe no one anything, except to love one another; for the one who loves another has fulfilled the law. The commandments, "You shall not commit adultery; you shall not murder; you shall not steal; you shall not covet"; and any other commandment are summed up in this word, "Love your neighbor as yourself." Love does no wrong to a neighbor; therefore, love is the fulfilling of the law.* — Romans 13:8-10

On the basis of texts like this, I believe it is appropriate to affirm same-sex couples in committed relationships and that those who are otherwise qualified can rightly be affirmed for ordination.

Affirmation for the Day:
Believing that God affirms life-giving relationships of faithful love and commitment, so will I.

August 2

Right sex requires a right relationship.

Sexual acts that are physically or emotionally harmful are certainly sinful, but sexual morality has more to do with the relationship between the people than with the specific sexual activity.

I once heard a young woman on a television talk show say, "Making love is what you do with your partner; having sex is just for fun." Masters and Johnson were far wiser when they pointed out that such promiscuity is "ultimately boring." If sex is to be not only fun, but joyfully life-fulfilling in the long run, it requires a relationship of love, respect, faithfulness, and commitment. The Bible acknowledges "the fleeting pleasures of sin" (Hebrews 11:25). Lasting joy is not found in such superficial sexuality.

Affirmation for the Day:
I will beware of purchasing short-term delight at the cost of long-term regret.

August 3

Learn something about sex from Sacks.

Even after having come to accept persons of same-sex orientation, it was difficult for me to understand those who said that "gay is good" and that they wouldn't change to straight even if able to do so. Then I read Oliver Sacks' story of "The Color-Blind Painter," in his book, *An Anthropologist on Mars*. It tells of an artist who, because of an accident, became totally color-blind. He was, at first, devastated and desperately sought help to regain his sense of color. Everything failed and he continued to see only black and white and shades of gray. Then as time passed he discovered that he began to appreciate his new vision. He saw tone and texture he had not seen before and began to paint again. He came to regard his new vision as "a strange gift" and confessed that he no longer desired to change back to colored sightedness.

That story helped me, with my bias in favor of heterosexuality, to see my gay and lesbian friends' orientation as "a strange gift" and to affirm them in their confession that it was good and in their desire to remain as they are.

Affirmation for the Day:
Since my orientation must seem as strange to them as theirs does to me, I will encourage us to learn from and affirm each other.

August 4

Masturbation is God's gift to the celibate.

Today's thought comes from a Roman Catholic priest who told me years ago that, since it is contrary to the policy of his church, he would have to deny saying it if I were to quote him by name. Therefore, I won't tell his name but will confess to believe that he spoke truth and that I think that his church might have been saved from much misconduct and misery if this bit of wisdom had been affirmed for its clergy.

I believe, as Herb Chilstrom and I state in *Sexual Fulfillment*, that God has created all of us for sexual fulfillment and that self-pleasuring is a good gift that God has provided for people for whom relational fulfillment is not possible or proper.

There is nothing in the Bible concerning masturbation. When Jesus spoke about adulterous, lustful looking, I think that what he was really condemning was the desire to possess another's spouse and that this sin has more to do with covetousness than with normal sexual desires and fantasies. Our ability to fantasize is also a gift from God. There is no doubt a fine line between sinful and sinless fantasies, but I don't think that God who has created our capacities to imagine and daydream condemns them all.

Affirmation for the Day:
I thank God for giving us more than one way of enjoying sexual fulfillment.

August 5

Sexual fulfillment is God's gift to elders as well as to "youngers."

Many young people dread the advancing years because, among other misunderstandings, they believe that they will soon be over the hill sexually. The fact is, however, as many studies have shown, that healthy couples often continue an active and fulfilling sex life into their sixties, seventies, and eighties. There is even evidence that the sexual responsiveness of women often increases with age and that many experience greater sexual fulfillment in their sixties and seventies than they did in their twenties and thirties.

To be sure, all senior citizens are not chronologically advantaged sexually speaking. There are sexual problems that come with aging including those that are by-products of illness, surgery, and certain medications. Such difficulties, however, need not be endured with stoic resignation. Help is available. Those experiencing such frustrations will wisely consult with a competent physician or therapist.

Affirmation for the Day:
I will seek to be a good steward of my health — physical, mental, emotional, and sexual.

August 6

"But he did — he got sick!"

Clarifying today's thought requires a story.

While participating in a program of clinical pastoral education, I visited with a man in the hospital who was suffering from an affliction that is often significantly psychosomatic. He told me that his problem was that as a lay leader in his congregation he was totally frustrated by his inability to get along with his pastor. "I've tried everything," he told me, "but I can't do anything about it!" When I shared this conversation with my supervisor, Dr. David Belgum, he replied, "But he did — he got sick!"

That insight reminds us that we are doing something consciously or unconsciously with our emotions. Our attitudes and actions contribute to both our sickness and health and to the health and hurt of others. When emotionally distressed, it is far wiser to share it with a counselor, therapist, or trusted friend than to silently stew in the acidic juices of resentment. Such stewing can really be sickening to ourselves and to our relationships.

Affirmation for the Day:
When troubled by stress and distress, I will share and not stew.

August 7

Thought for the Day:

"Three people can keep a secret if two of them are dead."

This thought comes from Benjamin Franklin and if we really wish to keep something secret, we do well to remember and to heed it.

It must have happened in Franklin's day as it does now — a person entrusted with a confidence says to someone, "I have been asked not to tell anyone but I am sure I can trust you to keep this secret." Then that person says the same to someone else and before long it is a secret no longer.

I even wonder if it is likely that three people will keep a secret when two of them are dead. The one still alive often lacks the wisdom and will to refrain from telling someone else. At any rate, if we really want something to be kept secret, we had best keep it to ourselves and if we must tell someone to share it only under the seal of the confessional.

Affirmation for the Day:

When I don't want something known, I will keep it to myself.

August 8

We don't affirm one good thing by denying another.

Today's thought comes from my experience of dealing with clergy and congregations with different kinds of ministries. Some, for example, focus on the pastoral care of the people in the congregation while others have a strong emphasis on prophetic ministry to relieve oppression and to work for justice and peace. People in both camps sometimes defend themselves by criticizing those whose emphasis is different from their own.

Such efforts to tear down another's ministry do nothing to build up our own. Wouldn't it be wiser, kinder, and far more constructive for each to affirm the other? Aren't both the pastoral and the prophetic vital aspects of life-giving ministry?

Similar examples abound from other kinds of work and volunteerism. Every good work is to be affirmed and no one of us can do it all. Therefore, let's be affirmers of all and detractors of none.

Affirmation for the Day:
I will refrain from trying to build myself up by tearing others down.

August 9

"Every theological statement that stands by itself is a lie."

I recall this thought from Professor Olaf Hanson at Luther Seminary. He was making the point that no sentence can say everything, and that every truth needs to be balanced by another, and sometimes even opposite, truth. Politicians, preachers, and others who are tempted to issue pontifical proclamations of absolute truth should be especially mindful of our thought for today. The limits of both our language and our understanding preclude the creation of statements that say all that can be said on any subject.

However, on the other hand, if Hanson is correct, it is, of course, true that his statement, by itself, is also a lie. Therefore, we should refrain from taking it as an absolute maxim. Nevertheless, we are wise to be aware of the fact that there is another side to almost everything and that we should be open to hear and to say, "on the other hand."

Affirmation for the Day:
I will remember that no statement can say everything about anything.

August 10

Talk back to the devil.

It is reported that someone once wrote to Martin Luther saying in effect, "I know that God is merciful but I can't believe that God has enough forgiveness to cover all my terrible sins." Luther replied that such thoughts were not the voice or God or Christian conscience but came from the devil. He then advised the person that if such thoughts came again the person should talk back, saying, "Devil, you don't know the half of my sins! I have many sins that are far worse than any of which you have accused me. God knows them all and God still loves and forgives me!"

Luther's response does not minimize our sinfulness. It gives vivid expression to the fact that though our sins be great, God's grace is greater still.

Affirmation for the Day:
I thank God, who knows all my sin, that I am still loved and forgiven.

August 11

Many of us are more troubled by shame than by guilt.

Guilt is regret over moral failure and usually relates to something we have done or failed to do. Shame is a kind of embarrassment over who we are and relates to things like how we look, our size and shape, or our lack of a particular ability.

As a result of having had polio when I was two years old, my right leg below the knee is much thinner than the other. While growing up in a rural community and attending a small one-room country school for the first eight grades, I don't think anyone ever said anything about my leg. When I started high school in Blue Earth with about seventy classmates who had never seen me before, I was bombarded with questions like "How come you limp?" and "What happened to your leg?" I must confess to feeling great shame over having such a deformity.

Many years later when our daughter, as a child, spoke of me as having "a chicken leg," I could laugh about it. And now, when our grandchildren ask me to show their friends "my chicken leg" I am no longer ashamed. I also know that if someone had described me that way when I was in high school or college, I would certainly have been shamed and angry.

Affirmation for the Day:
I pray for freedom from shame over things I can't change, and for strength to change any shameful thing that can be changed.

August 12

Also remember 1 John 3:16.

One of the first Bible verses many of us learned in Sunday school is John 3:16. It's from the gospel of John and tells us, "For God so loved the world that he gave his only Son, so that everyone who believes in him may not perish but may have eternal life." That's great good news. It assures us that God loves every person in this whole wide world and that all of us are invited to rest our lives in God's mercy and power.

That's great but it is not all — we are also to remember 1 John 3:16. Speaking of Jesus, it says, "We know love by this, that he laid down his life for us — and we ought to lay down our lives for one another." Then the next verse asks, "How does God's love abide in anyone who has the world's goods and yet sees a brother or sister in need and yet refuses to help?" And a little later John says, "Beloved, since God loved us so much, we also ought to love one another" (1 John 4:11).

This reminds me of a cynical comment that was reportedly made to a pastor who was extolling the amenities of a new parsonage. He was shocked to be told, "Just think, Jesus died to make all this possible!" Without suggesting that every Christian, and especially every pastor, take a vow of poverty and live with only the minimum necessities of life, we are reminded by 1 John 3:16 that Jesus didn't die to enable us to live in luxury. While basking in the love of God, we are to be acting with love toward others.

Affirmation for the Day:

I pray for courage to honestly examine my way of living in light of Christ's way, and for awareness that every situation is an occasion for acting with Christlike love.

August 13

"It's true that 'where there is no vision the people perish' (Proverbs 29:18 KJV). But it is also true that where there is no action the vision will perish."

Today's thought from Pastor Philip Dybvig affirms both dreamers and doers.

We need visionaries who, with Robert Kennedy, ask not only, "Why?" but, "Why not?" They are not content with the status quo but in imagination see a better world for themselves and their children.

Unless they and others who catch their vision are people of action, little or nothing will come of it and the visionaries themselves will be derided as utopian dreamers who are out of touch with reality.

Dybvig's wisdom relates not only to grand visions of global peace and justice but also to our personal lives. It is well to dream of being trim, in shape, free from addictions to nicotine or alcohol, well-educated, or whatever our good goals may be. But if we never take specific action to achieve our good goals our good visions will perish.

Affirmation for the Day:
I will seek to be a doer as well as a dreamer.

August 14

We often judge ourselves by our motives and others by their actions.

As I ponder this thought in the aftermath of September 11, 2001, it is clear that we judge the terrorists by what they did and regard them as barbaric murderers who are the virtual incarnation of evil. In evaluating our response to terroristic actions, we focus primarily on our motives and see ourselves as defenders of freedom, democracy, and the American way of life.

The terrorists and their supporters, we can be sure, judge similarly from their perspective. They see themselves as motivated by a God-given challenge to destroy the "Great Satan" that they believe threatens their way of life. They regard our lofty motives with the same contempt that we hold for theirs and point to our massacre of retreating soldiers in the first Persian Gulf War, imposing sanctions on Iraq, maintaining military bases near their sacred cities in Saudi Arabia, and our supporting Israel in suppression of Palestinian rights as acts of terrorism worse than, and fully justifying, their own.

Similar judging happens when a parent berates or beats a child "for your own good" thereby justifying the action. The child, on the other hand, feels the pain of the berating and beating and judges the parent to be hateful and cruel.

Affirmation for the Day:
When evaluating my behavior, I will pay attention to both my motives and the impact of my actions in the lives of others.

August 15

Practice gift-evoking leadership.

Our thought for today was inspired by a talk given by Mary Schramm, who with her husband, John, were leaders of the Holden Village Retreat Center in Washington state. Her talk was not about leadership but about gifts. She spoke about "evoking" — calling forth — the gifts of people for all kinds of service and ministry. That image of someone evoking gifts for accomplishing things has come to symbolize an activity that is essential for all kinds of effective leadership.

Such leaders seek to select talented people and then to focus far more on the exercise and development of their abilities than on criticism of their limitations. When practiced effectively, such leadership gives leaders many opportunities to express gratitude for work well done and reduces the occasions for criticism and correction.

Since varieties of gifts are dispersed in the lives of members of congregation and business community, wise executives will seek to create an atmosphere of such gift-evoking leadership throughout the entire organization. The productive capacity of such affirmed and appreciated individuals is likely to far exceed that of those who labor in an atmosphere of criticism and duress.

Affirmation for the Day:
Since I am encouraged and strengthened by those who affirm my gifts, I will seek to be a gift-evoking leader.

August 16

In staff relationships, the boss is "the first assistant to each of the subordinates."

I encountered this thought in Stephen Covey's book, *Seven Habits of Highly Effective People*, and became increasingly thankful for this understanding during my years as bishop. If we have been smart enough to select staff who are no less talented than ourselves and are not threatened by their competence, our job need not be detailed, dictatorial micromanagement but rather to encourage and assist each of them in doing their work.

Such a working relationship is expressive of the "gift-evoking leadership" that we considered yesterday. This arrangement is, I believe, more harmonious and productive than any other of which I am aware.

Affirmation for the Day:
When I am the boss, I will seek to be an assistant and not a dictator.

August 17

"He was my pastor."

Today's thought comes from a story told by Reinhold Niebuhr about a pastor in the South during the civil rights crisis who got into trouble with his congregation because of his strong affirmation of integration. Some members of the congregation organized a petition drive to get rid of him. When they came to the home of an elderly gentleman who was known to be supportive of segregation, they were surprised when he refused to sign their petition. "Why won't you sign it?" they asked him. "I'm not persuaded to favor integration," he replied, "but you are forgetting something. You are forgetting that my wife died a year ago and he was my pastor."

I have often shared this story with pastors as a reminder of the importance of their being bonded with their people and especially so when situations call for prophetic dealing with critical controversial issues. Such bonding requires compassionate and caring ministry, time spent with the sick, sorrowing, and respectful, relating with those whose opinions are different from our own.

If this is true for pastors, it is equally important for anyone who is a teacher or leader of any kind who seeks to guide and influence the thinking and living of others.

Affirmation for the Day:
If I want to motivate people to be more caring, I must sincerely demonstrate that I care for them.

August 18

Thought for the Day:

When we open our mouths, we let people look into our hearts and minds.

I think our thought for today gives us a clue as to why we are often fearful of public speaking. I have seen surveys that indicate that fear of speaking in public is almost universal and is greater for some people than the fear of dying.

Most of us would be anxious about walking fully clothed onto a brightly lit stage even if we had to say nothing. How would be feel if we had to do that without our clothes?

When we open our mouths and speak, we reveal far more about ourselves than we could ever do by taking off our clothes. We really do let people see into our hearts and minds. When insecure and fearful of such exposure we may become actors filling roles to prevent revelation of our true selves. When that happens, we may succeed only in revealing how phony we are. It is frightening to simply be who we are but there is no other way to be an authentic human being.

Affirmation for the Day:

Although it is scary business, I will seek in my speaking, and all my living, to be true to myself and be who I am.

August 19

Writers and speakers have an advantage over readers and hearers.

Those of us who do a lot of writing and speaking are sometimes distressed to discover that our readers and hearers have failed to understand what we said, but when we stop to think about it, that should not surprise us.

As writers and speakers we go from thoughts to words. Assuming that we have something to say, our heads are full of ideas that are usually pretty clear to us. When we put them into words, their intended meaning should naturally be obvious to ourselves. But the experience of our readers and hearers is exactly the opposite. They have to go from words to thoughts and that is a far more difficult matter.

In the first place, our words have to distract them from whatever other thoughts are floating in their heads and then those words have to be understood in a way that corresponds to the thought we are trying to express. All this is especially difficult when we have failed to order our thoughts carefully and have been sloppy in the selection of our words. Readers have an advantage over hearers in that they can go back and read a complex sentence over again but hearers must "go with the flow" or risk missing whole chunks of thought.

Affirmation for the Day:
In my speaking and writing, I will strive for easy listening and easy reading.

August 20

Public speaking is a natural extension of private speaking.

James Winans gives an imaginative illustration, suggesting that we imagine a time when no one had ever heard or given a speech. Then a person who is excited about some great news meets a friend on the street and begins to tell about it. Attracted by the animated conversation others stop to listen:

> *Five, ten, twenty, 100. Interest grows. He lifts his voice that all may hear; but the crowd wishes to hear and see the speaker better. "Get up on this truck!" they cry; and he mounts the truck and goes on with his story.*
>
> *A private conversation has become a public speech; and under the circumstances imagined it is only thought of as a conversation, enlarged conversation. It does not seem abnormal but quite the natural thing.*
>
> *There is no change in the nature or spirit of the act; it is essentially the same throughout, a conversation adapted as the speaker proceeds to the growing number of his hearers ... I wish you to see the speechmaking, even in the most public place, is a normal act which calls for no strange artificial methods, but only for an extension and development of that most familiar act, conversation.*

When speaking publicly, I pray to be so engrossed in my message and attentive to my hearers that I will be spared the self-consciousness that corrupts natural "enlarged conversation."

When speaking in public, my goal will be to share a significant message and not to be a great public speaker.

August 21

Let your preparations and problems "stew in the juices of your subconscious mind."

Today's thought is adapted from a suggestion from T. F. Gullixsen who was president of Luther Seminary during my first years as a student. He was lecturing against Saturday night sermon preparation and in favor of pondering upcoming texts and themes several weeks in advance. I've tried to practice what Gullixsen preached and have discovered that it often results in the happy problem of having far more than enough to say instead of the sad problem of last-minute scrambling to find something to say.

What is true of sermonizing is, I believe, equally true of all kinds of other preparing and problem-solving. There is wisdom in "sleeping on" things. Our brains seem to work best when relaxed and at rest but they can't work at all unless we provide an abundance of food for thought.

Affirmation for the Day:
I will remember that conscious reflection and subconscious stewing work well together.

August 22

Preparation for comes before preparation of.

From my perspective, there are two stages involved in preparing anything to be written or spoken. To take an example from the world I know best — the preparation for a sermon (which I call the jotting stage) comes before preparation of the sermon. For those who base their sermons on the Bible, "preparation for" centers on the study of a specific biblical text or theme. It also includes everything up until that moment that is part of the life experience of the preacher.

My old friend and Luther Seminary colleague, John Hilbert, often said that "There are two kinds of preachers — those who have to say something and those who have something to say." It may also be true that the chief cause of writer's block is that the writer has nothing to say.

A trip to the grocery store comes before the preparation of the meal. In a similar way, a significant "jotting stage" involving reflection, research, and jotting down everything that might be relevant to the work in process, saves speakers and writers from being among those who "have to say something" even when they have nothing to say.

Affirmation for the Day:
I will work at preparation *for* before attempting preparation *of*.

August 23

Focus on the selection and ordering of thought.

When asked how he found time to prepare all the talks and sermons he was giving, one pastor told me years ago, "I just open my mouth and listen to myself talk!" In contrast, I recall Harry Emerson Fosdick's confession, "I never speak in public without first attempting to carefully order my thoughts." Which preacher would you prefer to hear Sunday after Sunday?

After having at least a couple of pages of jottings in "preparation for" a talk or an article, we move on to the "preparation of" what we are going to say. I sometimes call this "the think stage" of preparation because it centers in the selection and ordering of thought.

Thinking is hard work and a lot of what I hear and read gives evidence that a lazy presenter didn't do much thinking but went directly from "preparation for" to stream-of-consciousness ad-libbing on a computer or in front of an audience.

In my own "preparation of," I start by putting the words, "introduction," "development," and "conclusion," spaced out on a piece of paper and then sketch out the first of usually several possible ways of beginning, developing, and ending. After settling on a specific plan, I flesh it out in more specific detail but, when preparing to speak, never write a formal manuscript.

Affirmation for the Day:
Preparing involves writing, but writing should never be a substitute for careful selection and ordering of thought.

August 24

At least one!

Our thought for today is the best answer I have ever heard to the question, "How many points should there be in a sermon?" and I believe it applies equally to all kinds of other speaking and writing. If there isn't at least one point to a presentation, it is not only by definition but also in the experience of hearers and readers essentially pointless.

Even when a presentation makes several specific points, I believe that it should have a central theme — one main point to which all other points are clearly related. Without the careful preparation of a clearly ordered plan of development our stream-of-consciousness presentations are often an insult to the hearer or reader.

Specifically concerning sermons, I am an advocate of what might be called "textual/thematic preaching." That is, I believe that a sermon should be grounded in the message of a biblical text, understood in light of God's central revelation in Jesus, and that it should focus on one central theme. This conviction prompts me to encourage preachers to title their sermons. The discipline of having to come up with a title forces us to get clear concerning the main thing we are trying to say.

Affirmation for the Day:
When preparing to speak and to write, I will ask myself, "What's the point of it?"

August 25

"The secret of good writing is rewriting."

Today's thought comes from Australian author, Mem Fox, who tells of how she wrote and rewrote each of her children's books. I think she's right and would add to her wisdom a couple of similar maxims — "The secret of good thinking is rethinking" and "The secret of good ordering of thought is reordering of thought."

Someone told me that "Shakespeare never rewrote a line," but I don't believe it! I read that Dostoevsky wrote eight full-draft revisions of his long novel, *The Idiot*, plus hundreds of minor revisions. Although this seems almost unbelievable from the pen-and-pencil era, it strikes me as probably true.

I saw a facsimile of the page on which John Keats wrote the poem containing "A thing of beauty is a joy forever." His handwritten notes in the margin indicated he considered such alternatives as "a lasting joy" and "an eternal joy." As one who explores alternative wordings in the attempt to write a clear sentence, I was encouraged to be in the good company of such a struggling poet.

Years ago, Paul Scherer warned us against preparing talks and drafts of things to be published with a typewriter or pen and ink "because," he said, "it may look so nice you will be tempted not to change it." He encouraged us to "work with a pencil and eraser" and, while I could use a computer, I still follow his suggestion. Working with paper on which I can draw lines, scratch out, erase, and make jottings in the margin is, for me, more conducive to rethinking, reordering, and rewriting than is working at a keyboard.

Affirmation for the Day:
Whenever preparing anything written or spoken, I will practice the great arts of rethinking, reordering, and rewriting.

August 26

"Vital communication happens when the speaker is thinking of the thought at the moment of utterance."

While attempting to teach preaching at Luther Seminary, it took me a long time to figure out what was wrong with preachers *reading* their sermons. I thought at first that they hadn't practiced enough or that they looked too much at their manuscripts and too little at their hearers. Then I read today's thought in a book by James McCroskey and realized that those sermon readers were not thinking of their thoughts at the moment of utterance. Their minds were focused more on their words and sentences than on the thoughts they were seeking to express.

To be sure, quoting a sentence or two that expresses a great thought is an effective part of vital communication but, for most of us, reading or reciting words from memory is more likely to be dull, if not deadly, than lively, life-giving communication.

Therefore, as a professor of preaching, I changed the assignment and told the students to stop writing manuscripts and to prepare a detailed plan of carefully ordered thought that would enable them to think their thoughts while they were speaking.

Affirmation for the Day:

In my preparation, I will prepare to speak and to neither read nor recite.

August 27

Preaching without feedback is like driving golf balls in the dark.

Nobody goes to a driving range to hit golf balls at midnight with the lights turned off, but a lot of pastors preach that way. They, metaphorically speaking, hit homiletical golf balls in the general direction of the congregation without knowing if any of them ever hits the green.

As a golfer needs light to know where the ball is going, preachers need feedback to learn if our sermons are meaningful. A lot of helpful feedback is provided informally. When a parishioner shakes our hand and says, "Thanks for a great sermon," it apparently landed in at least one person's arena of meaning. But most people aren't likely to tell us much about our preaching unless we ask them.

I personally found it helpful to ask ten kind, honest people to meet with me once a month to provide specific feedback on my preaching. The first session was always a sharing of their lifelong experiences with preaching. Since it seemed easier for them and on me, I asked that the second session focus on things they appreciated in my sermons and that subsequent sessions center on suggestions for improvement plus questions and concerns raised by what I'd said. I treasure memories of those meetings and commend such a process to all preachers and to kind and honest parishioners.

We also had feedback cards in the pew racks that invited people to tell 1) what they appreciated, 2) what they found distracting, and 3) their suggestions for improvement.

Affirmation for the Day:
As a preacher, I need help from my parishioners; as a parishioner, I want to help my pastor.

259

August 28

When critiquing preaching and people, general positive comments are welcome, but general negative comments are forbidden.

This thought grew out of my attempts to teach preaching. As I reflected on comments made following seminary students' sermons, it became obvious that statements like, "That was a good sermon," were encouraging while others such as, "I didn't like your sermon," were worse than useless. The general positive comments provided support and encouragement. The general negative comments created discouragement and despair.

To be helpful, negative criticisms of both preaching and people need to be focused specifically on things that can be improved. A comment like, "An illustration or example would have helped clarify your point," gives the preacher something to work on. Similarly, even an angry, "Clean up this mess," to a child is far better than, "You are a hopeless slob."

It's easy, but hurtful, to slam someone with a negative generalization. It's often harder, but wiser and far more helpful to share a concrete, constructive comment.

Affirmation for the Day:

When it is necessary to be negative, I will seek to be helpfully specific.

August 29

"Preachers should talk about the gospel the way a farmer talks about a Holstein cow."

Although today's thought is directed to clergy, I have a hunch that most laity will affirm its wisdom. It comes from Alvin Rogness and we, as preachers, should take it to heart. We often speak more naturally during the announcements than during our sermons. We are talking then about real events. It's natural, direct, person-to-person conversation.

When we step into the pulpit, some of us speak differently. Some recite words from memory or read a manuscript. Others take on a "pulpit manner" and speak with an other-worldly "preacher's voice" as if acting a part or filling a role. When we talk this way we must believe, or feel, that we can't simply be ourselves while doing something as solemn and holy as "preaching the sermon."

Yet the effect of such unnatural communication is to give the sermon an aura, not of splendor and holiness, but of unreality. It can even sound like the phony pitch of a salesperson who, we are convinced, never uses the product being promoted.

Stanley Jones confessed gratitude for having been told after a sermon, "You didn't preach at us, you just told us things." We have a story to tell. The gospel is good news and the love of God is as real as a Holstein cow!

Affirmation for the Day:

The grace of God is as real as cows, cats, and cars, and I will seek to speak of it as of them.

August 30

Good preaching evokes desires to pray.

I once heard a moving sermon that strongly encouraged all of us to be people of prayer and expected the preacher to then lead us in prayer. When that didn't happen, I must confess to having felt a bit deprived.

That experience also reminded me of Paul Scherer's comment and suggestion that "The sermon should bring the people to the point of wanting to pray and the preacher should, therefore, lead the congregation in prayer at the close of the sermon." Post-sermon prayers of thanks, trust, surrender, intercession, and petition for power to do what the sermon has proclaimed can be a vital part of our worship experience. Such prayers strike me as a natural and appropriate response to the sermon's message. I have followed Scherer's suggestion for forty years and continue to commend it.

Affirmation for the Day:
A sermon should evoke trust, thought, and action, but there is something wrong if it doesn't also evoke a desire to pray.

August 31

"I know that Jesus said 'Feed my sheep,' not 'feed my giraffes' but I think it well to encourage the sheep to stretch their necks."

John Sheldon Whale is the source of our thought for today and I remember well the point of it. It was addressed to clergy who were accused of failing to challenge their people to study and to think not only about the Bible and things long ago and far away, but about the most vital and often controversial concerns that confront us now.

There are those who suggest that the way to build a growing congregation is to gather like-minded, and even like-looking, people; give them what they are looking for, and insofar as possible, stay clear of talking about things that are complex and controversial. After several years in such a congregation, one of the members shocked me by saying, "I belong to a growing and dying church!" When I asked, "What do you mean by 'growing and dying'?" he replied, "The people keep coming and the congregation is getting bigger, but we are seldom challenged to examine our lives, to change and to grow, to think new thoughts and to act in new ways."

Affirmation for the Day:

I will seek to be a lifelong learner, grower, changer, and challenger.

September 1

When we feel that we are being crucified, we should remember that there were three crosses on the hill that day.

There may be times in our lives as pastors and lay people when we feel that we are being crucified by our congregations. Stubborn people reject our vision and refuse to support our plans for the parish. We may feel personally despised and rejected. When that happens it is easy to identify with Jesus, and to see ourselves as being crucified with Christ.

That may sometimes be true, but on such occasions it is well to remember that there were two others on crosses that day. Jesus was crucified for being so good, the other two for being so bad! That may suggest that when we are being crucified the chances are two to one that we are more like those thieves than we are like Jesus! Are we suffering because of our Christlike compassion and wisdom or because we have been tactless, loveless, and even in some measure senseless in our dealing with people?

After hearing one pastor's complaints about being crucified by a congregation the bishop is reported to have replied, "The trouble with you, my friend, is that you are not dead yet!" When we, as pastors or parishioners, are rejected by others because of our tactlessness and arrogant self-righteousness we cannot credit our miseries to our faithfulness in following Jesus.

Affirmation for the Day:
While seeking to follow Jesus, I will not blame him for problems of my own creation.

September 2

Thought for the Day:
Give me my flowers while I live.

My earliest memory of today's thought comes from my mother who said it after returning from a funeral at a church filled with flowers. She was not a crusader against funeral flowers but made a point that I have never forgotten. We shouldn't wait until the funeral to tell people of our affection and appreciation with words and flowers.

Mother died very unexpectedly only a couple of days after a stroke from which she never regained consciousness. My brother and I always had a wonderful relationship with our mother but we had no opportunity to share our final thoughts of love or to say good-bye. Had we known that her time would be so short, I am sure we would have more often heeded her invitation and given her many more flowers, both literally and figuratively, while she lived.

Affirmation for the Day:
I will seek to thank for, and to tell of, love before it is too late.

September 3

Have a place for everything and put everything in its place.

Some of these thoughts convict me of failing to live up to the good advice I've been given. Today's thought was dinned into me by my dad and convicts me as I share it because I don't always do it. The folly of my failure comes home to me when I look for something and can't find it because I either hadn't provided a place for it or hadn't put it back in its place.

This is especially true in terms of my dealing with paper. I have been blessed by great secretaries to whom I could hand things in confidence that they could be retrieved when needed. But when I'm on my own, I'm better at piling than filing, which often results in frustrating and sometimes futile searching. I've taken comfort from Gerhard Frost's line that "my messy office is a symbol of my messy life" but confess to believe that people, beginning with me, would be better off if they followed Dad's instruction rather than my example.

Affirmation for the Day:

Since a few minutes of planning and placing can save hours of searching, I will seek to practice what my dad preached.

September 4

Muddle through!

During a meeting the other day, someone remembered my having said that "One of my mottoes for survival is 'muddle through'" and I had to confess that he remembered correctly. I am not proud of that motto but honesty compels me to admit that it is sometimes the best that I can do.

My dictionary defines "muddle through" as a "chiefly British" expression that means "to push on to a successful conclusion in a disorganized way." That definition is two-thirds positive. "To push on" witnesses to steadfast determination. "A successful conclusion" tells us that things turned out well. "In a disorganized way" is not a compliment. It witnesses to confusion and lack of careful preparation.

When confronted with a problem or challenge, I like to be well prepared. Disorder and disorganization are distressing to me but in my life and work it is impossible to be well prepared for every challenge and crisis that knocks at my door. At such times, the best we can do is to muddle through and to hope and pray for "a successful conclusion."

Affirmation for the Day:
Even when I can't do well, I will try to do my best.

September 5

Don't just agonize, organize!

I understand that today's thought is an old labor union slogan but I don't recall hearing it until recently. I share it because it convicts me and because I believe it contains a truth we all need to remember.

Some of us, beginning with me, are great agonizers. We lament the state of the world, deplore injustice, grieve over the suffering of the impoverished and oppressed, but too often don't do anything very significant to help make things better.

None of us can solve all these problems by ourselves, but one thing we can do is to organize and to support existing organizations of like-minded people who are working to create a more just and peaceful world. Organizing and raising funds to support our churches and world-betterment organizations such as The United Nations Association, Bread for the World, Citizens for Global Solutions, and World Citizen, Inc. is hard work. It is a lot easier to agonize than to organize but is also a lot less effective in changing the world.

Affirmation for the Day:
I won't just talk the talk, but will work with others who are walking the walk.

September 6

Thought for the Day:

"The best day in my life was when I resigned from being chair of the board of the universe."

E. Stanley Jones told of hearing our thought for today as a confession of gratitude and went on to affirm it for all of us.

We live poorly as make-believe gods. That job is a bit too big for any of us! Nevertheless, we are tempted to think and act as if we were gods ruling our little corner of the world or at least our own lives. Even that job is too big for us. The fact is that however talented and able we are, we are still frail, fallible, one-day-to-die human beings.

When we face this reality, we can go on to discover that we can live amazingly well as limited but greatly blessed people with capacities often beyond our own awareness. Resigning from our roles as make-believe gods enables us to live out our lives as authentic, gifted human beings.

Affirmation for the Day:

I will trust God to do God's work and concentrate on doing my work.

September 7

In everything God works for good.

Today's thought comes from Romans 8:28 in the translation of the Revised Standard Version. Other translations say, "We know that all things work together for good." But, having had an imaginary conversation with the apostle Paul, I know that is not what he meant. Paul was not a Christian Scientist who believed that sin and sickness are illusions of the mind and that evil is goodness in disguise. Paul believed that evil is evil, that sin is hurtful, and that death is the "enemy to be destroyed" (1 Corinthians 15:26). I don't believe that sin, sickness, evil, and death, in and of themselves, work for good even for those who love God.

But I do believe that in everything good, bad, and indifferent, God is at work for good to bring joy out of sorrow, health out of sickness, good out of evil, and even life out of death. That's the good news that the apostle Paul invites us to believe.

Affirmation for the Day:
In everything, I will trust the working of a life-giving God.

September 8

God took the worst and made the best.

E. Stanley Jones liked to say, "God took the worst thing that ever happened, the crucifixion of Christ, and made it into the best thing that ever happened, the redemption of the world."

It may be generally true, as Professor Paul Sponheim of Luther Seminary has said that "God is able to bring more good out of goodness than out of evil." This conviction asserts that what we do and fail to do really does count for something including with God, and that our goodness gives God more to work with than does our sin.

Whatever our theories of the atonement, the cross of Jesus assures us that the world's worst is not beyond the transforming power of God. It also reveals God's gracious redemption of the world to be an extremely painful and costly business.

Such thoughts concerning our redemption are speculative and clouded with mystery, but they can help us avoid temptations toward what Dietrich Bonhoeffer called "cheap grace." While thanking God for forgiving grace we need to remember that it is neither cheap nor conditional, but exceedingly costly, even for God.

Affirmation for the Day:
I thank God that even my worst is grist in God's mill for creating goodness.

September 9

We live in God.

Many understand God to dwell in a heavenly realm far beyond us and to intervene only now and then in our lives. Some Christian theologians object to this view. They call themselves "panentheists" and believe that we live in God every moment of our lives. Please note the spelling of that word. These people are not "pantheists" who think that everything is God. They are panentheists who think that all things, including our lives, exist in God.

This is not a new notion. It echoes the line the apostle Paul quotes in Acts 17:28: "In him we live and move and have our being." It affirms an understanding of the Holy Spirit as the presence of God with us and within us.

As an illustration, I suggest that living in God is like living in gravity. We seldom think about it but we live in it every moment. Gravity is beyond us in the farthest reaches of the universe but we are never apart from it. Even if we seldom think about God, we live in God's presence every moment and are held and sustained by God's love and power.

This also suggests that we live in God as a fish lives in the water. Marshall McLuhan once said, "I don't know who discovered water but I am sure it wasn't a fish." We live and move in realities that are so near and so basic that we take them for granted without conscious awareness. There are mystics who tell of times they experience an almost sensual awareness of God's presence. Such moments come rarely, if at all, to most of us. Most of our days are lived not by perception, but by promise.

Affirmation for the Day:
I will ponder again and again "In God I live and move and have my being."

September 10

Honest confessing requires honest confession.

When nearing seminary graduation, several of us met with Professor Warren Quanbeck to ask if confessing allegiance to the creeds meant that we had to agree with everything in them.

We focused on the Athanasian Creed which is seldom, if ever, used in most of our churches but to which we were asked to "subscribe." It tells in great detail how we are to think about the doctrine of the Trinity and concludes by saying, "This is the catholic faith. One cannot be saved without believing this firmly and faithfully." When asked his opinion, Dr. Quanbeck confessed, "Of course, I don't believe that!"

He went on to point out that we are saved by the grace of God and not by our theology and that we confess the creeds "historically" in the sense that we see ourselves as part of a community that struggled long ago to sum up its understanding of the God we know in Jesus. Marcus Borg affirms a similar understanding of creedal confession. He points out:

> *Credo [I believe] does not mean "I hearby agree to the literal-factual truth of the following statements" ... when we say credo at the beginning of the creed, we are saying "I give my heart to God" ... the rest of the creed tells the story of the one to whom we give our heart: God as the maker of heaven and earth, God as known in Jesus, God as present in the Spirit.*

Believing in doctrines is not a ticket to salvation. A candidate for ministry who believes that agreeing with creeds is essential for salvation lacks understanding of the unconditional grace of God and is not yet ready for ordination.

Salvation by grace frees me to be honest in confessing my problems with the confessions.

September 11

Things that are urgent, but not important, often crowd out things that are important but not urgent.

For me, the "urgent" is symbolized by the ringing of a telephone that must be answered immediately and the "important" by the stack of significant books that I have purchased but not found time to read.

Our problem is that some things, including that telephone call, can be both urgent and important which leaves us with the difficult task of sorting things out. Distractions often keep us from focusing on things that really matter. Many of us live like the famous person who "mounted a horse and rode off in all directions." We fail to concentrate on anything long enough to accomplish something significant and in the process become increasingly frazzled and frustrated.

If that is descriptive of any of us we need to order our priorities and begin to live a more focused life. One way of doing this is to make a list of the "musts" and the "maybes" that we would like to accomplish in life. Another, that is a bit more specific, is to use an A, B, C, rating system. The A's are both essential and urgent. They get top priority. The B's are important but not urgent, and the C's are things that we would like to do but are neither very significant nor urgent.

After such ordering we may need to be almost tyrannical in disciplining ourselves to deal first with the "musts" and the A's and then with the B's, without being distracted by the C's and maybes.

Affirmation for the Day:

After selecting a significant goal, I will ride in that direction until I reach it.

September 12

"I was troubled by interruptions until I realized that interruptions are my work."

Henri Nouwen shares this thought from a priest who was blessed to realize that interruptions were not always distractions but often an essential part of his work.

Unless we are working in a place like a hospital emergency room where our total responsibility is to deal with one crisis "interruption" after another, it is important that we order our lives to include time for reflection, meditation, study, and planning so that we are not devoured by distractions. But we also need to live a bit loosely with our daily agendas.

I believe Gerhard Frost was correct in encouraging teachers, for example, to carefully prepare lesson plans but also be ready to abandon them in order to deal with the spontaneous, unplanned opportunities for teaching and learning that frequently occur in the classroom. Responding to a significant question from a student may be far more important than getting through the plan for the day.

Affirmation for the Day:

I will be open to interruptions, but won't let them order my life.

September 13

When the sun sinks in the west, the lazy work the best.

These words speak to procrastinators of all kinds. The thought came from my dad and the image from life on the farm. After loafing through the day, the sinking sun reminds the lazy farmer of work that must be done and inspires late afternoon energy. A student who goofs off until the night before the big exam or the due date of a term paper and then devours NoDoz© to keep awake to study or complete the paper is another obvious example.

Some people seem to thrive and be amazingly productive under such pressure but most of us fare better when operating with more responsible stewardship of time. While heeding Jesus' admonition, "Do not worry about tomorrow" (Matthew 6:34) we wisely remember that planning for tomorrow is today's work, and that Jesus also said, "We must work the works of him who sent me while it is day; night is coming when no one can work" (John 9:4).

Affirmation for the Day:

I will seek to live "not as unwise people but as wise, making the most of the time" (Ephesians 5:15).

September 14

We need to learn to do nothing well.

We can be blessed by pondering a little poem and a one-word quotation that I once heard from Gerhard Frost. Frost first shared this poem:

> *There are times for doing nothing, but be sure you do it*
> *   well.*
> *And listen, for God in silent spaces has something great*
> *   to tell.*

After sharing the poem, Dr. Frost went on to tell of how someone once asked an old saint what he had learned through all his many years. The person expected a long answer — at least a few sentences or perhaps a little speech, but received only one word — *presence.*

"And my question is," said Dr. Frost, reflecting on that answer near the end of his own life, "have I learned *presence*? Do I always count one more than I can see?" And then he added, "When we are doing nothing, that's the time to remember *presence*."

We are called to be busy and active in life-giving work, but we also need quiet times for reflection, study, and prayer, and even times of doing nothing.

When stressed and distressed by demands and details, we do well to pause and pray with John Greenleaf Whittier:

> *Dear Lord and Father of Mankind,*
> *Forgive our fev'rish ways!*
> *Reclothe us in our rightful mind;*
> *In purer lives thy service find,*
> *In deeper rev'rence praise.*

Drop thy still dews of quietness,
Till all our strivings cease;
Take from our souls the strain and stress,
And let our ordered lives confess
The beauty of thy peace.

Affirmation for the Day:
I, too, will seek to practice the great art of doing nothing well.

September 15

Thought for the Day:
"All leaves must fall."

Like Jesus, Gerhard Frost took lessons from nature that have meaning for our lives. Here is one taught by the falling of leaves.

> *We sat on the bank,*
> *high above the beautiful lake,*
> *my beloved and I.*
> *It was August,*
> *and one leaf fell,*
> *just one,*
> *but as it fell,*
> *it spoke.*
> *We thought we heard it say,*
> *"All leaves must fall.*
> *come September and October.*
> *All must fall."*
> *It is far past August*
> *in our life together —*
> *at least November.*
> *Dear Lord of falling leaves,*
> *of far-spent and flowing rivers,*
> *help us, your frail and fragile ones,*
> *to look serenely into the sunset glory*
> *of this, your given day.*

Affirmation for the Day:
Wherever I am in the seasons of life, I will pause to remember that "all leaves must fall."

September 16

Numbering our days adds wisdom to our years.

Centuries ago, the psalmist wrote, "Teach us to number our days that we may get a heart of wisdom" (Psalm 90:12). Our days are numbered. We do well to ponder the truth inscribed on the rotunda of the Colorado State Capital: "Today is going to be long, long ago."

Such awareness is sobering, but it need not be morbid. It can teach us the wisdom of treasuring each moment of joy and beauty and love. In this beautiful poem, A. E. Housman sets an example for all of us to follow:

> *Loveliest of trees, the cherry now*
> *is hung with bloom along the bow,*
> *and stands about the woodland ride*
> *wearing white for Easter tide.*
>
> *Now, of my three score years and ten,*
> *twenty will not come again,*
> *and take from seventy springs a score,*
> *it only leaves me fifty more.*
>
> *And since to look at things in bloom*
> *fifty springs are little room,*
> *about the woodland I will go*
> *to see the cherry hung with snow.*

Each of us can amend these lines to reflect our age. Here is how I shared them, with generous life-expectancy, at our St. Olaf College fifty-year reunion:

Now, of my four-score years plus ten,
seventy will not come again,
and take from ninety springs ten less four-score
it only leaves me twenty more.
And since to look at things in bloom
twenty springs are little room ...

I encourage you to rewrite them to fit your age.

Affirmation for the Day:
**No matter how old or how busy, I will take time
for beauty, friendship, and love.**

September 17

"It's dangerous to talk with us old-timers because everything reminds us of something."

Memory is a magnificent, wondrous gift. Try to imagine life without memory. There would be no language, no learning, no human life as we know it. Destruction of memory by dementia is truly tragic and grounds for great grief.

As Gerhard Frost reminds us in our thought for today, a mind filled with memory can sometimes overflow into conversations that can go on almost forever and overwhelm even the most patient listeners.

Therefore, with all our remembering we are wise to face the fact that not everyone is interested in everything we can remember. At the very least, we should give others a chance to share some of their favorite memories and be mindful again that "God has given us two ears and one mouth and we should take the hint!"

Affirmation for the Day:
Although it's fun for me to share memories, I will try to remember that it's not always fun for others to hear them.

September 18

"It's the last time."

As I search my memory for thoughts to share, I am a bit surprised that so many of them relate to ordinary life experiences that stick in memory like the cockleburs I remember from back on the farm.

Such is our thought for today. I remember Paul Scherer telling us of walking into his church in New York City and observing the cleaning woman washing the chancel steps. As he greeted her, he noted that she was crying. When he gently inquired concerning the source of her sorrow, she replied, "It's the last time." She had scrubbed those steps for years. It was a dull and dreary task and we can be sure that she wasn't sorrowful at the end of each scrubbing. Even now, she probably felt relief that she wouldn't have to scrub those steps again, but still there were tears. That job had been her life. It had given her meaning and purpose. She had been needed and useful and now it was over. She could rightly rejoice but it was also right to grieve.

Most of us have complained about boring repetitive tasks like mowing the lawn, shoveling the snow, changing diapers, washing dishes, and taking out the garbage. But, when last times come, there is not only relief and joy, there is also loss and sorrow, and a time for tears.

Affirmation for the Day:
I will remember to be grateful even for drudgeries that enable me to be useful for something.

September 19

Polyactivity can be both a vice and a virtue.

I am sometimes accused of being polyactive and don't think it is always a compliment. It is certainly frustrating to visit with someone who is only half listening while reading a book or magazine at the same time. Car accidents have been caused by driving while talking on a cell phone. There is no doubt that polyactivity in many forms is a dangerous and bad thing.

At the risk of being accused of being both defensive and polyactive, I believe that some forms of polyactivity are good stewardship of time. I don't think it is sinful or dangerous to pray or listen to a taped lecture or radio address while driving the car. During my bishop days, I dictated lots of letters while driving. That seemed safer to me than talking on the phone. All I had to do in heavy traffic was to turn off the machine, which we are less prone to do while visiting via phone.

After getting an exercise bicycle, at first I found hardly any time to use it. Then I got a reading stand for my bike and, in effect, added about 45 minutes to many days by reading and riding at the same time instead of reading and riding at different times. After over 20,000 miles of such riding and reading, it is a practice that I highly commend.

Affirmation for the Day:
When it risks no harm and does some good, I will be open to practice polyactivity.

September 20

Thought for the Day:
Work when you work and play when you play.

This thought is another that comes from my childhood. I heard it often and although I can't remember all the specifics, I believe it was prompted by my goofing off with my twin when we were supposed to be working. On such occasions, Dad would tell us again, "Work when you work and play when you play."

I recall an occasion when Dad had hired a neighbor boy to help my brother and me clean out the chicken house. Dad came back near the end of the day and observed that we hadn't accomplished much. When he expressed his disappointment that the job wasn't closer to completion, the neighbor boy, who was getting paid by the hour, replied, "Well, I put my time in." To that comment, Dad shook his head, paid what had been promised, and never hired him again. My brother and I only earned Dad's disappointment and another reminder to "Work when you work and play when you play."

Some of us, on the other hand, really work when we work but don't always play when we play. Preoccupation with work so fills our minds and controls our time that we miss the joy of total playfulness. We are equally in need of what many old prayers called "amendment of life."

Affirmation for the Day:
Working and playing are both vital parts of life, but seldom go well when mixed up together.

September 21

Steady and slow gets the job done.

Today's thought surfaced in memory while preparing to shovel snow from our walk and driveway. My wife warned me as I was going out that shoveling snow is dangerous and that she didn't want me to have a heart attack. I assured her that I would seek to shovel as Dad had taught me and as he had demonstrated when he was a decade older than I am now.

"Steady and slow" was his motto for such tasks, which he said gets a lot more done than working by "fits and starts." Although he was a farmer, and not a doctor, I am sure that he was also aware of the fact that working at a slow, steady pace is much healthier for our nerves and hearts than rushing and straining to get the job done as quickly as possible. Many who plunge ahead with such stressful vigor have done themselves in and never finished the job at all!

Affirmation for the Day:

"Steady and slow when shoveling snow" strikes me as a good motto with multiple applications in many dimensions of life and work.

September 22

Our childhood should last at least sixty years.

Our thought for today expands the wisdom of Ashley Montagu who says in his book, *Growing Young,* "The ideal should be to prolong childhood up to sixty years." My expansion to "at least sixty" in our thought for today is based not only on the thought of Sigmund Freud that "In our inmost soul we are children and remain so for the rest of our lives" but especially on the teaching of Jesus who also says, in effect, that we are to live life-long with childlike qualities. (See Matthew 18:1-4.)

Among those qualities, one of the most striking and significant to me is a child's eagerness to grow and to learn — to become bigger, stronger, and wiser. I have never met a child who didn't want to grow up. Some adults seem to live with the sense of having arrived. They have learned all they need to know and spend far more time talking about the past than about the future.

Children, and childlike adults, aren't like that. They are eager for more learning, more growing, and more living. Whatever their specific wants, they don't want to stay as they are. Perhaps this is part of what Jesus had in mind when he said, "Truly, I say to you, whoever does not receive the kingdom of God like a child shall not enter it" (Mark 10:15).

Affirmation for the Day:
I think E. Stanley Jones was onto something when he said, "We don't grow old — we get old when we stop growing!"

September 23

"No! No! No! Read slowly!"

While a student at Luther Seminary, I took a course in efficient reading at the University of Minnesota at the end of which I received a certificate indicating that I had learned to read at 1,000 words per minute. Shortly after receiving that certificate, I was visiting with Dr. Edmund Smits who was one of our most learned seminary professors. During a lapse in humility, I told him of my having learned to read at 1,000 words a minute. In my naiveté, I expected him to commend and congratulate me. But his response was closer to horror — "No! No! No!" he said. "Read slowly! Great minds have recorded lifetimes of wisdom on those pages. You must ponder every word!"

With that admonition, Smits reminded me of a significant truth. Pages containing lifetimes of wisdom should certainly be read slowly. To skim such profundity is likely to miss its meaning altogether.

At the same time, 1,000 words per minute is sometimes too slow. Some things aren't worth reading at all! The key, therefore, is to adjust the speed to the content.

In a sense, reading is like driving a car. Thirty miles per hour is too fast in some places while 75 is okay on some super highways. Someone who drove the same speed everywhere would certainly be an ineffective driver. Same-speed-drivers and same-speed-readers are both inefficient.

Affirmation for the Day:
I will read the significant slowly and the trivial swiftly, if at all!

September 24

If we are early, we are anxious; if we are late, we are hostile; if we are on time, we are compulsive.

Our thought for today, from an unknown humorist pretending to be a psychoanalyst, reminds us that there are times when we just can't win. Whatever we do, we will be criticized by someone.

It also reminds me of the old fable about a man, a boy, and donkey. No matter who rode or who walked, passersby were so severely critical that the man and boy ended up carrying the donkey.

Beyond all that, there is both truth and error in our thought for today. Anxious people may tend to be early, the hostile to be late, and the compulsive to be on time, but these tendencies aren't true of everyone. I don't think, for example, that my frequent lateness is the result of hostility but of my tendency to try to do too much in too little time which often results in my rushing to finish something when I should be leaving to be somewhere else.

Affirmation for the Day:
While respectful of the time and opinions of others, I will not be enslaved by their criticisms.

September 25

Thought for the Day:
Welcome to the older generation.

Mother died first, very unexpectedly at age 69. Dad died in a nursing home three years later when he was 83. Following his death, one of the first things my twin brother said to me was, "Welcome to the older generation," since our parents didn't marry until Dad was nearly fifty and Mother nearly forty. My brother and I were then in our early thirties. It didn't strike me then as it does now that we were pretty young when we joined the older generation. We have friends in their sixties and seventies who still have a living parent. They are still in the younger generation.

At whatever age, the experience of entering the older generation is a bit of a jolt and I can only wonder at what it means for those who lose both parents in childhood. Beyond the grief of loss, it meant for me that I no longer had these wise and caring mentors to turn to and rely upon. I abruptly came of age and felt a lot older than I had before.

As I meet Mom and Dad now only in imagination and memory, I sometimes wonder what it would be like to visit with them, and others of their generation as adults all of the same age as I am now, and not as one younger talking with an elder. I would certainly ask about many things that I wish we had talked about before they died.

Affirmation for the Day:
While there is time, I will ask and listen and speak.

September 26

I won't live long enough to do everything I'd like to do.

Today's thought is prompted by the arrival, far sooner than expected, of my 73rd birthday. As the time that has been lengthens and the time to be shortens, I am compelled to confess that I will never do everything I'd like to do.

I'm reminded of a sermon by my friend, Ted Vinger, that dealt with "The Art of Living with Unfinished Business." That is certainly a much needed art in the business of daily living. We often come to the end of a day, or week, or month, or year with a lot on our "things to do" list still undone. For many of those things we can look to a new day, week, month, or year and to the possibility of their still being accomplished. It may be healthy realism, or pathological morbidity, to recognize, however, that the time will come when there will be no tomorrow and on that day it will be well for us if we have gained a bit of wisdom concerning "The Art of Dying with Unfinished Business." I don't claim such wisdom, but I have a hunch that it has something to do with living each day as fully as we can and letting go of fantasies of earthly immortality.

Affirmation for the Day:
As long as I live, I will try to do my best and to learn to leave the rest.

September 27

Snow on the roof doesn't mean that the fire has gone out in the furnace.

I recall reading somewhere of Mark Twain's musing to himself, "Will I ever stop feeling young?"

After moving into my seventies, I must admit that there are times when I don't feel as vigorous and energetic as I once did, but I have been surprised to discover that most of the time I still feel about as young as ever! I get groggy if I miss my nap, but there is nothing new about that. I have been a napper for years and still awake from a fifteen-minute snooze with a feeling that it is the start of a new day.

When blessed with the incomparable gifts of health and strength of body and mind, feelings of youthfulness can last far beyond age seventy. Perhaps this reminds you, as it does me, of a story told earlier of my visit with Helen Mathiesen on the occasion of her 102nd birthday. When I asked, "How old are you now?" she smiled broadly, held up two fingers and replied, "I'm two years old. I'm starting over again!" That's more youthfulness than any of us has a right to expect, but it is a reminder that fires of life and love can co-exist with snow on the roof.

Affirmation for the Day:
While vitality lasts, I will gratefully rejoice in my youthfulness.

September 28

"That time of year thou mayst in me behold."

Even while rejoicing over feelings of youthful vitality, we old-timers do well to ponder the fact that the days ahead are far fewer than the days that have been. No one of whom I am aware has poetically pictured that reality more beautifully than Shakespeare in "Sonnet #73." As you ponder these lines, take time to visualize the magnificent metaphors of the dying of the leaves, the day, and the fire. Then pause to reflect on the wisdom of the last two lines:

> *That time of year thou mayst in me behold*
> *When yellow leaves, or none, or few do hang*
> *Upon those boughs which shake against the cold*
> *Bare ruined choirs where late the sweet birds sang.*
>
> *In me thou seest the twilight of such day*
> *As after sunset fadeth in the west,*
> *Which by and by black night doth steal away,*
> *Death's second self, which seals up all in rest.*
>
> *In me thou seest the glowing of such fire*
> *That on the ashes of his youth doth lie,*
> *As the deathbed whereon it must expire,*
> *Consumed with that which it was nourished by.*
>
> *This thou perceiv'st, which makes thy love more strong,*
> *To love that well which thou must leave ere long.*

Affirmation for the Day:
When love is deep, a lifetime is too short for loving.

September 29

"It's time to get in line."

Our thought for today is the title of the first chapter of *Final Gifts: Understanding the Special Awareness, Needs and Communications of the Dying* by Maggie Callanan and Patricia Kelley. The authors are hospice nurses who share wisdom learned from their dying patients.

In one sense, all of us are already "in line." "Every one of us," as Dr. Gerhard Frost reminded us, "is old enough to die." Yet most of us most of the time are experts at ignoring or denying that fact. We are like a famous celebrity who is reported to have said on his deathbed, "I've always known that everyone dies but I really didn't think it would happen to me."

Many of us hope that death will come quickly without misery for ourselves and the prolonged burden of painful and often exceedingly expensive caregiving for our loved ones. But the time will likely come for many of us when we are compelled to realize that our days are truly numbered. If that happens, I pray that we, too, in continued trust in God's mercy and promises, will have the realistic wisdom to say, "It's time to get in line."

Affirmation for the Day:
While standing in the lines of life, I will remember that I am also in line for death.

September 30

Thought for the Day:
"O why should the spirit of mortal be proud?"

Our thought for today is the first line of a long poem titled *Mortality* by the eighteenth-century Scottish poet, William Knox. Its claim to fame is that Abraham Lincoln called it his favorite poem, which tells us much about Lincoln. It begins with this "cheerful" thought:

> *O why should the spirit of mortal be proud?*
> *Like a fast-fleeting meteor, a fast-flying cloud,*
> *A flash of the lightning, a break of the wave,*
> *He passes from life to his rest in the grave.*

And continues for fifty lines with thoughts like these:

> *The hand of the king that the sceptre hath born,*
> *The brow of the priest that the mitre hath worn,*
> *The eye of the sage, and the heart of the brave,*
> *Are hidden and lost in the depth of the grave.*
> *The peasant whose lot was to sow and to reap,*
> *The herdsman who climbed with his goats to the steep,*
> *The beggar that wandered in search of his bread,*
> *Have faded away like the grass that we tread.*

It ends as it begins:

> *Yea! Hope and despondence and pleasure and pain,*
> *Are mingled together like sunshine and rain;*
> *And the smile and the tear, and the song and the dirge,*
> *Still follow each other, like surge upon surge.*
> *'Tis the wink of an eye, 'tis the draught of a breath*

From the blossom of health to the paleness of death,
From the gilded saloon to the bier and the shroud,
O why should the spirit of mortal be proud?

Affirmation for the Day:

When tempted to arrogance, I will ponder my mortality.

October 1

"The curfew tolls the knell of parting day."

Since it is honorable to identify with Abraham Lincoln, I will confess that some of my favorite poems are also a bit morbid. One from which we had to memorize when I was in high school, is Thomas Gray's "Elegy Written in a Country Churchyard." The first stanza is clearly symbolic of the twilight of life as of the dying day:

> *The curfew tolls the knell of parting day,*
> *The lowing herd wind slowly o'er the lea,*
> *The plowman homeward plods his weary way,*
> *And leaves the world to darkness and to me.*

The poem's most famous lines witness to a reality we are all tempted to deny or ignore:

> *The boast of heraldry, the pomp of pow'r,*
> *And all that beauty, all that wealth e'er gave,*
> *Await alike th' inevitable hour:*
> *The paths of glory lead but to the grave.*

Pondering such lines reminds me of hearing Paul Tillich say that the most profound insights and expressions of the meaning of life come not just from philosophers and theologians but from poets, including not only makers of verse but also from novelists, dramatists, and even some movie-makers who are revealers of reality.

Affirmation for the Day:
I, too, will remember to ponder the poets.

October 2

"Even to live 100 years is not to live very long."

When we look ahead from the perspective of childhood, 100 years seems to be an exceedingly long time. It is almost beyond imagining. But as we look back from the closing decades of a century we wonder how those years could have passed so quickly. We then say "Amen" to today's thought which was shared with me by Ray Solseth as he was dying not long after the death of his wife.

It reminds me of these little poems — Steven Vincent Benet's "Thirty-Five":

> *The sun was hot, the sky was bright,*
> *And all July was overhead.*
> *I heard the locusts first that night*
> *"Six weeks 'til frost," they said.*

and Robert Service's "Just Think!":

> *Just think! Some night the stars will gleam*
> *Upon a cold, grey stone,*
> *And trace a name with silver beam,*
> *And lo! 'Twill be your own.*
>
> *A little gain, a little pain,*
> *A laugh, lest you may moan;*
> *A little blame, a little fame,*
> *A star-gleam on a stone.*

"Six weeks 'til frost" — "A star-gleam on a stone" — that is the story of life and death.

Affirmation for the Day:
I've often sung it and now must face it: "Swift to its close ebbs out life's little day." (*Lutheran Book of Worship* #272)

October 3

"Please don't hire anyone until you have visited with me."

Today's thought is the punch line of a story that I heard Norman Vincent Peale tell years ago. It was about a young man who went to apply for a job. When he got there, he discovered a long line of people waiting to be interviewed. After pondering a few minutes, he took a piece of paper out of his pocket on which he wrote a brief note, walked to the front of the line, and handed it to the person who was checking in the applicants. Then he returned to his place in the line and waited to be interviewed.

Peale then told us, "He got the job!" and went on to ask, "What do you think he had written on that note?" We sat in silence and I don't recall anyone attempting to answer his question. Then he gave us the answer you already know, for it is our thought for to-day. I share it with you as an example of the power of creative thinking and of the importance of being assertive without being arrogant or offensive.

Affirmation for the Day:

I pray for wisdom and courage to put aside my modesty and to be as assertive as the situation requires.

October 4

We are all to be animators.

While visiting Christian communities in Central America several years ago, I discovered that many of them designated someone to be "the animator." Until that time, I understood animators to be cartoon technicians who brought characters to life. While in Central America, I learned that these animators were people who worked and witnessed to enliven a Christian community.

As disciples of Jesus who came to give us life "in all its fullness" (John 10:10 NEB), I think that each of us is created and called to be an animator and that this is, in an especially focused way, central to the life and work of pastors. We aren't just teachers of religion. We are to be proclaimers and bearers of life-giving love.

As pastors, we are sometimes tempted to be envious of doctors, engineers, architects, and others who have such concrete and obviously useful vocations, while we are dealing with ancient things that may seem remote from life. But if we see ourselves as animators with Christ, we realize that no one else has a more lively and life-giving vocation.

Affirmation for the Day:

Whether clergy or lay person, I will remember that Christ calls me to be an animator.

October 5

God doesn't bake bread.

The Bible tells of God providing a kind of bread, called manna, to the people wandering in the wilderness, but in our time God depends on bakers to prepare our bread. Their task would, of course, be impossible apart from other people and the gifts God provides.

A little poem recalled from long ago puts it well:

> *Back of the loaf is the snowy flour,*
> *Back of the flour, the mill;*
> *Back of the mill are the wheat and the shower*
> *And the sun and the Father's will.*

When we stop to think about it, a loaf of bread is a wonderful symbol of how we and God work together. God provides the basic resources and we prepare the final product. When we ask God to "give us this day our daily bread," we are not asking for loaves from heaven but for wisdom and strength to do the farming, milling, and baking that turns the love of God conveyed through sunshine, rain, earth, seed, and human labor into the bread that sustains our life.

Affirmation for the Day:
When savoring my daily bread, I will thankfully remember all that makes it possible.

October 6

Hope for the best but be prepared for the worst.

A line from an old hymn reminds us that "we walk in danger all the way." We need to be aware of the fact that trouble and tragedy can strike at any moment. None of us, no matter how pious or rich or successful, has any immunity against suffering and sorrow. Ponder again Gerhard Frost's blunt observation that each of us "is old enough to die." Faced with such realities, we certainly need to be prepared for the worst.

At the same time, the joys of life and benedictions of blessing like these words from the apostle Paul invite us to live with hope and joyful expectation: "May the God of hope fill you with all joy and peace in believing, so that by the power of the Holy Spirit you may abound in hope" (Romans 15:13 RSV). When empowered by the Holy Spirit we may sometimes feel helpless but we are never hopeless.

Affirmation for the Day:
Trusting "the God of hope" enables me to be prepared for the worst and to hope for the best.

October 7

Thought for the Day:

Our attitudes reveal what we are at heart.

Attitudes are difficult to define or to describe. They arise from our state of mind and have to do with our feelings, moods, and basic disposition, and in that sense tell a lot about what we are like in our heart of hearts.

Are we warm- or cold-hearted? Are we kind or cruel? Caring or careless? Compassionate or indifferent? Joyful or sullen? Loving or hateful? Such qualities are often subtle but we know they are powerfully real in ourselves and in others, and that they exert great influence, both good and bad, in our life together.

Affirmation for the Day:

Thinking about attitudes prompts me to pray, "Create in me a clean heart, O God, and put a new and right spirit within me" (Psalm 51:10).

October 8

"*Borta bra men hemma bast.*"

Our thought for today comes from a little red heart that hangs on our kitchen wall. It's in Swedish and means, "Away is good but home is best."

Carol love to travel and, thanks to our daughter's employment with a major airline, we have had great trips all over the country and to several places in distant lands. We are truly grateful for this experience and affirm as does our thought for today that "away is good."

But even after returning from the best of those wonderful journeys, we have never been moved to argue with the assertion that "home is best." To walk into one's own home, to sit together at the kitchen table, to sleep in one's own bed, to enjoy again that "at home feeling," these are joys that cannot be experienced anywhere else on the planet.

Affirmation for the Day:
Whatever my happy wanderings, I will always look forward to the joy of being home again.

October 9

Thought for the Day:

There are few honors greater than that of being trusted.

Although it didn't surprise me at the time, I now marvel at something that Dad did a few days before my twin brother and I left home for our freshman year at St. Olaf College. He took us with him to the State Bank in Frost, Minnesota, and had us sign signature cards that enabled us to write checks on his bank account. Dad was not a rich man and it was the only checking account that he had. He asked us to keep him informed concerning the checks that we wrote but set no limit on the number or amount of those checks. He trusted us to spend no more than we needed.

At the time, this arrangement struck me as nothing more than a convenient way of doing things. We didn't have to write home for money, and he didn't need to send us checks in the mail. In retrospect, I can only wonder how many students at St. Olaf have been trusted in this way by their parents? I'd guess that there have been mighty few.

Our parents honored us with such trust and I am grateful to report that we did not betray it. We had been brought up in such a way that we weren't tempted to abuse the privilege that had been entrusted to us and I am sure our parents never lost a minute's sleep worrying about it. For that kind of upbringing and that kind of trust I will always be grateful.

Affirmation for the Day:

I pray for wisdom to be responsibly trusting and trustworthy.

October 10

"Don't miss the benediction!"

Professor Herman Preus told us when we were his students at Luther Seminary long ago, that when we went to church and the singing was terrible, the scripture poorly read, the sermon bad, and the prayers mumbled, "Don't miss the benediction! It's very difficult," Preus said, "for a pastor to ruin the benediction."

I don't think I have ever participated in a worship service that was so awful that there was nothing to be received from it except the final word of blessing, but I do think it is wise to pay close attention to those final words of benediction.

Here is one of those most commonly used in our worship services:

> *The Lord bless you and keep you;*
> *the Lord make his face to shine upon you,*
> *and be gracious to you;*
> *the Lord lift up his countenance upon you,*
> *and give you peace.* — Numbers 6:24-26

If we listen and take that in, it really does give us a great sendoff for the week ahead.

Affirmation for the Day:
Whatever else I don't get from a worship service, I will be sure to get the benediction.

October 11

Thought for the Day:
We can pray without words.

When I heard Charles Whiston tell a group of pastors that he prayed for 6,000 people every day, I was shocked into disbelief. When asked, "How in the world do you do that?" he told of visioning the cosmic Christ with open arms welcoming him to an embrace of love. Then he thought of Christ turning him around and standing with hands on his shoulders saying, "Look with me at the people I love." In that context Whiston called to mind, with the help of lists of people for whom he had promised to pray, the names and faces of those 6,000 people. It took him, he said, about two hours a day and since it was part of his work of prayer, he confessed that he didn't do it on Saturdays and Sundays.

Praying for 6,000 people a day is far beyond my capacity or desire, but I can manage about sixty. They include members of our extended family recalled from memory and a list of others for whom I have been asked or moved to pray. Such praying is not entirely without words. For someone known to be in special need, personal petitions come naturally to mind, but for most it is a prayer of remembrance and concern without a verbalized petition.

Affirmation for the Day:
I will remember that "Prayer is the soul's sincere desire, unuttered or expressed."

October 12

"Never lose a holy curiosity."

Today's thought comes from Albert Einstein and is the last sentence of a longer statement that says:

> *The important thing is not to stop questioning. Curiosity has its own reason for existing. One cannot help but be in awe when contemplating the mysteries of eternity, of life, of the marvelous structure of reality. It is enough if one tries merely to comprehend a little of this mystery every day. Never lose a holy curiosity.*

It strikes me as significant that Einstein called such curiosity "holy." It reflects reverence of three great mysteries that he singles out for special contemplation: "Of eternity, of life, and of the marvelous structure of reality."

When he goes on to say that it is enough if we try "merely to comprehend a little of this mystery every day," it is obvious that he regards none of the three to be fully understandable and yet not beyond partial comprehension.

We live with these mysteries day-by-day. We stand on the surface of the planet with knowledge of atoms spinning within and around us, and of galaxies spinning far beyond us. It is certainly more than enough to make our heads swim with awe and wonder, and to evoke within us day-by-day a sense of "holy curiosity."

Affirmation for the Day:
I will never cease to marvel at the mysteries within and around me, and to seek day-by-day to comprehend a little more.

October 13

"Now I know only in part."

Here is an analogy from Leo Tolstoy with which I fully agree:

> *We live in this world like a child who enters a room where a clever person is speaking. The child did not hear the beginning of the speech, and he leaves before the end; there are certain things which he hears but does not understand. In the same way, the great speech of God started many, many centuries before we started learning, and it will continue for many centuries after we turn to dust. We hear only part of it, and we do not understand the biggest part of what we hear, but nevertheless, a bit vaguely, we understand something great, something important.*

Tolstoy's illustration reminds me of this reflection from the apostle Paul from which our thought for today is taken:

> *When I was a child, I spoke like a child, I thought like a child, I reasoned like a child; when I became an adult, I put an end to childish ways. For now we see in a mirror, dimly, but then we will see face to face. Now I know only in part; then I will know fully, even as I have been fully known. And now faith, hope, and love abide, these three; and the greatest of these is love.*
> — 1 Corinthians 13:11-13

One of our greatest hypocrisies is in pretending to know things that we do not know. Temptation to such hypocrisy may be especially close to those of us who have been called to reveal the mind and heart of God.

A professor put a small dot on a large blackboard and told the students, "This dot represents the sum total of human knowledge. The rest of the blackboard represents human ignorance." If that is true of all humanity, how much smaller is the dot of my personal knowledge?

Affirmation for the Day:
While thankful for my knowledge, I am mindful of my ignorance.

October 14

"We live in the eighth day of creation."

Today's thought from the Russian philosopher, Nikolai Berdyaev, wisely adds a day to the biblical story of creation. It is as if God, after resting a bit, had said to Adam and Eve and their descendants, "You will discover that the world beyond Eden is imperfect and incomplete. I want you to join me in the creative work of making it better."

I believe that God rejoices over every discovery and good work that makes life better. Having had polio in childhood, I think that creation got better and that God smiled when Salk and Sabin developed the vaccines that saved the world from this crippling and sometimes deadly affliction.

At the same time, I believe that God grieves over the misuse of human creativity and resources that are directed toward the denial and destruction of life rather than toward fullness of life for all God's children. I wonder what the state of the world would be if humanity had spent as much money and brainpower on finding ways of curing and preventing cancer and other diseases as we have spent on war and war-making.

Affirmation for the Day:
I will affirm all life-giving creativity and oppose all that is life-degrading.

October 15

Evolution is a necessary but insufficient explanation of the origin and diversity of life.

I believe that evolution is for real and that it explains and helps us to understand many things, but I am not persuaded that it explains everything.

When I visit an aquarium or a zoo or walk through a meadow, forest, or flower garden, I often ponder the amazing and mysterious potentiality for life that is built into the structure of the universe. From whence does that potentiality come? Belief that the physical universe and the diversity of life within it is the result of "pure-chance" evolution alone, seems far less likely than believing Michaelangelo's *David* and the Mount Rushmore monument could have been created by wind and weather alone. The odds of that are, for me, beyond belief!

I confess to being intrigued by the reflections of scientists like Stephen M. Barr, Michael Behe, S. Conway Morris, Paul Davies, Michael J. Denton, John F. Haught, Kenneth R. Miller, John Polkinghorne, Keith Ward, and Arne Wyller. All affirm evolution as a true but inadequate explanation of a life-giving universe. As I understand them, they all, in effect, witness to what William James called "The More." Some affirm "intelligent design," while others, like Haught, believe that "Cosmic purpose is more appropriately thought of in terms of nature's promise" and that "the idea of 'promise' serves more suitably than 'design' to indicate life's and the universe's inherent meaning."

Affirmation for the Day:
I will not assume theories that explain something explain everything.

October 16

There are questions that science cannot answer.

The scientific method and an abundance of scientific discoveries are from my perspective great gifts from God. Starting from the assumption that all truth is God's truth, I believe that scientists should be encouraged to continue exploration of everything that is amenable to scientific inquiry.

At the same time, however, I am aware that there are exceedingly significant questions to which science cannot give an answer. To cite just one example, I frequently find myself asking, "Why is there something instead of nothing?" When I observe the world, it strikes me that everything comes from something, and that only nothing can come from nothing. Pushing that point leads to the logical conclusion that there should be nothing.

When believers in God, of whom I am one, respond by saying, "It all comes from God," there is something within me that goes on to ask, "Where did God come from?" to which I have no answer. We seem to have a choice between believing in an uncreated universe or an uncreated God. This compels me to face the fact that there are realities utterly beyond my comprehension. I don't know why there is something instead of nothing. But to my mind it is more reasonable, as well as more comforting and purposeful, to believe that our origin and destiny are in God than to believe that our magnificent universe somehow happened by accident and that our lives are meaningless.

Affirmation for the Day:
Science can tell me a lot about who, what, where, when, and how, but it can't tell much about why.

October 17

We are visitors to planet earth.

Although it may seem a bit bizarre, I sometimes imagine myself as a visitor to planet earth from somewhere in a distant galaxy. To set the stage for such imagining, I wonder how I would feel if someone with a Star-Wars-type transporter were to invite me to visit a thriving civilization on a beautiful planet somewhere else in the universe. What if they were to promise me a safe, swift, round-trip journey with enough time on that new planet to check things out?

I will never, of course, be invited to such an adventure, but thinking about it reminds me that each of us is really such a privileged explorer of life on planet earth. I have already been given nearly three-quarters of a century for exploration of this place and I continue to be amazed at what I have discovered. Perhaps there is more intelligent, more compassionate, wiser, and less violent life on another planet somewhere in this universe, but I must confess to find much joy and beauty on this little sphere. In spite of all our problems, it is a place of promise and possibility and I am immensely grateful for the privilege of visiting this planet.

Affirmation for the Day:
I'd like to visit all the lively planets in the universe but since that's impossible, I will try to make the best of my pilgrimage on planet earth.

October 18

"What are you doing with my world?"

My twin brother tells of the time when he was leaving to attend a meeting at which he was to give a speech. To be able to point out the location of several countries, he decided to take along a globe he had given to one of his children. As he was walking out the door, his son spied him with the globe under his arm and called out, "Hey, Dad, what are you doing with my world?"

When we look about us and observe activities that pollute, waste, desecrate, and even threaten to destroy the life of this planet, we can almost hear both God and millions of people asking, "What are you doing with my world?" We are stewards and trustees not only of our money, abilities, and time but also of the life of this planet. Responsible exercise of this stewardship has many social and political dimensions but it is essentially a moral matter. We cannot rightly rejoice and give thanks to God for "life and health and every good" and at the same time be indifferent to evils that threaten to destroy it all.

Early in the 1800s the American revivalist, Charles Finney, declared that he did not believe it was possible to clearly proclaim the saving gospel of Jesus Christ while at the same time supporting, or even being silent, concerning the great abomination of slavery. In a similar way, I do not believe it is now possible for us to be clear in our witness to Jesus Christ while we support (by sound or silence) the wasting, warring, and desecration of the planet.

Affirmation for the Day:
I will seek to live as a faithful steward of the present and future life of this planet.

October 19

"A miracle is the natural law of an unusual event."

Today's thought, from Eugen Rosenstock-Huessy, reminds us that it is not necessary to think of miracles as events contrary to the laws of nature. They may be in accord with laws of nature that we do not yet fully understand. Leslie Weatherhead imagined visitors from another planet watching the traffic patterns at a busy intersection. When the light was green the traffic moved; when it was red the traffic stopped. They recorded this as the natural law of our planet. Then all traffic stopped or moved aside while a vehicle with a flashing red light sped through the intersection while the traffic light was red. Since it was contrary to their understanding of our planet's laws they recorded it as a miracle. What they had observed was, however, fully in accord with a law, of which they were unaware, that permits emergency vehicles in urgent situations to run red lights.

With our knowledge of radio waves, we think nothing of holding little devices in our hands and talking with someone in China or listening to a symphony from London. For our ancestors who knew nothing of radio waves, that would have been utterly miraculous.

Interpreting biblical miracles is challenging and difficult. Some may be metaphorical signs similar to parables. Some healing miracles may have been psychosomatic. But whatever they are, we don't need to think of them as God suspending the laws of the universe but as the "natural law of unusual events."

Affirmation for the Day:
All miracles are mysterious, but all mysteries are not miracles.

October 20

We won't get another house!

When my wife was an elementary school librarian, she would sometimes bake a loaf of bread (using a special recipe she had picked up at the San Diego Zoo) and place it in an empty aquarium tank in the library. She would cut a couple of small holes in the loaf and then place two white mice in the tank. They quickly made their home in the loaf which was also their only source of food.

Things looked good for several days and most of the kids thought the mice could live in that loaf for a very long time. But before long signs of trouble began to appear. It soon became evident that those stupid mice were wrecking their beautiful home. They seemed more intent on digging holes and polluting instead of preserving the place. Before long the "roof" of their beautiful, life-giving home collapsed, and the floor of the aquarium became an unsightly mess with two little mice scurrying about looking for a place to hide. When that happened, my wife would either bake a new loaf and start the process over again or give the mice to one of the children who was eager to give them a new home.

Although we are certainly more intelligent than those dumb mice, we may be in the process of doing something similar to the earthly "loaf of bread" in which we live. In fact, our wasting and polluting may be worse for us than it was for those mice. There won't be someone to bake us a new loaf nor will someone whisk us away to set up happy housekeeping on another planet. If we are smarter than mice, we will learn to take better care of the only house we will ever have.

Affirmation for the Day:
Those who care for their families take good care of their homes.

October 21

Beware of *post hoc ergo propter hoc.*

This line in Latin says: "After it, therefore because of it." The warning is to beware of thinking that just because something follows something else it has been caused by it.

The classic example is the rooster who crows at the first light of dawn and is sure that his crowing causes the sunrise. Why shouldn't he think that way? He crows and the sun rises! It hasn't failed yet!

The rooster may be pardoned for such thinking but how about ourselves? Prosperity abounds and the president and all politicians take credit for it. They may have done nothing more to cause it than did the rooster the sunrise. The reverse is also true. Times of recession come and whoever happens to be in office gets blamed for it, even though it may be far more the fault of previous administrations or of factors beyond anyone's control. Warriors who take credit for all good things that follow their conquests are sometimes as irrational as a person who credits present health to a previous illness.

We are tempted to similar fallacious thinking in relation to the good and bad fortune of our personal lives. When we prosper and enjoy good health we are tempted to think it is totally the result of our virtue and wisdom, and when we come upon bad times we may blame ourselves for afflictions that come to good and bad alike.

Since we live in a cause-and-effect world, we do experience results and consequences that follow from good and bad, wise and foolish behavior. But things that follow after are not always the result of things that went before.

Affirmation for the Day:
I will try to be more discerning than the rooster who takes credit for the sunrise.

October 22

Thought for the Day:
"Don't go empty-handed."

Today's thought is from my mother and is a reminder to do something useful while on the way to or from doing something else. Although it is a bit embarrassing to think of it, my earliest memory of its meaning was her encouragement to bring in an armload of firewood when returning from the outhouse which was around the corner and a bit beyond the woodshed. I am sure that many mothers today give similar encouragement inviting children and husbands to return food to the refrigerator and dishes to the kitchen sink following meal times.

Although it is hardly a momentous admonition, today's thought is a reminder of at least two things that we frequently forget. One is of the importance of planning ahead so that we don't need to make two trips when one would suffice. The other is to be mindful of the needs of those with whom we live and work and to do our best to be helpful. Such helpfulness often requires only a bit of thoughtfulness and a little effort, and especially when habitual, contributes immensely to the harmony of life at home and at work.

Affirmation for the Day:
I will seek to combine thoughtfulness and kindness in all my living.

October 23

Trust, because everything depends on God; work, because everything depends on you.

Our double thought for today is a modification of a statement heard long ago from someone who said, "Trust as if everything depends upon God and work as if everything depends upon you." Since the "as if" smacks of pretending and make-believe, I have replaced it with "because." I do so also because I think both statements are true.

When I first heard this saying, I puzzled over how both statements could be true. If everything depended on God, how could everything also depend upon me? For me, the paradox is resolved by two of my favorite illustrations that have been shared earlier. One is to liken life to an ocean liner that does two things at the same time — it trusts and it works. It is 100 percent dependent upon the sea and, if it is to get anywhere, it is 100 percent dependent upon its engines. A similar illustration is of a lifeguard who also trusts and works at the same time. A lifeguard who doesn't trust the dependable buoyancy of the water couldn't save anybody. Nor would anyone be saved without the lifeguard's energetic activity.

With ships, lifeguards, and in daily living, trusting and working go together. Trusting the living, loving, lifting presence of God sustains and strengthens us. Working with all the energy that is in us gets things done.

Affirmation for the Day:
Being both dependent and dependable sounds good to me.

October 24

Good people love people and use things. Bad people love things and use people.

Our thought for today is adapted from this paragraph from Sidney J. Harris' book, *Pieces of Eight*:

> *The difference between a good person and a bad person (and each of us, naturally is a little of both) is really very simple at bottom: the good person loves people and uses things, while the bad person loves things and uses people.*

Remembering Alfred North Whitehead's maxim, "Seek simplicity and distrust it," prompts me to be a bit wary of Harris' wisdom. I am not fully persuaded, for example, that it's always wrong to use people. When a seminary student made an eloquent statement about how terrible it is for Christians to "use God," Dr. Edmund Smits replied, "Ah, yes, but in his love, God invites us to use him." So, too, doctors and nurses, lawyers and counselors, friends and family members, invite us to use them and their wisdom and love, especially in the troubled times of our ventures of living.

Granting all that, I still think Harris is on to something important. Our lives are certainly messed up if our central focus is on loving things and using people. We are not only far better off but also are far better people if we are loving people and using things. Loving things is close to idolatry. Loving people is reflective of the compassion of Jesus.

Affirmation for the Day:

I will seek to do no more than like things, and no less than love people.

October 25

Thought for the Day:
"Our extremities are God's opportunities."

I am moved to think of today's thought in two ways. The first is in terms of our extremities of trouble that come in many forms — guilt, grief, sickness, failure, misunderstanding, anger, resentment, financial and family problems, and the list goes on. I remember Gerhard Frost saying that for the first half of his life he was a "coper." Then he encountered an extremity that was beyond his ability to cope. It was then, he said, that he really learned what it is to live by the grace of God. During open meetings of Alcoholics Anonymous and other twelve-step groups, I have heard similar stories of people who said, "I came to the end of my rope" and discovered that God and people were there to lift and carry me into a new way of living.

I think it is also true that extremities of joy as well as trouble are God's opportunities. One of the definitions of extremity in my dictionary is "the greatest or utmost degree" and that can apply to gladness and ecstasy as well as trouble. When surprised and moved by love and beauty, feelings of joyful gratitude rise within us.

Repentance can occur in moods of gaiety and ecstasy as well as guilt and grief. To repent is to have a change of mind and to turn from centering in ourselves to centering in the presence and promises of God. Our extremities, both good and bad, are often times of such change and turning.

Affirmation for the Day:
When beyond myself in horror or happiness, I will be open to a new encounter with God.

October 26

"Every person who belongs to Christ belongs to every person who belongs to Christ."

At first hearing, this line from E. Stanley Jones may sound like double talk, but please take time to reflect on it. When we look to Christ for life and salvation, we are united with every other person who looks to Christ for life and salvation. Whether we know them, or like them, share or differ in denominational, national, racial, political, or whatever affiliation, has nothing to do with it. Belonging to Christ, we belong to each other.

I believe that Jones' statement captures the essence of Christian unity. Many of the debates about differences in details of doctrine and specifics of ecclesiastical practice strike me as, at best, distracting diversions and, at worst, anti-ecumenical denials of our unity in Christ. Every person who belongs to Christ does belong to every person who belongs to Christ.

Affirmation for the Day:

I will seek to live in consistent affirmation of our unity in Christ.

October 27

Every person loved of God belongs to every person loved of God.

E. Stanley Jones' statement that "Every person who belongs to Christ belongs to every person who belongs to Christ" witnesses to the essence of Christian unity. Today's thought witnesses to the essence of human unity. Since we will never meet a person whom God does not love, it reminds us that we are brothers and sisters with every person on the planet.

During previous generations, Christians frequently spoke of "The Fatherhood of God and the brotherhood of man." I now reject that sexist language but still affirm its essential truth. As Christians, our unity is in Christ. As human beings, our unity is in the love of God who cares for non-Christians as much as for Christians. Pondering this truth reminds me that all war is civil war and that all killing is fratricide — the killing of a brother or sister.

All of us have local allegiances. It's great to cheer for the home team. But it would be tragic for those allegiances to become so strong and exclusive that neighboring communities started killing each other. Yet we see this tragedy played out again and again on the global scene. Our thought for today may sound platitudinous but taking it in and then living it out would make this a far more just and peaceful world.

Affirmation for the Day:
I will seek to think and act in remembrance of the fact that "Every person loved of God belongs to every person loved of God."

October 28

Thought for the Day:

"If thine heart is right, as my heart is with thy heart, give me thine hand."

Our thought for today comes from a sermon preached by John Wesley on 2 Kings 10:15. It is an affirmation of unity in the midst of diversity. Here is part of his sermon on Christian cooperation:

> *The two grand, general hindrances are, first, That they cannot all think alike; and, in consequence of this, secondly, They cannot all walk alike.*
> *Though we cannot think alike, may we not love alike? May we not be of one heart, though we are not of one opinion? Without all doubt we may. Herein all children of God may unite, not withstanding these smaller differences.*

He goes on to speak specifically of differences in theology, worship, and church government, and points out that just as we are not required to accept the opinions and practices of other Christians, we should not attempt to impose ours upon them.

I believe that if Christians lived by Wesley's wisdom, we would have many more celebrations of our unity in Christ and far fewer occasions of divisive discord.

Affirmation for the Day:

I will remember that even when we don't "think alike" or "walk alike" we can still "love alike."

October 29

We are one family.

We have thought of how "Every person who belongs to Christ belongs to every person who belongs to Christ" which makes us part of the Christian family, and of how "Every person loved by God belongs to every person loved by God" which makes us brothers and sisters in the human family.

Matthew Joseph Thaddeus Stepanek, who has been writing poetry since he was three years old, captured that family spirit in this little poem that he wrote at the advanced age of six:

> *We are growing up.*
> *We are many colors of skin.*
> *We are many languages.*
> *We are many ages and sizes.*
> *We are many countries ...*
> *But we are one earth.*
> *We each have one heart.*
> *We each have one life.*
> *We are growing up, together,*
> *So we must each join our*
> *Hearts and lives together*
> *And live as one family.*

If a six-year-old can grasp the importance of our being "one family" so clearly and express it so beautifully, those of us who are older certainly "must each join our hearts and lives together" and find, or create, better ways to "live as one family."

Affirmation for the Day:
I will remember the words of Isaiah, "and a little child shall lead them" (Isaiah 11:6).

October 30

There is a place to meet again.

The story of the prodigal son and the elder brother in Luke 15:11-32 has good news for those of us who are alienated from someone by conflict and discord. It tells us that there is a place where we can meet again.

We aren't told why the prodigal left home, but a good guess is that he couldn't get along with his pompous, self-righteous elder brother. We do know that the elder brother didn't want to come to the party celebrating his brother's return. The main character in the parable is the loving father who not only runs down the lane to welcome and embrace his wayward son but also goes out into the field to invite home his angry son and to remind him that the prodigal is still his brother.

Here we see the father's mercy and compassion covers both sins of self-indulgence and self-righteousness and that both the prodigal and the proud have a place to meet again in their father's love.

Shortly after the second World War, a relief worker was asked how she was able to work so cooperatively with her former enemies. She answered, "We meet at the place of tears." That is a great place of meeting but there is one even better and that is to meet again in the mercy, compassion, and grace of God.

Affirmation for the Day:
When embraced by God's love, we can also embrace each other.

October 31

Live with reverence for life.

Today's thought became the motivating force in the life of Albert Schweitzer who came to sense a vital connection between himself and all living things. Without elevating it to the level of human relationships, Schweitzer was aware of a kind of kinship with the ants crawling across his deck and with all other creatures in whom there was the breath of life.

Those who live with reverence for life are not compelled to be vegetarians, but they cannot affirm cruelty to animals including that of so-called "factory farming" that cages and controls animals to maximize production and profit. It was gratifying to learn recently that McDonald's, one of the nation's largest "consumers" of eggs and chickens, had pressured the poultry industry to adopt more chicken-friendly practices.

Above all, they will live with reverence for human life. They may affirm a woman's right to abortion in tragic, exceptional circumstances, but not as a standard method of birth control. They must, it seems to me, stand against the killing of prisoners who can be restrained from harming others. They will seek alternatives to abortion, war, mercy killing, and the death penalty and will be deeply committed to providing food, health, education, equal opportunity, security, and justice for all.

Affirmation for the Day:
Remembering my kinship with all living things, I will seek to live with reverence for life.

November 1

Thought for the Day:

Jesus rejects capital punishment.

Even when told that Moses commanded that a woman caught in adultery should be stoned to death, Jesus stopped the execution and declared, "Let anyone among you who is without sin be the first to throw a stone at her" (John 8:7). In light of the fact that only the sinless are qualified to carry it out, I am both amazed and saddened that many Christians continue to affirm the barbaric practice of capital punishment. Do they really believe that we show it is wrong to kill people by killing people? Does that make any more sense than trying to show that rape and torture are wrong by raping and torturing people?

John 8:1-11 is the only account of Jesus writing something but it doesn't say what he wrote. I once heard Roman Catholic Sister Joan Chittister tell a group of pastors, "I know what he wrote! He wrote, 'Where is the man?' " I think her guess is as good as any. If that woman was "caught in the very act of committing adultery" (John 8:4), she was not alone, but she alone was being condemned to die. The man had gone free. Then, as now, the use of the death penalty was notoriously unjust.

Affirmation for the Day:

As a follower of Jesus, I affirm Jesus' clear rejection of capital punishment.

November 2

We will end war or war will end us.

Today's thought reflects the cynical wisdom of someone who said, "War will be abolished from the face of the earth either before or after the next world war." War, as Norman Cousins often said, is "like drilling a hole in the bottom of the boat on which we are all riding." War and violence in all their forms are not just against our enemies but against the whole human family and the fabric of life itself.

Years ago, Daniel Maquire stated, "If current trends continue, we will not." As our little planet continues to be ravished by seemingly endless terrorism and war, we are forced to wonder: "What will be the end of all this?" I fear that unless "current trends" are changed, the last human act may be to erect a monument with the inscription: "All who take the sword will perish by the sword" (Matthew 26:52) with the name of the author "Jesus of Nazareth" inscribed beneath it.

Advocates of nonviolent alternatives to war are often criticized as idealistic dreamers, but they may be the true realists. What they propose does not threaten the survival of the human species and offers a far brighter human prospect than do the advocates of violence and war. It is also far more in harmony with the way and teachings of Jesus.

Affirmation for the Day:
In the face of trends that move toward death, I will affirm alternatives that offer hope of life.

November 3

"As he died to make men holy, let us kill to make men free."

During the first World War, Harry Emerson Fosdick went to Europe and preached patriotic sermons to American troops in support of that war "to end all war" and "to make the world safe for democracy." Years later, Fosdick repented of such preaching and delivered sermons on "Putting Christ into Uniform" and "To the Unknown Soldier" in which he asked for forgiveness for having been a cheerleader for war.

He denounced the line, "As he died to make men holy, let us die to make men free," from the Civil War's "Battle Hymn of the Republic" as a false and sentimental comparison of soldiers going to war with Christ going to the cross. He suggested that if we were realistic and truthful we should sing, "As he died to make men holy, let us kill to make men free." Then he went on to say, "Alas, that spoils the song."

It is interesting to note that Julia Ward Howe's original version had "let us die," but most contemporary hymnals now have "let us live." Apparently we don't care to sing about either such dying or killing.

Affirmation for the Day:

I will refuse to equate the life-giving love of Christ with the life-degrading violence of war.

November 4

Jesus affirms a metaphorical sword but rejects a literal sword.

Many understand Jesus' statement, "Do not think that I have come to bring peace to the earth; I have not come to bring peace, but a sword" (Matthew 10:34), as an affirmation of violence and war. It is clear, however, from the parallel passage in Luke that says, "Do you think that I have come to bring peace to the earth? No, I tell you, but rather division!" (Luke 12:51) that "sword" in Matthew 10:34 is a metaphor for the division Jesus brings even to members of a family.

However, when Jesus says, "Put your sword back into its place; for all who take the sword will perish by the sword" (Matthew 26:52), the "sword" to which he refers is clearly literal, not figurative. In the parallel passage in Luke, Jesus' rejection of the use of a literal sword is even stronger. There he says, "No more of this!" (Luke 22:51).

I have often said that it is easier, on the basis of the New Testament, to prove that Jesus was a pacifist than that he was a Lutheran or member of any other denomination. Some Christians will almost go to war to defend literal interpretations of Jesus' words concerning holy communion, which may have been metaphorical, while ignoring or reinterpreting Jesus' clear rejection of literal use of the sword and his ominous warning to those who do so.

Affirmation for the Day:
As a follower of Jesus, I pray for wisdom to hear and courage to heed what Jesus teaches.

November 5

"We don't defeat the devil with the devil's weapons."

During my childhood and youth, I don't recall ever hearing a pastor, or anyone else for that matter, discuss the possibility that conscientious objection to participation in war was a viable option for Christians. During those days of World War II people were singing, "Praise the Lord and Pass the Ammunition," and it seemed unquestionably the right thing to do.

While a freshman at St. Olaf College, I attended a lecture by a Quaker named Howard Lutz who had been a conscientious objector during World War II. I went to hear him out of curiosity but was profoundly challenged by what he had to say, which included our thought for today. It raised questions that I have been pondering for decades. Are we really to follow Jesus in loving our enemies? Do we love them by killing them? Do we stop killing by killing people? Do we end terror by terrorizing people? Can bad means produce good ends? Do we overcome evil by evil? Is it really possible to overcome evil with good? Would we and all the world be more secure if the human race spent as much time and money sharing bread and life-giving compassion as we now spend on death-dealing weapons of war?

Affirmation for the Day:

I am compelled to ask, "If the way of Christ is right, must not the way of war be wrong?"

November 6

"War is a monstrous failure of imagination."

According to classic Christian thinking, war and violence are always to be used only as a last resort after all other possibilities for peace have been tried and exhausted. As I survey wars and violent conflicts past and present, I am persuaded that Franz Kafka is right: "War is a monstrous failure of imagination," and that the same is true for other acts of violence whether perpetrated by parents against their children or terrorists against their hated enemies.

Carol and I recently watched a documentary on World War I and found ourselves saying to ourselves and to each other, "This war was crazy and utterly irrational! It was sold as 'the war to end all wars' and 'the war to make the world safe for democracy,' but it began the most bloody century in human history. Surely there must have been, and must now be, better ways of resolving conflict than the way of war." As I ponder the history of past wars, I find myself thinking again and again "this war, too, was a monstrous failure of imagination."

We are often locked into militaristic modes of thinking that keep us from exploring possibilities "outside the box" of violence and war. Among other things, I believe that this means working for peace through justice, reconciliation, global security, and nonviolent action, instead of relying primarily on military power.

Affirmation for the Day:
When dealing with conflict, I will seek to exercise creative imagination and to think "outside the box" of violence and war.

November 7

War is a drug that gives fleeting meaning.

At first sight, the title of Chris Hedges' book, *War Is a Force that Gives Us Meaning*, looks like an affirmation of war. We don't read far, however, before discovering that almost every page is a powerful denunciation of the drug of war. Here are a few of his thoughts:

> *The rush of battle is a potent and often lethal addiction, for war is a drug, ...We must guard against the myth of war and the drug of war that can, together, render us as blind and calloused as some of those we battle ... Wars that lose their mythic stature for the public ... are doomed to failure for war is exposed for what it is — organized murder ...*
>
> *The message that the nation is good, the cause just, and the war noble is pounded into the heads of citizens in everything from late-night talk shows to morning news programs to films and popular novels. The nation is soon thrown into a trance from which it does not awake until the conflict ends.*
>
> *Stay long enough in war, and real love, real tenderness and connection, becomes nearly impossible. Sex in war is another variant of the drug of war ... In times of peace, drugs are war's pale substitute. But drugs, in the end, cannot compare with the awful power and rush of battle ... War is necrophilia ... The necrophilia is hidden under platitudes about duty or comradeship.*

Affirmation for the Day:
I renounce addiction to the drug of war.

November 8

"War and Christianity are not compatible."

Our thought for today comes from Leo Tolstoy who became an ardent opponent of war and militarism. "War," he said, "is one of the worst, most terrible things in this world." He considered war to be "mass murder" and was critical of those who "think that if they call mass murder 'war' then mass murder will stop being a murder, a crime ... murder is always a crime, no matter by whom and how it is justified." He affirmed the statement of Blaise Pascal that "Is there anything more absurd than a person having a right to kill me because we live on two opposite banks of the river and our kings quarrel with each other?"

At the same time, Tolstoy had little hope that national leaders and international peace conferences would end the abomination of war-making. "War in this world can be stopped," he said, "not by the ruling establishment, but by those who ... will do the most natural thing: stop obeying orders," and refuse to participate in such mass murder. He believed that war would not end until vast numbers of people were so horrified and fed up with this madness that they would no longer participate in or support it.

Tolstoy's conviction was created and sustained by Jesus' affirmation of love of enemies and his "No more of this" (Luke 22:51) rejection of the sword. If all Christians followed Tolstoy in rejecting violence and war, there would probably be many martyrs but, in the long run, this would almost certainly be a far better and far safer world.

Affirmation for the Day:
If Tolstoy is right concerning war, most of Christianity is wrong.

November 9

"How many does it take?"

Today's thought is the title of an article by Adin Ballou quoted by Leo Tolstoy in his book, *The Kingdom of God and Peace Essays*. In one sense, Ballou's question seems simple-minded. He wonders how many people does it take to transform "wickedness into righteousness"? He points out that when one person kills another, it is murder and that:

> ... *two, ten or one hundred men acting on their own responsibility must not kill. If they do, it is still murder. But a state or nation may kill as many as it pleases and it is not murder. It is just, necessary, commendable and right. Only get enough men to agree to it and the butchery of myriads of human beings is perfectly innocent.*

Ballou then asks, "But, how many does it take?" Although it may sound a bit bizarre, I believe that his question is exceedingly profound. It challenges basic assumptions concerning war and the rights of nations.

I recall a comment from the hired man we had on the farm when I was a child during World War II. I asked him, "How come there is so much killing going on when we have a commandment that says, *Thou shalt not kill*"? He replied, "That commandment doesn't count in wartime!" Ballou's question challenges such thinking and I'm grateful to Tolstoy for encouraging us to ask it.

Affirmation for the Day:
I, too, wonder — why are one, ten, or 100 people condemned as murderers when they kill, while vast numbers of people are praised and honored for doing so?

339

November 10

"Soldiering is more shameful than prostitution."

In *Pro-Life, Pro-Peace*, I recognized that a case can be made for justifiable warfare in tragic exceptional circumstances, and therefore military service may be necessary. Tolstoy, on the other hand, is scathing in his condemnation of all forms of military service which he likened to prostitution:

> *Shame is the position of the prostitute who is always ready to give her body to be defiled by anyone her master indicates; but yet more shameful is the position of the soldier always ready for the greatest of crimes — the murder of as many as his master indicates ... And therefore if you do indeed desire to act according to God's will, you have only to do one thing — to throw off the shameful and ungodly calling of the soldier, and to be ready to bear any sufferings which may be inflicted upon you for so doing.*

Branding military service as "shameful and ungodly" will neither win many votes in the next election nor enhance a preacher's popularity. But might Tolstoy be right? Is there something wrong with those of us who call for the abolition of war while honoring, or at least failing to criticize, those who participate in it? Is that, to use Tolstoy's analogy, like deploring prostitution while pinning medals for meritorious service on prostitutes? Since I recognize the possibility of heroic action in justifiable warfare, I cannot fully affirm Tolstoy's analogy. But I think it is worth pondering and agree with Nicholas Berdyaev that "the romanticism of war is equivalent to the romanticism of death" and that "all romanticism about war should be finally and irrevocably destroyed." General Sherman was

closer to the truth when he said that "War is hell" than are those
who glorify war and make a hero of every warrior.

Affirmation for the Day:
**Killing may sometimes be necessary, but it is never
glorious and is often shameful.**

November 11

The idea that violence is redemptive is a Christian heresy and a human delusion.

In *Jesus Against Christianity*, Jack Nelson-Pallmeyer sets his understanding of Jesus against the belief that violence and war are creative of a better world. He will grant that in the short run they may seem to decrease evil and increase good but is persuaded that Jesus rejects belief in such "redemptive violence" and calls us to a wiser and better way.

While pondering his book, I was struck by the fact that belief in redemptive violence is a dominant idea in the minds of people who in other ways are far different from one another. The list is long and includes Adolf Hitler, the 9/11 terrorists, Palestinian suicide bombers, Ariel Sharon, George W. Bush, and a host of Christian, Jewish, and Islamic religious and political leaders including many of the writers of their sacred texts. They all affirm violence and war as a means of creating a better world. Nelson-Pallmeyer's Jesus commands us to reject this notion wherever it is found and to follow Jesus in the way of nonviolent love even if it means suffering and the cross.

This is a powerful challenge that few have been willing to accept and follow. But as violence and war now threaten the survival of civilization and even of humanity, it seems essential that we ponder the possibility that Nelson-Pallmeyer may be right about Jesus, and that Jesus may be right about what is truly redemptive.

Affirmation for the Day:

Jesus seems so right about everything else, might he also be right in rejecting redemptive violence and affirming redemptive nonviolent love?

November 12

War brings out the best and the worst.

War stories abound with tales of valor, bravery, courage, and self-sacrifice. From one point of view, it can be argued that war brings out the best in people among whom are many of our greatest heroes.

Without detracting from anyone's heroic self-sacrifice, we need to remember that in times of war such personal nobility is often in the service of terrible barbarity. From their perspective terrorists and suicide bombers give their lives in heroic self-sacrifice to destroy what they believe to be satanic forces oppressing their people. We see them, rightly I believe, as misguided murderers.

We need to remember that war brings out the worst, as well as the best, in people. I concur with a historian heard long ago that the Nazi Holocaust could not have occurred apart from the twisted mentality and corrupted morality created by the ravages of total war. I think also of atrocities on our side — incinerating Dresden and Japanese cities, the atomic annihilation of Nagasaki that was surely unnecessary after Hiroshima, and the Mi Lai massacre. I recall the confession of a Vietnam veteran who told me that their times of R and R (rest and recuperation) were more commonly known as I and I (intercourse and intoxication). Many of those in our veteran's hospitals have stories to tell, not of the glories of war but of the effects of the military's condoning, and often encouraging prostitution and behavior that led them into nicotine and alcohol addiction. It is sheer sentimentality and romantic nonsense to regard war and military service as bringing out only the best in people.

Affirmation for the Day:
Morality is the frequent victim of militarism.

November 13

Selective conscientious objection is inherent in justifiable war theory.

Many governments, including our own, have required conscientious objectors to confess that they are conscientiously opposed to participation in any and all war in order to be granted CO status. This places an unfair requirement on all Christians who affirm historic justifiable/unjustifiable war principles.

Those principles declare that while some wars may be justifiable, others are not, and that Christians should not participate in unjust wars. Many, for example, who said they would have fought against Hitler in World War II, declared themselves to be selective conscientious objectors and refused to participate in the Vietnam War, which they regarded as unjust. I believe that our government should offer such selective conscientious objection. When it fails to do so, it creates conditions of justifiable civil disobedience.

Affirmation for the Day:
Even if not a pacifist, I will refuse to support any war I believe to be unjustifiable.

November 14

"Patriotism is the last refuge of a scoundrel."

Patriotism is often wonderful. It's great to fly the flag, sing the National Anthem, and join with fellow citizens in joyous celebration of the blessings of the country we call our own.

As Dr. Samuel Johnson points out in our thought for today, patriotism can also be the refuge of scoundrels. Misguided leaders of democratic societies as well as tyrannical dictators can rally their citizens around the flag and with patriotic frenzy send them off to kill and die in wars that time will tell to be utterly unnecessary and unjustifiable.

I am surprised and distressed by the almost automatic, almost universal support our presidents receive in support of acts of war in times of crisis, and I am grateful for those who raise voices of concern and caution.

George Bernard Shaw was bold enough to say, "You will never have a quiet world 'til you knock the patriotism out of the human race." That's too much for me. I think proper patriotism is a good thing but I also believe that knee-jerk, idolatrously nationalistic patriotism is a terrible thing. The best patriotism lives in awareness that we are citizens not only of our country but of the world.

Affirmation for the Day:
I will fly the flag proudly but wave it cautiously.

November 15

Beware of the doctrines of preemptive and preventive war.

Our government's arguments affirming preemptive war are similar to those that have been used for centuries in support of justifiable warfare. It is not difficult in the abstract imagination to make a plausible case for both. Aren't we justified as innocent victims in defending ourselves against ruthless aggressors? If we know that someone is going to attack us tomorrow shouldn't we attack today? It is hard to answer an emphatic "No!" to such questions.

When we leave abstract imagination and return to concrete reality, we discover that as a practical matter justifiable war theory has been used to bless virtually every war that any nation has ever wanted to fight. Now, having used the doctrine of preventive war to justify attacking a nation because we feared that it could someday acquire the capacity to attack us has set an example that, if followed by the nations of the world, would result in global disaster.

The law of the land does not justify killing our neighbors because we fear that they may someday have the capacity and desire to kill us nor should the law of the nations allow such arrogant, aggressive barbarism.

Affirmation for the Day:
The golden rule applies to nations as well as persons and stands clearly against the doctrine of preventive war.

November 16

Beware of unintended consequences.

Harry Emerson Fosdick told a story of a man who boarded a bus intending to go to Detroit but, after a long day's journey, he discovered that he was in Kansas City. He had caught the wrong bus! Fosdick used this as an illustration of the fact that our destinations are not determined by our intentions alone but by the roads we travel. It is sadly too often true that "The road to hell is paved with good intentions."

Well-intended actions often result in unintended consequences. The signers of the Versailles Treaty, which placed heavy burdens on Germany following World War I, had no intention of creating a Hitler and another World War, but many believe they helped to do so. Placing U.S. troops in Saudi Arabia and supporting Israel's oppression of Palestinian people was certainly not intended to incite hatred and terrorist attacks against the United States, but they have.

Students who teased and bullied classmates had no intention of inciting school shootings, but that has happened. I have never known anyone who married with the intention of getting a divorce, but attitudes, words, and actions created that unintended result.

Thinking about unintended consequences reminds us again that "when we pick an apple we shake the tree." That should teach us to ponder the possible unintended consequences of everything we say and do. We need the mindset of top-notch chess players who are always thinking several moves ahead in anticipation of what each of their moves will prompt from their opponents. In life, as in chess, those who think only of the next move are bound for trouble.

Affirmation for the Day:
Before acting, I will watch out for unintended consequences.

November 17

"The dogmas of the quiet past are inadequate to the stormy present."

Our thought for today comes from Abraham Lincoln who said it in 1862. He went on to say, "The occasion is piled high with difficulty, and we must rise to the occasion. As our case is new, so we must think anew and act anew."

Albert Einstein had similar thoughts. He said, "The unleashed power of the atom has changed everything save our modes of thinking, and we thus drift toward unparalleled catastrophe." As early as 1946, Einstein had come to believe that "A new type of thinking is essential if mankind is to survive and move toward higher levels," and that "to maintain the threat of military power" is to cling to an outmoded method in a world that had "changed forever."

September 11, 2001, shocked us into awareness of having entered a century in which suicidal terrorism may be the greatest threat to our peace and security. When tempted to respond with violence and terrorism of our own, we need to ask if such methods are adequate "to the stormy present." Even if we succeed in killing ringleader terrorists and dispersing their forces, will we have ended the threat of terrorism or only created martyrs who will inspire endless cycles of future terrorism?

Affirmation for the Day:
In confronting new situations, I will be open to "think anew and act anew."

November 18

International terrorism is a crime against humanity.

Since September 11, 2001, we have been waging "a war against terrorism." I believe, however, that those acts of terrorism were a crime against humanity and not just a war against the United States.

This is not just a matter of semantics. With the "war against the United States," understanding our response has been primarily unilateral and military. Billions more were immediately added to the military budget, and we challenged other countries to join us — "Are you with us or against us?" — in fighting this war.

With "a crime against humanity," understanding the threat of terrorism would have been seen and presented as a global, not primarily American, problem. We would have told the nations of the world, "We are with you and commit ourselves to provide increased support for the United Nations, the International Criminal Court, and other multinational efforts to outlaw and prevent terrorism."

We would have been as diligent in asking and as honest in answering, "Why do they hate us?" as we were in probing, "What went wrong?" following the space shuttle disasters. We would have faced the fact that our policies concerning Palestine and Israel, stationing troops in Saudi Arabia, and imposing sanctions that resulted in the death of thousands of innocent children and civilians in Iraq, helped fuel the suicidal anger of 9/11. Overall, our response would have been less militarily defensive and more humanitarianly offensive. Our focus would have been on the elimination of injustice, oppression, and needless suffering that foments hatred and spawns terrorism.

Affirmation for the Day:
Internationally, as medically, mistaken diagnoses result in faulty treatment.

November 19

"War is a way people have of settling their indifferences."

When Bruce Bernu wrote that answer on a confirmation quiz, I think he meant to say "differences" but in a profound sense he got it right. It is our indifference as well as our differences that get us into trouble and create conflict, violence, and war.

This came home to me in a very poignant and moving way while reading dozens of articles in the magazine, *World Press Review*, after the September 11, 2001, terrorism attacks. They were selected from newspapers and magazines from around the world.

Without blaming the United States for such barbarism, many commentators from other countries were candid in pointing out that we, the American people and our government, have often been callously indifferent to the world suffering, hunger, poverty, and other acts of terrorism including some of our own. Some said, in effect, "You may now begin to understand what we have been going through for so long and may even catch a glimpse of why misguided hatred and powerlessness are expressed in such a murderous way."

Affirmation for the Day:
I pray to be more aware, more compassionate, and less indifferent toward the suffering of others.

November 20

"One death is a sorrow; 100 deaths is a tragedy; a million deaths is a statistic."

Today's thought is attributed to Josef Stalin. Few of us would be as blunt in expressing it, but all of us are tempted to share his perspective. We sorrow when a friend or family member dies. We feel the tragedy of 100 people killed in a plane crash. But when we read or hear news of millions dying from AIDS and from hunger, malnutrition, and related diseases, we may shake our heads and change the channel or turn the page. Their deaths become just another statistic in the grim story of human suffering.

In one sense, this is certainly understandable. Such tragedy is more than we can take in or do anything about. The victims are nameless and faceless. They have become only a number too big for us to comprehend. The result is what Robert Lifton has called "psychic numbing." It cuts us off from realities too painful to face.

Although understandable, such thinking and lack of feeling is to be strongly resisted, lest we succumb to a kind of statistical immorality manifested by monstrous mass murderers like Stalin and Hitler. We need to raise voices of protest and to band together with others who are caring and courageous enough to call for change. None of us can alleviate all of the world's suffering, but individually and together we can make a difference.

Affirmation for the Day:

I pray for courage to face and to fight statistical immorality that tempts us all.

November 21

We don't cure our headaches by cutting off our heads.

For centuries, philosophers and theologians have debated the question, "Does the end justify the means?" In some situations, the answer may be difficult but in others, including our thought for today, it is certainly obvious. A person suffering from painful, chronic headaches is not likely to be comforted by a doctor who offers the guaranteed cure of decapitation!

Yet, is such a solution any less irrational than that of the military expedition during the Vietnam War that reported, "We had to destroy the village in order to save it!" Or is it less tragically misguided than the thinking of those at the height of the Cold War arms race who were willing, in effect, to destroy the world in order to save it from Communism!

As Gandhi and many others have pointed out, ends and means are bound up together. Evil means do not produce good ends. We do not defeat the devil with the devil's weapons. The apostle Paul offers a wiser strategy when he says, "Do not be overcome by evil, but overcome evil with good" (Romans 12:21).

Affirmation for the Day:
Ends justify many, but not all, means.

November 22

"Do not be overcome by evil, but overcome evil with good."

The majority of Americans confess to being Christians of one kind or another, and to believing that the Bible reveals God's will for their lives. Yet, if told that we are to love our enemies and to respond to terrorism with bread not bombs, most would regard such advice as foolish, weak, un-American, and even traitorous. But isn't this what the Bible tells us to do? Jesus said, "You have heard that it was said, 'You shall love your neighbor and hate your enemy.' But I say to you, 'Love your enemies and pray for those who persecute you' " (Matthew 5:43-44). Similarly, the apostle Paul says:

> *Do not repay anyone evil for evil, but take thought for what is noble in the sight of all ... never avenge yourselves, but leave room for the wrath of God, for it is written, "Vengeance is mine, I will repay, says the Lord." No. "If your enemies are hungry, feed them; if they are thirsty, give them something to drink ... Do not be overcome by evil, but overcome evil with good."*
> — Romans 12:17-21

Might this be the new thinking that the world needs to more wisely counter suicidal terrorism? What would happen if the United States led a coalition of nations that would spend as much time, money, and energy feeding the hungry, caring for the oppressed, and working for justice as we now spend on violence and war? Would we and the world be more or less secure?

Affirmation for the Day:

I pray for courage to follow Jesus in loving my enemies and by seeking to overcome evil with good.

353

November 23

"Remember Rehoboam!"

We have been taught to "Remember Pearl Harbor" and to "Remember Munich." Those are good things to remember. They remind us to beware of surprise attacks and disastrous compromises.

But we also need to "Remember Rehoboam!" In her book, *The March of Folly*, Barbara Tuckman reports that this was the advice that John Wesley gave the British prime minister at the time of the American Revolution. She believes he would have been wise to have heeded it.

Rehoboam was the son of Solomon and became king when his father died. When the people asked to be relieved of some of the burdens Solomon had imposed upon them, Rehoboam first consulted with "the older men who had attended his father." They advised him to listen to the people and to lighten their burdens. Then he "consulted with the young men who had grown up with him." These young "Rambos" told him to get tough. Rehoboam heeded their foolish advice and sent his "taskmaster" to impose new burdens. The people stoned him to death, Rehoboam fled to Jerusalem, and the united kingdom was divided. (See 1 Kings 11:43—12:19 and 2 Chronicles 9:31—10:10.) To all of which, Tuckman comments that the entire history of Israel from that time forward would have been different if Rehoboam had been smart enough to follow the advice of the wise old men.

Affirmation for the Day:

I will remember that just as there are times to stand firm, there are also times to compromise.

November 24

To those who have only a hammer, every problem may look like a nail.

A physician once told me of a surgeon who was labeled, behind his back, as "Gallbladder Bill." With humorous hyperbole I was told of how this surgeon, following a brief examination, would tell almost every patient that whatever the symptoms, the cure was gallbladder surgery. I hope such doctors are rare but it is no doubt true that there may be some specialists tempted to hit the patient's "nail" with their "hammer."

Even more tragically, I fear that our country with its massive military "hammer" tends to see global problems like nails to be pounded with that tool. We are tempted to use war, and threats of war, to cure social, economic, and political problems that could be more wisely dealt with by nonmilitary means. Just as antibiotics are safer and more effective than surgery in the treatment of many afflictions, patient diplomacy and strenuous efforts to correct the root causes of injustice are more likely to produce lasting solutions to international problems than military action. From personal to international life, we, like a well-equipped carpenter, need lots of tools to get the job done.

Affirmation for the Day:
Those with hammers, scalpels, and weapons must beware of using them unwisely.

November 25

Perhaps you can be the 100th monkey or the 3,741,953rd snowflake.

Two stories illustrate our potential for effecting change.

One story from Ken Kesey Jr. tells of a colony of monkeys in which few washed their food. Over many days, others take up the food washing habit. At a certain point — perhaps when "the 100th monkey" begins to wash her food — the idea catches on and they all start food washing.

Slavery and male dominance held sway for centuries; then some questioned, doubted, and disbelieved. The brave started talking and acting in new ways. Many hated them. But one day, someone became "the 100th monkey" and the community was transformed.

The other story from Ron Sider and Richard Taylor tells of a chickadee sitting on the branch of a fir tree. It begins counting the snowflakes falling on the branch and when flake number 3,741,953 fell, the branch broke off and the chickadee flew away. A dove, who had watched the counting thought to herself, "Perhaps there is only one person's voice lacking for peace to come about in the world."

Affirmation for the Day:
Perhaps even I can do something to help create a more just and peaceful world.

November 26

"If we are to have real peace on earth we must start with the children."

Today's thought from Mahatma Gandhi is a central motto of World Citizen, Inc., with which I have been involved for many years. World Citizen, Inc., is perhaps best known for the establishment of Peace Sites, of which there are now about 200 in Minnesota and over 700 worldwide, and for the Nobel Peace Prize Festival held each year at Augsburg College in Minneapolis.

These are great, but from my perspective, our Peace Education Program, which encourages and works with teachers and public schools to infuse mutual respect, nonviolent conflict resolution, and global perspective into the lives of teachers and students, is even more significant. In the wake of the schoolhouse killings and September 11, there is great interest in effective peace education. We hope that what we and others are doing will be an example and model that will inspire other schools, not only in our own community but across the country and around the world, to start with the children in creating a more just and peaceful world.

Affirmation for the Day:
I will do what I can to help teach children the things that make for peace.

November 27

Every church should be a peace church.

Several years ago, a group of Roman Catholics started a movement that now includes Christians of many denominations called "Every Church A Peace Church." This movement encourages clergy and laity alike to lift up the teaching and example of Jesus in ways that reject violence and war and affirm things that make for peace. They stress that Jesus didn't say, "Blessed are the peace *lovers*" or "Blessed are the peace *keepers*," but "Blessed are the *peacemakers*" (Matthew 5:9).

In secular, public school, peace education programs like that of World Citizen, Inc., we can lift up the examples of Mahatma Gandhi, Martin Luther King Jr., Nelson Mandella, and others whose lives witness to the potential and power of nonviolent actions. But we cannot present Jesus-centered peace education that includes emphasis on love of enemies and encouragement of divine obedience expressed through civil disobedience. No government wants, nor would long tolerate, public school programs that encourage students to obey God rather than human authority (see Acts 5:29), by refusing to participate in any war they believed to be unnecessary and unjust. But isn't this something that every church that is faithful to Jesus should be teaching to both children and adults?

Affirmation for the Day:
I will affirm churches that affirm the way of the Prince of Peace.

November 28

Distrust your inner compass.

Perhaps because I grew up on a farm, I live with a strong sense of geographic direction. Wherever I am, something within me conveys a sense of north, south, east, and west. This is usually helpful but it is sometimes wrong.

Thanks to our daughter's employment with a major airline, we enjoyed a great trip to Australia where I had a problem. My inner compass couldn't adjust to the sun being in the north and for the first week or so my sense of direction was completely reversed. I knew it was wrong but I was powerless to change it. I didn't see Sydney correctly until we returned three weeks later. It was weird to discover that the world-famous Opera House had "moved" to the other side of the bridge.

What can we learn from such an experience? One lesson is that a strong sense of being right is no guarantee against being wrong. It also teaches that when wrong it sometimes takes more than an act of will to set things right. We need to be corrected from the outside and that can take time plus openness to see things differently.

Sometimes we don't realize that our inner compass is wrong. On a trip home from a college debate tournament, the driver turned south instead of north and we went fifty miles in the wrong direction. That reminds us that groups as well as individuals can have faulty compasses. When that happens we need the sunrise of a new day and the confrontation of people who see things rightly to set us straight.

Affirmation for the Day:
While grateful for my inner compasses of direction, conviction, and conscience, I will remember to distrust them.

November 29

The good is the enemy of the best.

"It's good enough" is a terrible motto for people who are too easily satisfied with imperfection.

The cabinetmaker who built the cabinets in our kitchen was apparently such a person. We noticed when they were installed that some of the doors failed to match by fractions of an inch. They worked fine but didn't look quite right. Since we wanted to get along with our builder, who had been helpful in many ways, we decided not to make an issue of such a little thing. Now, in retrospect, I think we were wrong. The cabinetmaker, who had been hired by our builder, shouldn't have been allowed to get away with such imperfections. Those cabinets were good but they were not what they should have been.

Proper pride in excellent workmanship should have kept that cabinetmaker from making such easily avoided mistakes. Years later, another cabinetmaker corrected them all in a couple of hours.

Each of us needs a measure of proper pride in the work we do and when tempted to be careless should beware of saying too quickly, "It's good enough."

Affirmation for the Day:
When the best is required, I will not settle for the good.

November 30

Thought for the Day:
The best is the enemy of the good.

"It's good enough" is a good motto for those who are never satisfied with anything less than absolute perfection.

In my life pilgrimage, I have met people who are paralyzed by perfectionism. Sometimes it is relatively harmless. They can't enjoy tennis or golf because they don't think they play well enough. At other times it is more serious, even tragic. They can't complete projects for school or at work because nothing they do is ever good enough. There are Ph.D. advisers, for example, who have driven students to desperation by always insisting that there is always something more that they need to do to complete their thesis. The tyranny of such perfectionism is even worse when it comes not from an outside advisor but from an internal obsessive compulsive perfectionism that is not able to say, "This is really good enough!'

Affirmation for the Day:
I will try to stay on the road between the ditches of perfectionism and carelessness.

December 1

"When supper is going to be late, remember to set the table."

This is a lesson I learned from my mother in childhood. When supper was going to be a bit late, we always set the table before Dad came in from work. And now in retirement, when I am the househusband and Carol is working, it is a practice I still follow.

Some might accuse my mother and me of deception, but I see it as a signal that tells the weary worker that preparations are under way and that it won't be long until it is time to come to the table.

It is certainly true that appearances can be deceiving but it is no less true that appearances can also be reassuring, and I see nothing significantly sinful about doing things that give a good impression. To my way of thinking it is one way of expressing tact and common sense.

Affirmation for the Day:
If I have a choice between making a good impression and a bad one, I will seek to make it good.

December 2

In times of grief, be bold to speak and be kind to listen.

"Give sorrow words," said Shakespeare. "The grief that does not speak whispers the o'er fraught heart and bids it break." This reminds us that times of grief are times for telling and times for listening. Bereaved people need to talk and that means that friends and family need to hear.

In the shock of sorrow we may not feel like talking and may rightly have the impression that others feel uncomfortable when we do start sharing our sorrow.

I can still remember an awkward visit with a dear friend that took place shortly after the death of our first baby who lived only an hour. My friend, who apparently didn't know what to say, chose to say nothing and we visited only about other things. I could have said something but was waiting for him to say, "I'm sorry about your baby," or some such. When that didn't happen, I said nothing. The result was one of those dumb conversations during which, as the saying goes, "We talked about everything except the elephant in the room."

In times of loss, we have both the need and right to talk about it, and those who care have the responsibility to listen. It takes only a few words of sharing and condolence to begin such a conversation and a gentle inquiry to keep it going. We may fear loss of control but should be more wary of bottling things up. We need to remember that tears are therapeutic and that willingness to tell and hear the pain of sorrow is essential to relationships of love.

Affirmation for the Day:

When grieving, I will talk and when caring, I will ask and listen.

December 3

Be a builder.

The New Testament encourages us to "encourage one another and build up each other" (1 Thessalonians 5:11). Ponder this from a speech by Robert Byrd in the U.S. Senate:

> *I saw them tearing a building down*
> *A group of men in a busy town.*
> *With a ho-heave-ho and a lusty yell*
> *They swung a beam and the side wall fell.*
> *I said to the foreman, "Are these men skilled —*
> *The type you would hire if you had to build?"*
> *He laughed and said, "No, indeed.*
> *Common labor is all that I need.*
> *I can easily wreck in a day or two*
> *That which takes builders years to do."*
> *I said to myself as I walked away*
> *"Which of these roles am I trying to play?*
> *Am I a builder who works with care,*
> *Building my life by the rule and square?*
> *Am I shaping my deeds by a well-laid plan,*
> *Patiently building the best that I can?*
> *Or am I a fellow who walks the town*
> *Content from the labor of tearing down?"*

The apostle Paul likens himself to "a skilled master builder" (1 Corinthians 3:10). This reminds us that our basic business is to build up and not to tear down, to be constructors and not wreckers, to be encouragers and not criticizers, to be affirmers and not complainers.

Affirmation for the Day:
I will seek to be a "builder-up" and not just a "tearer-down."

December 4

Thought for the Day:
"Don't sign anything you haven't carefully read."

Today's thought was advice from my dad received decades ago. Many have come to grief for failing to follow that counsel. They relied on glowing sales pitches and trusted bold print promises without reading the fine print. They didn't realize that what the big print gives the little print sometimes takes away, and discovered to their sorrow that the contract or insurance policy they had signed contained fine print exclusions that didn't meet their expectations.

Most sales people are honest enough to point out small print meanings but some are so eager to secure a signature that they maliciously or carelessly fail to tell the whole story. An old saying warns, "Let the buyer beware." If we don't heed such wisdom we may find ourselves someday sadly confessing, "I didn't realize...!"

Affirmation for the Day:
In all my business dealings, I will seek to realize first and sign later.

December 5

"Believe what you can."

In times of doubt, it doesn't do any good to try to believe things that we don't think are true. It is far better to be honest with ourselves and to settle back in confidence that it is sufficient to believe what we can.

Herman Olson, a grand old saint at Farmington Lutheran Church, told me of having received this advice as a young man. He had confessed his doubts to a Bible camp counselor and was told, "Believe what you can." Those words set him free to be honest with himself and enabled him to become not only a lifelong doubter but also a lifelong learner who ventured his life in trust of God's promised grace.

In my study of Harry Emerson Fosdick, I discovered that he shared the same advice with doubters who came to him for counsel, and I am now pleased to join him and that Bible camp counselor from long ago in commending it to you.

Affirmation for the Day:
In trust of promised grace I, too, will believe what I can.

December 6

Thought for the Day:
Jesus might be right!

Years ago, Harry Emerson Fosdick preached a sermon titled, "On Doubting our Doubts," in which he encouraged people to "set their doubts alongside the faith of Jesus" and then to ask themselves, "Who is more likely to be right — me in my doubts, or Jesus in his faith?"

Fosdick presented Jesus as a great doubter who questioned a lot of commonly held convictions. Jesus was also a great disbeliever who did not believe, for example, that we should hate our enemies or that life consists in the abundance of our possessions.

Jesus was also a great believer. He lived with unshakable conviction that our lives are sustained and empowered by the love of God and that in trust of that love we are to give ourselves in love to others. By setting our doubts alongside those convictions, said Fosdick, we can be renewed in our trust of the love of God and be strengthened in our compassion to care for one another. Since Jesus seems so right about everything else I'm betting that he was also right about God!

Affirmation for the Day:
I will seek to exchange my doubts and disbeliefs for the beliefs and convictions of Jesus.

December 7

"Jesus' teachings aren't true because Jesus said them. Jesus said them because they are true."

I heard this statement about sixty years ago from my mother's brother and I have never forgotten it.

At the end of the Sermon on the Mount it says that the crowds were astonished at Jesus' teaching because "He taught them as one having authority" (Matthew 7:28-29). The Greek word for "authority" can also be translated "out of the nature of things." Jesus' teachings reveal the nature of things.

Jesus is authoritative without being authoritarian. He does not burden us by imposing arbitrary rules and regulations. He liberates us from ignorance and error by exposing reality. This is what the New Testament means when it says, "Jesus came into the world to testify to the truth" (John 18:37).

Some non-Christians, in their quest for truth, have been more serious students of Jesus than most Christians. The Jewish political commentator, I. F. Stone, confessed, "I study Jesus just as I study the prophets of the Old Testament." Mahatma Gandhi, who never made a Christian confession, frequently acknowledged his gratitude for the life and teachings of Jesus. In our quest for truth, we do well to follow their example.

Affirmation for the Day:
Since I want to know how best to live I, too, will study Jesus.

December 8

"Take your burdens to the Lord and leave them there."

Some of us have sung "What a Friend We Have in Jesus" hundreds of times. We know its repeated refrain, "take it to the Lord in prayer," and may have also done that hundreds of times. When burdened by sins and griefs, trials and temptations, discouraged by troubles and sorrows and weaknesses, we have taken it all to the Lord in prayer. Then, we have often picked up those burdens and taken them back home with us.

Our thought for today reminds us not only to take our burdens to the Lord but also to leave them there. That's not always easy, but it is what God invites us to do. John Bunyan's *Pilgrim's Progress* tells that when Pilgrim Christian came to the grave of Christ, the heavy burden he was carrying fell from his back and rolled into the tomb, never to be seen again. So, too, we are to let go of our burdens and leave them with the Lord.

That's what the apostle Paul did. He tells of being burdened by an affliction he calls "a thorn in the flesh" and goes on to say, "Three times I appealed to the Lord about this, that it would leave me, but he said to me, 'My grace is sufficient for you, for my power is made perfect in weakness' " (2 Corinthians 12:9). Paul prayed three times — not thirty or 300 or 3,000 — three was enough! After that, he left his burden with the Lord and went on to live by the promised sufficiency of the grace of God.

Affirmation for the Day:

I will let go of my old burdens and trust grace sufficient to bear my new ones.

December 9

"What kind of car would Jesus drive?"

Lots of people these days are wearing WWJD bracelets as a reminder to ask themselves, "What would Jesus do?" Many confess to having found it helpful to ask that question in times of temptation. They tell of being saved from lying, cheating, stealing, swearing, and from unkind words and actions by modeling their lives on what they believe Jesus would do.

That's great, but I think we need to go beyond issues of occasional temptation and wonder individually and together about how Jesus would react to our American way of life. The question, "What kind of car would Jesus drive?" that I heard raised by Tony Campalo in a lecture at Luther Seminary leads us into that kind of thinking and conversation. Would Jesus drive a new Cadillac or a used Ford Escort, or would he refuse to own a car at all and rely only on public transportation? I certainly don't know the answer to such questions but as one who taught us that our lives do not consist in the abundance of our possessions (see Luke 12:15) and who practiced what he preached, it seems highly likely that Jesus would refuse to participate in a lot of the materialistic overindulgence most of us have come to take for granted.

Affirmation for the Day:
I don't know what Jesus would do, but I will try to do what I think he would do.

December 10

"If the teachings of Jesus aren't true, they ought to be true!"

In times of doubt, we are sometimes encouraged to trust and act as if the promises of God are true and are told that we will then find them to be true in our own experience. I think that's good advice. Today's thought, which is another from E. Stanley Jones, is similar but goes a bit beyond it.

Jones dares to ponder the possibility that the gospel of God's love and promises in Jesus may be a great illusion, or even deception, and not true at all! It's in that context that he says that, for him, "They ought to be true" because, after a worldwide search, he found no other way of life that brings with it such meaning, joy, and fulfillment not only for ourselves but for others.

Then he goes on to ponder the unbelievable oddity of such a deception making such sense of life and returns to the conviction that Jesus must, after all, be a revealer of reality.

Affirmation for the Day:
True or false, I will live the way of Jesus for I know no better way.

December 11

"The worst thing about being an atheist is having no one to thank."

Today's thought is another from Alvin Rogness who spoke of how he thought it was possible for people to endure immense suffering and difficulty with a kind of stoic courage and resignation without reliance on God. Even when they couldn't "grin and bear it" they could grit their teeth and somehow muster strength to carry on.

But, Rogness wondered how is it possible for someone to be overwhelmed by gratitude for joys in life that came from somewhere beyond the capacity of any person to provide and then to have no one to thank? That was just too much for Rogness to comprehend.

Some see religion, including the Christian faith, as a refuge for the weak and infantile who have not learned to get through life on their own. I certainly thank God for being with us in our weakness but am equally grateful that God is with us in our strength and in our joy as well as in our sorrow. Each of us is blessed with gifts far beyond our own creation. The apostle Paul's questions are addressed to all of us: "What do you have that you did not receive? If then you received it, why do you boast as if it were not a gift?" (1 Corinthians 4:7). For "life and health and every good" each of us needs someone to thank.

Affirmation for the Day:

Gratitude for all good things moves me to give thanks to God.

December 12

Thought for the Day:
Many who commit suicide die from an illness.

Among the sad stories from church history are those of pastors and members of congregations who condemned persons who committed suicide. Some churches even denied them burial in their cemeteries.

Martin Luther was wiser and more compassionate. He wrote to a family grieving the death of a person who had taken his own life saying that he did not believe that everyone who committed suicide was condemned by God because "they do not do this of their own free will but are like someone who is struck down by a robber in the woods."

A dear friend of ours committed suicide. She had suffered from depression for many years and had received the best treatment available at that time. During my sermon at her funeral, I told the congregation, who knew that she had committed suicide, that I believed she had died from an illness and I believe that today. Her depression was a brain disease as deadly as any that can afflict other parts of our bodies. Thankfully, new understandings, new medications, and new treatments are now available to help prevent such tragedies.

Affirmation for the Day:
I will not condemn anyone who suffers from physical or mental illness.

December 13

"The older we become, the more we become associated with the dead."

This thought was an aside by Dr. Theodore Jorgensen during his course on the dramas of Henrick Ibsen at St. Olaf College over fifty years ago.

Although it may seem morbid, it is also most certainly true. During childhood our personal associations may be 100 percent with the living but then someone, perhaps a grandparent, relative, or famous person, dies and we begin our association with the dead. Now in my seventies, my acquaintances among the dead must be about as numerous as those among the living. If I live another decade or two, their number will rapidly increase. If I don't live that long, many others will then have this new association with me.

Jorgensen confessed to finding wisdom in imagined conversations with some from whom he was now separated by death. He would wonder, "How would so-and-so deal with this situation?" and told of receiving much good counsel from such "conversations."

Affirmation for the Day:

I will ponder my associations, not only with the living but also with the dead.

December 14

Thought for the Day:

"Welcome to the company of those who are soon to die."

Although I heard it over forty years ago, I was sufficiently shocked that I have never forgotten it. It is our thought for today and was the first sentence in a speech by Jacob Tanner addressed to T. F. Gullixsen during his retirement dinner at Luther Seminary. Tanner, himself then about ninety, apparently believed that he was well qualified to begin with such a greeting. Since I am now close to Gullixsen's age at that time, it seems fitting for me to share it, especially with others of similar vintage.

I often ponder the passing of time. When we are young, future events seem far away. To have to wait a year before learning to drive seems like an eternity. But as we grow older, the time between anticipation and realization seems to become increasingly shorter. We look forward to a vacation trip. It happens and is soon over and we are moved by the realization that this will soon be true of life itself. We wonder to ourselves and others, "Where have all those years gone?" We reminisce with old friends and say, "Good grief! That was fifty years ago!"

My cousin once told me that we have passed middle age when we don't know anyone twice as old as we are. It's been a long time since I have known anyone as old as that!

Affirmation for the Day:

Realism compels awareness that my years yet to be are far fewer than those that have been.

December 15

"What you are, we were; what we are, you will be."

This statement from a sign over the gate to a cemetery speaks from the dead to the living. It tells a profound truth, but it is hard for us to take it in. We don't like to think about being dead and when we do it is difficult to imagine ourselves in a cemetery and our corner of the world without ourselves in it. Yet, sooner or later, that day will come and the world will go on without us.

Such thoughts may make us depressed but they can also be an answer to the psalmist's prayer:

> *Lord, you have been our dwelling place in all generations.*
> *Before the mountains were brought forth,*
> *or ever you had formed the earth and world,*
> *from everlasting to everlasting you are God.*
> *The days of our life are seventy years,*
> *or perhaps eighty, if we are strong ...*
> *they are soon gone, and we fly away ...*
> *So teach us to count our days*
> *that we may gain a wise heart.*
> — Psalm 90:1, 2, 10, 12

Affirmation for the Day:

Since it is a way to wisdom, I will dare to ponder my death and dying.

December 16

The living say good-bye one by one; the dying say good-bye to all.

To lose a loved one is a great grief. To say good-bye to a grandparent, parent, spouse, child, or friend is a great loss for which it is right to grieve. To love well and to live long is to guarantee many such grief experiences across the years.

As long as we are healthy and look forward to more of life, it is difficult to even imagine the grief of the dying who must say good-bye not just one by one, but to all at one time. Yet, unless death comes so swiftly that we have no time to say good-bye to anyone, that great grief will be the experience of all of us who retain our ability to know and to love. Contemplating it now can deepen our gratitude for the love and friendship we treasure and help prepare us for saying those sad good-byes.

Affirmation for the Day:
Grief comes to all who live, and most profoundly, to us in our dying days.

December 17

"Rage, rage, against the dying of the light."

Today's thought is a line from the poem that Dylan Thomas wrote at the death of his father: "Do not go gentle into that good night. Old age should burn and rage at close of day, rage, rage, against the dying of the light." It reminds us that the apostle Paul describes death as "the last enemy to be destroyed" (1 Corinthians 15:26) and that it is right and proper to rage against death.

At the same time, when life has ebbed slowly away and the misery of suffering has been intense, death may be experienced more as friend than enemy. There are those who take their lines not from Dylan Thomas but from William Cullen Bryant's *Thanitopsis*: "Sustained and soothed by an unfaltering trust" they "approach their graves like one who wraps the drapery of his couch about him and lies down to pleasant dreams." They are well aware that death is the enemy of life but for them its power has already been broken.

As the apostle Paul's thorn in the flesh was both "a messenger of Satan" and also a means of grace so, too, with death — the conquered enemy can become a friend ushering us into new and even greater life with God.

Affirmation for the Day:
Even while raging against the dying of the light, I will look for the dawn of a new and brighter day.

December 18

"When Jesus prayed, 'Father, into your hands I commend my spirit' he taught us everything we need to know about how to die."

We would like to know a lot more, but I think Gerhard Frost got it right when he expressed our thought for today. To commit our lives to the hands of a loving God is all we need to know about how to die.

Jesus really lived that prayer every day of his life and when our dying day comes it will be helpful if we have lived it, too.

When I think of those who know how to die, I go back in memory to my first experience of being with a dying person. I was only about ten years old. Although I don't know why, Dad took me with him to visit his uncle who was soon to die. Like most of us in proximity with death, Dad was probably ill at ease and may have felt that my presence provided a little companionship and comfort.

We sat together by his uncle's bed in the little house where he and his wife lived. I don't recall a word of what Dad or I had to say, but I have a vivid memory of five words from his uncle. He was frail but his mind was clear. There must have been honest acknowledgment that he was dying because he said with quiet confidence: "We get a better place."

Dad's uncle didn't quote Jesus but, in retrospect, it was clear that he had commended his life and spirit to a merciful God, in whom he trusted to bring him to a better place.

Affirmation for the Day:

In life and in death I, too, will pray, "Father, into your hands I commend my spirit" (Luke 23:46).

December 19

"Resurrection is the final healing."

When sickness strikes, we pray for healing and thank God for healing that comes through the recuperative powers built into our bodies, the help of medical practitioners, and the direct touch of God's healing spirit upon our lives.

But there are times when healing does not come as we hope. Agonizing illnesses are often prolonged. Human medicine fails, our prayers seem worthless, and death triumphs over life.

When that happens, we need not despair that God has failed to hear or heed our prayers. In Christ, God does promise the healing of all our diseases, but it is important to remember that sometimes such healing must await what E. Stanley Jones liked to call "the final healing of resurrection."

There is much mystery here. Someone has said that we know about as much about heaven as an unhatched chick knows about a henhouse or unborn baby knows about life in this world. Yet, we are invited to trust that in God's grace this world is the womb of greater life to be and that the healing of resurrection is birthing into that reality.

Affirmation for the Day:
Although I can't comprehend it, I am apprehended by promises that invite and enable me to trust in God's final healing.

December 20

"Ultimately, hell will be empty and heaven full."

Our thought for today expresses the conviction of Leslie Weatherhead and is the logical conclusion of his belief in the final fulfillment of the ultimate will of God. Although he affirms human freedom and might agree with someone who said, "God loves us so much he lets us go to hell if we want to," Weatherhead believed that the infinite love of God will some way, some time, finally win the trust of the coldest, hardest heart. Since God "desires everyone to be saved and to come to the knowledge of the truth" (1 Timothy 2:4), he was confident that this would be the ultimate fulfillment of God's intentional will.

Although some believe that such hope of universal salvation undercuts the motivation for Christian evangelism and global mission, that need not be true. Christian witness is not just to save people from hell beyond our dying. It is to proclaim graceful love and power for living each day of our lives in this world, right here, right now!

Reflection concerning hell enters a realm of mystery and raises questions to which none of us can give for-certain answers. But, of one thing I am sure — if Weatherhead is right and hell will be empty and heaven full, I am certainly not against it!

Affirmation for the Day:
If God desires universal salvation, I will rejoice in that prospect and do what I can to help it happen.

December 21

Even if there were no promise of heaven, I'd still follow Jesus.

Some accuse Christians of following Jesus only because he offers a ticket to heaven but, as I understand Christianity, it's much more about now than then.

I must confess to wondering about a sentence in the apostle Paul's great chapter on the resurrection. He says, "If for this life only we have hoped in Christ, we are of all people most to be pitied" (1 Corinthians 15:19). I understand and affirm his emphasis on the centrality of the resurrection of Christ to our life and salvation but "most to be pitied"? If there is no life beyond our dying, should we feel sorry for people who follow Jesus in lives of trust and love and who die in hope? Is there any better way to spend the days of our earthly pilgrimage? Is there any better way of dying? If the promises of heaven are true, we will have an eternity for rejoicing. If they are not true, we will not be alive and aware to lament our loss.

Affirmation for the Day:

Whatever will be then, I know of no better way than to follow Jesus now in a life of faith, love, and hope.

December 22

"The purpose of life is to express love in all its manifestations."

Today's thought is again from Leo Tolstoy who said with characteristic concreteness:

> *Everyone can recall a moment, universal to all, perhaps from early childhood, when you wanted to love everyone and everything — your father, your mother, your brothers, evil people, a dog, a cat, grass — and you wanted everyone to feel good, everyone to feel happy; and even more, you wanted to do something special so that everyone would be happy, even to sacrifice yourself, to give your life so that everyone should feel happy and joyful. This feeling is the feeling of love, and it must be returned to, for it is the life of every person.*

"There is only one thing in this world," said Tolstoy, "which is worth dedicating all your life. This is creating more love among people and destroying barriers which exist between them." And again: "Love provides a person with the purpose of life. Intelligence shows the means to achieve that purpose." This means that we are not only created to love but also that we have been given brains to figure out ways of loving.

Affirmation for the Day:

Whatever my circumstances, I will pray for the wisdom, compassion, and strength to love.

December 23

One candle can light 1,000.

The illustration in our thought for today is another from Leo Tolstoy who said:

> *Just as one candle lights another and can light thousands of other candles, so one heart illuminates another heart and can illuminate thousands of other hearts. Good books are a good influence. Good art is a good influence. Prayer is an influence as well, but the strongest influence is the example of a good life. A good life becomes a blessing for people, not only for those who live good lives but those who see, know and understand such lives.*

Such thoughts remind me of the old saying that "It is better to light a candle than to curse the darkness." We sometimes feel discouraged and defeated by the darkness of personal and global troubles that indwell and surround us. We feel helpless and wonder "What good can one person do?" Then it helps to remember that we can light a candle and that candle can light another and another and another and another and another....

Affirmation for the Day:
When I can't do a lot of good, I will still do a little.

December 24

Thought for the Day:

"Prayer is the key that opens the day and secures the night."

Today's thought from a source beyond recall encourages the wonderful habit of beginning and ending the day with prayer.

Charles Wiston suggested that we begin each day with what he called a "prayer of preacceptance of God's blessing" such as "Thank you, gracious Father, for every good gift this day will bring. Thank you for grace sufficient for every moment. Thank you that nothing in life or death this day can separate me from you and your love in Christ Jesus." He encourages us to include such thanksgiving among our first waking thoughts and to follow it with prayers of surrender and intercession.

Thinking of bedtime prayers that secure the night reminds me again of the one we taught our children: "Now I lay me down to sleep. I pray thee, Lord, thy child to keep. Thy love guard me through the night and wake me to the morning bright." This was followed by free prayers entrusting family, friends, hurting people in all the world to the care of God. Following such prayer we can rest in the security affirmed by the psalmist who said, "I will both lie down and sleep in peace; for you alone, O Lord, make me lie down in safety" (Psalm 4:8).

Affirmation for the Day:

When I open the day and secure the night with prayer, I discover that I can live the day with an attitude of prayer "without ceasing." (See 1 Thessalonians 5:16-18.)

December 25

"Christmas always comes at night."

My mother died unexpectedly on December 14, which made for a sad Christmas for our family and especially for our father. He then lived alone in what our five-year-old daughter called "the lonely house." During those days, Herman and Della Olson gave us a copy of a magazine article with the title "Christmas always comes at night."

It was a reminder of a fact that what was true for us that particular Christmas had always been true for others every Christmas across the centuries. Millions around us and before us knew in their personal experience that Christmas comes at night. It has been and will always be so, and that's what gives Christmas such depth of meaning and joy.

The good news is not that there is no more darkness but that Christmas came and Christ was born and "in him was life, and the life was the light of all people. The light shines in the darkness, and the darkness did not overcome it" (John 1:4-5).

Affirmation for the Day:
In my darkest hours, I still walk in the light of Christ.

December 26

Christ is our wisdom.

The apostle Paul speaks of Christ as "the wisdom of God." (See 1 Corinthians 1:18-31.)

That description of Jesus reminds me of hundreds of conversations over many years with a wonderful, intelligent friend who suffers from schizophrenia. She hears voices and calls frequently to tell me the latest message she has "heard" from God. Since she visits regularly with a psychiatrist and is receiving the best medication that is available I do not attempt to be her psychotherapist. But, with her doctor's blessing, I do repeatedly assure her that schizophrenic voices that speak condemnations contrary to everything we know in Jesus are not the voice of God. That usually helps for a time, but those voices are so powerful (Dr. Scott Sponheim, a clinical psychologist doing research in schizophrenia, describes them as "omnipotent") that repeated reassurance of this fact has so far been necessary.

Thankfully, most of us don't suffer from the terrible affliction of schizophrenia, but we, too, need to be repeatedly reminded that every voice from within and without that tells us things that are contrary to what we know in Jesus is neither the voice nor the wisdom of God. Some of the thoughts and temptations that enter our heads from friends, family, teachers, pastors, presidents, and authorities of all kinds may sometimes sound close to omnipotent but if they are out of harmony with what we know of God in Jesus we are right to reject them as surely as my friend is right to reject the voices of schizophrenia.

Affirmation for the Day:
I will judge the wisdoms of the world by the wisdom of God that I know in Jesus.

December 27

We live with memory and anticipation.

This little poem illustrates our thought for today:

> *The covered wagon jostled on the prairie track,*
> *One sat looking forward,*
> *One sat looking back.*

Those lines create for me a vivid image of a man filled with anticipation as he holds the reins looking westward over the backs of a team plodding toward new life in a new land. At the same time, I see an immigrant wife seated at the rear of the wagon, perhaps cradling a child in her arms, filled with memories and fears as she looks back toward home and family left far behind.

Although that image is vivid for me, I know that the eager anticipation doesn't reside only in the man nor the memories in the woman. They are mixed in each of them and also in each of us. That is how I am sure it should always be. To live without some measure of joyful anticipation is really to settle into despair and depression. To live without memory, as in tragic cases of Alzheimer's and advanced dementia, isn't only to lose resources for going on but sometimes to lose the meaning of life itself.

Affirmation for the Day:
Treasuring both memory and anticipation, I look back with gratitude and forward with hope.

December 28

"It might have been otherwise."

Our thought and reflection for today come from this poem by Jane Kenyon:

> *I got out of bed*
> *on two strong legs.*
> *It might have been otherwise. I ate*
> *cereal, sweet*
> *milk, ripe, flawless*
> *peach. It might*
> *have been otherwise.*
> *I took the dog uphill*
> *to the birch wood.*
> *All morning I did*
> *the work I love.*
> *At noon I lay down*
> *with my mate. It might*
> *have been otherwise.*
> *We ate dinner together*
> *at a table with silver*
> *candlesticks. It might*
> *have been otherwise.*
> *I slept in a bed*
> *in a room with paintings*
> *on the walls, and*
> *planned another day*
> *just like this day.*
> *But one day, I know,*
> *it will be otherwise.*

I will live in gratitude for all the good things that have been, and now are, "but one day, I know, it will be otherwise."

December 29

Thought for the Day:
We venture together through the night.

I have been captivated by the imagery of this hymn stanza:

> *Through the night of doubt and sorrow*
> *Onward goes the pilgrim band,*
> *Singing songs of expectation,*
> *Marching to the promised land.*
> *Clear before us through the darkness*
> *Gleams and burns the guiding light;*
> *Pilgrim clasps the hand of pilgrim*
> *Stepping fearless through the night.*
> — *Lutheran Book of Worship* #355

In imagination, I see that pilgrim band venturing through a dark and gloomy night, holding hands, to strengthen and comfort each other as they walk in "the light of God's own presence ... brightning all the path we tread" as the next stanza puts it.

Perhaps I like this hymn because it is so realistic and hopeful, and because it doesn't sing of solitary travelers sneaking through the night but of a whole community venturing forward together.

If I were to edit that stanza just a little, I would substitute "onward" for "fearless" in the last line. Faced with the uncertainties of life and the certainty of death I doubt that most of us are truly fearless, and that's all right. Called and sustained by the presence and promises of God we take the hands of fellow travelers as we venture "onward through the night."

Affirmation for the Day:
Graced by God and God's people, I venture onward with confidence and hope.

December 30

Each moment is an added gift from God.

It is easy for us to think of time, as we have done in several of our recent reflections, as a possession that is being steadily diminished. Every day we lose another 24 hours and time-wise are literally becoming poorer by the minute. But there is another way to think about time — not as our possession but God's gift. Think of God as continually creating more time and then giving it to us moment by moment.

From this perspective, every minute is an added blessing that God gives us to enjoy. With this attitude, we greet the dawn saying, "This is the day which the Lord has made; let us rejoice and be glad in it" (Psalm 118:24). With this attitude, we cease clutching at time as something to keep and stop grieving its daily loss. Instead, we open our hands and hearts to receive the moments of each new day as a gift from God.

Letting go of time, we let God give us the time we need. As God's gift, time comes to us as a friend rather than fleeing from us as an enemy. And, when the gift of time is past, the gift of eternity in God's greater light and nearer love is promised to us.

Affirmation for the Day:
In the grace of God, time is not fleeting away but flowing in, not being subtracted, but added on.

December 31

In Christ, the best is yet to be.

Someone is reported to have said that what he liked about Napoleon was that he "had so much future in his mind." I don't know the source of that quality in Napoleon. Perhaps it came from his own self-centered ambition to be triumphant in conquest.

But I do know that we, like Napoleon, are also to live with future in our minds and that our confident hope and expectation come not from self-centered ambition, but from the promises of God.

In Christ we are assured, as we have reminded ourselves in these reflections, that nothing in life or in death can separate us from God's love, and that beyond the worst that sickness and death can do is the final healing of resurrection unto fullness of life in God's presence.

Affirmation for the Day:
In trust of the best yet to be I, too, will live with future in my mind.

Name Index

Covey, Stephen — August 16
Davies, D. R. — January 19
Dybvig, Philip — August 13
Eddy, Mary Baker — April 13
Einstein, Albert — October 12, November 17
Emotions Anonymous — February 7
Finney, Charles — October 18
Fisher, Roger — January 8, February 6, March 19
Fitzgerald, Edward — January 10
Flaten, Arnie — July 12
Fosdick, Harry Emerson — January 10, January 13, February 16, March 10, April 18, May 3, May 21, August 23, November 3, November 16, December 5, December 6
Fousek, Betty — January 29
Fox, Mem — August 25
Franklin, Benjamin — February 24, August 7
Freud, Sigmund — September 22
Frost, Gerhard — April 2, April 20, April 21, September 3, September 12, September 14, September 15, September 17, September 29, October 6, October 25, December 18
Gandhi, Mahatma — April 18, May 2, May 10, November 26, December 7
Gibran, Kahlil — July 11
Gornitzka, Reuben — April 29
Gray, Thomas — October 1
Gretsky, Wayne — March 28
Gullixsen, T. F. — August 21
Hansen, Phil — January 23
Hanson, Olaf — August 9
Harris, Sidney — February 28, July 2, October 24
Hedges, Chris — November 7
Helmstetter, Shad — June 30
Hilbert, John — January 4, August 22
Hombro, Edvard — June 16
Hong, Howard — January 9, February 18
Housman, A. E. — February 23, September 16
Howe, Julia Ward — November 3

Jackson, Don — July 15

James, William — October 15

Jefferson, Thomas — March 1, April 22, June 29

Johnson, Samuel — May 14, November 14

Johnson, Virginia — August 2

Johnson, Vivian — May 15

Johnson, Wendell — June 7

Johnsrud, Sherm — May 22

Jones, E. Stanley — January 5, January 16, January 19, February 1,
    February 14, March 17, April 5, April 6, April 24, May 2,
    May 19, August 29, September 6, September 8, September 22,
    October 26, October 27, December 10, December 19

Jorgensen, Theodore — December 13

Kafka, Franz — November 6

Kant, Immanuel — March 19

Keats, John — August 25

Keillor, Garrison — April 14

Kelley, Patricia — September 29

Kennedy, John F. — June 25

Kennedy, Robert — August 13

Kenyon, Jane — December 28

Kersten, Paul — January 21

Kesey Jr., Ken — November 25

Khayyam, Omar — January 10

Kildahl, J. N. — January 18

Knox, John — March 30

Knox, William — September 30

Koop, Steven — June 5

Landers, Ann — March 7, July 10

Lederer, William — July 15

Lifton, Robert — November 20

Lincoln, Abraham — March 20, July 18, July 20, September 30,
    November 17

Loy, David — May 12

Luther, Martin — January 12, January 15, January 16, January 17,
    January 20, February 16, February 27, March 29, May 12,
    July 6, July 16, July 21, August 10, December 12

Lutz, Howard — November 5
Maquire, Daniel — November 2
Masters, William — August 2
Mathiesen, Helen — March 27, September 27
McCroskey, James — August 26
McLuhan, Marshall — September 9
Miller, Alice — June 6
Moller, Jurgen — February 26, July 19
Montagu, Ashley — April 27, September 22
Morris, Colin — July 4
Myers, Ched — May 14
Nelson-Pallmeyer, Jack — April 11, November 11
Nessan, Craig — July 31
Niebuhr, Reinhold — January 25, January 26, June 17, June 27, August 17
Norstad, Fritz — July 21
Norwich, Julian of — February 17
Nouwen, Henri — September 12
Olson, Herman — December 5
Pascal, Blaise — November 8
Paulson, Arthur — March 9
Peale, Norman Vincent — October 3
Peck, M. Scott — April 6
Preus, David — February 24
Preus, Herman — October 10
Quanbeck, Warren — September 10
Robertson, F. W. — January 2
Rogness, Alvin — January 20, February 15, April 10, April 11, April 24, July 7, August 29, December 11
Rolston III, Holmes — June 19
Rosenstock-Huessy, Eugen — October 19
Rossing, Barbara — April 1
Rothkopf, David J. — May 13
Sacks, Oliver — August 3
Satre, Lowell — February 14
Scherer, Paul — February 11, May 23, June 19, June 23, August 25, August 30, September 18

Schiotz, Fredrik — February 25

Schopenhauer, Arthur — March 4

Schramm, Mary — August 15

Schweitzer, Albert — October 31

Service, Robert — July 18, October 2

Shakespeare, William — September 28, December 2

Sharp, Gene — June 24

Shaw, George Bernard — November 14

Sherman, William Tucumseh — November 10

Sibley, Mulford Q. — January 11

Sider, Ron — November 25

Smiles, Samuel — March 26

Smith, William (Bill) — January 31, February 29

Smits, Edmund — February 29, September 23, October 24

Solseth, Ray — October 2

Soros, George — May 13

Speidel, Iona — July 1

Sponheim, Paul — September 8

Sponheim, Scott — December 26

Spurgeon, Charles — July 24

Stalin, Josef — November 20

Stepanek, Mattie J. T. — October 29

Stevenson, J. W. — April 9

Stone, I. F. — December 7

Sverdrup, George — January 12

Swimme, Brian — May 7

Tanner, Jacob — December 14

Taylor, Richard — November 25

Temple, William — February 10, May 1

Thomas, Dylan — December 17

Tillich, Paul — March 17, October 1

Tolstoy, Leo — March 26, April 14, April 16, April 17, May 10,
    May 11, October 13, November 8, November 9, November 10,
    December 22, December 23

Tournier, Paul — February 23, March 6, May 27, June 1, July 21,
    July 23

Tuchman, Barbara — November 23

Twain, Mark — September 27
Vaagenes, Morris — May 9
VanDusen, Henry P. — May 20
Vinger, Ted — September 26
Voltaire — April 14
Walther, C. F. W. — January 15
Weatherhead, Leslie — June 12, December 20
Weil, Simone — April 7
Wesley, John — October 28, November 23
Whale, John Sheldon — April 1, August 31
Whiston, Charles — June 13, October 11, December 24
Whitehead, Alfred North — February 12, October 24
Whittier, John Greenleaf — September 14
Winans, James — August 20
Wolf, Sue — March 24
Yackel, John — May 15

Endnotes

Borg, Marcus. *The Heart of Christianity: Rediscovering a Life of Faith.* San Fransisco: HarperSanFransisco / HarperCollins Publishers, 2003, pp. 31, 40, 109

Harris, Sydney J. *Pieces of Eight.* Boston: Houghton Mifflin Company, 1982, p. 47

Hedges, Chris. *War is a Force that Gives Us Meaning.* New York: New York Public Affairs, 2002, pp. 3, 17, 21, 64, 101, 163, 165

Hildahl, J.N. *The Holy Spirit and Our Faith* (Minneapolis: Augsburg Publishing House, 1960) p. 43. Previously published under the title *Ten Studies on the Holy Spirit*, in 1937

Scharen, Christian Batalden. *Married in the Sight of God: Theology, Ethics and Church Debates over Homosexuality.* Lanham, Massachusetts: University Press of America, Inc., 2000, p. 25. Luther quote

Winans, James A. *Speech-Making.* New York: Appleton-Century-Crofts, 1938, pp. 11-12

Permissions